FESTIVALS
of Western Europe

FESTIVALS
of Western Europe

Dorothy Gladys Spicer

THE   H.   W.   WILSON   COMPANY

NEW   YORK   1958

FESTIVALS OF WESTERN EUROPE

Copyright © 1958
by
Gladys Spicer Fraser
First Printing 1958
Second Printing 1961
Third Printing 1967
Fourth Printing 1973
Printed in the United States of America

International Standard Book Number 0-8242-0016-0

Library of Congress Catalog Card Number 58-7291

Affectionately dedicated

to

LAURA MARY MOENCH, M.D.

and to

BLACK-FACED SAINT SARA
guardian of gypsies
and
patroness of a cherished friendship

PREFACE

"Tradition ties the past to the present and is the link which binds the past to the future," according to Camillo de Castello Branco, Portugal's great nineteenth-century novelist.

I have written FESTIVALS OF WESTERN EUROPE as one who loves the old in relation to the new, and looks upon the past as the heritage of the future. *Festas*, fairs, holy days, pilgrimages and patronal village feasts—all these events have come down through the centuries, and intermingled with the traditions of the church and the lives of peasant folk. Festivals once held to honor pagan deities have become associated in the course of time with the saints' days of the Christian calendar. Ancient fertility rites have been transmuted into parish ceremonies to welcome spring and ensure growth of crops and health to beasts. The fires once kindled to light the Sun God on his dark midwinter journey through the heavens now glow brightly in honor of the Christ Child's birth.

Thus it is that festivals and ceremonies observed in European countries today have origins which are lost in the mists of time. These traditional events are a treasury from which we draw knowledge of peoples, places and customs. Without the past there could be no present, just as without the present there can be no future. This is why tradition is important.

I have written about European festivals as a reporter who, through the years, has visited many countries and participated in many joyous traditional events. I have described customs and ceremonies as I have witnessed them or have learned of them through reliable sources. To make the book more practical festival descriptions are supplemented by reference material which includes a table of Easter dates and movable festivals dependent upon Easter, a glossary of some common festival terms and a list of sources in different languages.

vii

FESTIVALS OF WESTERN EUROPE

Numerous items in FESTIVALS OF WESTERN EUROPE are revisions or duplications of material that originally appeared in my earlier work, *The Book of Festivals*, published by the Woman's Press in 1937 and long out of print. The rights in this publication have reverted to the author.

FESTIVALS OF WESTERN EUROPE includes descriptions of some of the principal festal events of twelve different countries. The geographical basis of selection is an imaginary line, drawn from Stettin on the Baltic to Trieste on the Adriatic. Roughly speaking, everything to the left of this line is "western European," although at various points pieces of the different countries spill over the line on one side or the other.

The basis of festival selection has been more difficult than determining geographical areas. For each country the cycle of the Christian year has been followed as a skeleton to which local saints' days and regional celebrations have been added. In most countries each tiny hamlet has its own special fêtes. Each village celebrates its patronal feast with its own rituals, foods, and folkways. Since few "outsiders" ever hear of these feast days, customs practiced in one village often are totally unknown in the next. Out of hundreds of such days, especially in countries where "every day is a festa," I have tried to select events that are typical of certain localities or varieties of peasant culture.

No national or political holidays have been included, or "festivals" in the sense of those periodical seasons of entertainment so popular among European tourists. The festivals I have described are the religious feast days and the anniversaries of "days of joy" which occur in the annals of the church and are deeply rooted in the hearts of peasant people.

Since folklore is probably the most fluid of all sciences, inaccuracies are bound to occur, despite careful checking, in any book which depends largely upon folk tradition and folk memory for its source. Additional hazards are met in dealing with a variety of languages and dialects not only from one country to another, but often within the same country. Nuances of meaning and emotion are blurred or lost in translating from a foreign tongue. In many instances archaic words, or words known only to certain localities, occur in the folk rhymes and verses that accompany certain festivals. For this reason I have consistently sought to retain native flavor rather than give literal translations.

I have given the English version of the festival in parentheses immediately following each foreign title. When festivals local in significance or with special regional characteristics are described, the name of the town or village in which the celebration occurs follows the English title. In order that the locale may be accurately identified, I have also given the larger geographical area.

* * *

I wish it might be possible to acknowledge my indebtedness to the many people in many countries who have contributed to the making of this book; for wherever the festival trail has led me, I have met with friendliness and genuine eagerness to share time-honored traditions with someone from afar. Thus I have experienced the joy of "belonging," so to speak, to widely different lands and cultures, and a difficult research task has been lightened by the warmth of happy human relationships.

I wish to give special thanks for generous help in translating from foreign languages, checking manuscript and many other services to the individuals and organizations listed below under the various countries. I also acknowledge indebtedness for much material to the sources given at the end of the book under Some Helpful Books:

BELGIUM: Belgian Government Information Center, New York City.
DENMARK: Danish Information Office, New York City.
FRANCE: Mesdemoiselles Jeanne Pons and Henriette F. Liboz.
GERMANY: German Tourist Information. Office, New York City.
ITALY: Italian State Tourist Office, New York City.
LUXEMBOURG: Mr. George J. Kremer, in Echternach, who acted as my host and established many helpful local contacts, the late Mr. Corneille Staudt, Consul of Luxembourg, and Miss Yolande Loesch, Deputy Commissioner of Industry and Tourism, Consulat Général du Grand Duché de Luxembourg, New York City.

FESTIVALS OF WESTERN EUROPE

NETHERLANDS: The Netherlands Information Service, New York City. Dr. Jacomina Korteling, in Deventer, interpreted for me and I am indebted to her for research and translation. I am also indebted to Mr. J. M. Lentfest, De Twentsche Bank, in Denekamp, for interpreting and establishing contacts; Mr. Th. E. G. Looman, in Denekamp, for the Dutch version of the Denekamp Easter Hymn; Mr. Scholten Lubberink, *klompenmaker* in Denekamp, for information on the winter horn; Mr. Toon Borghuis, in Oldenzaal, for songs and information on Overijssel customs; Pastor Eerwaarde Jan Bolscher, in Beuningen, for local folk material.

NORWAY: Norwegian National Travel Office, New York City.

PORTUGAL: Mr. Joaquim G. de Vasconcellos, from Casa de Portugal, New York City; Sisters of Colégio do Sagrado Coração de Maria, in Guimarães, my hostesses during *Festas Gualterianas,* who made contacts for me and helped in many ways; Miss Juanita Parsons.

SPAIN: Spanish National Tourist Department, New York City.

SWEDEN: Mr. Holger Lundbergh and Mr. Stig Näsholm of The American Swedish News Exchange, Inc., New York City.

SWITZERLAND: Public Relations Department, Swiss National Tourist Office, New York City; Mrs. Maarten Bos, in White Plains, New York.

DOROTHY GLADYS SPICER

White Plains, New York
December 1957

CONTENTS

PART I
FESTIVALS

PART II
FOR FURTHER REFERENCE

INDEXES

xi

PART I

FESTIVALS

1

FESTIVALS OF BELGIUM

The fact that both French and Dutch are spoken in Belgium accounts for the mixture of the two languages in the place names and descriptions of Belgian festivals.

NIEUWJAARSDAG (New Year's Day)

January 1

For weeks before New Year's Day children begin saving their pennies to buy gaily decorated papers for writing holiday greetings to parents and god-parents. Often these papers are prettily embellished with motifs such as golden cherubs and angels, brightly-colored roses or ribbon-tied garlands. The children practice composing and writing their letters in school, until a final perfect, or nearly perfect, copy can be made on the fancy paper. Then they carefully hide the messages from their parents.

On New Year's morning the children read their little compositions before the assembled family. Not only do they wish health and happiness in the coming year; they promise to mend naughty ways and behave like angels during the next twelve months.

In the Walloon district of Liége children go about from house to house, or stop passers-by on the streets, to wish them a Happy New Year and offer *nules,* large wafers which are decorated with raised imprints of the crucifix. The children receive coins in exchange for the wafers, which people keep during the year as charms against evil and disease.

Walloon and Flemish farmers still observe the charming custom of rising early on January first and going out to stables and pens to say "Happy New Year" to the horses, cows, pigs and other domestic animals.

DRIEKONIGENDAG (Three Kings' Day)

January 6

Three Kings' Day, the great festival of boys and girls, usually is celebrated with a party and a *gâteau des rois,* or cake of the Kings. A bean baked inside the cake bestows royalty for the day on the child who finds it in his portion. The King chooses a Queen. Crowned with gold paper crowns and robed in finery borrowed from mother's scrap bag, the youthful sovereigns rule the merry party. Whatever the King and Queen do must be imitated by everyone else.

Often bands of children go from door to door singing ditties about the Kings and receiving coins in return. One favorite rhyme is:

> Three Kings, Three Kings,
> Give me a new hat.
> My old one is worn out.
> Mother must not know it:
> Father counted the money on the grille! [1]

SINT GUDULE or SAINTE GEDULE (Saint Gedula), Brussels, province of Brabant

January 8

The anniversary of Saint Gedula, patroness of Brussels, is observed with great ceremony at the Church of Sainte-Gedule. In 1045, Saint Gedula's relics were translated to the Collegiate Church of Saint Michael, which was thereafter called Sainte-Gedule.

Legend says that the seventh-century saint, who was noted for piety, used to walk barefoot several miles, morning and evening, to attend Mass at the church of Morzelle. One day, when on the way to early service, the devil extinguished her lantern. As the young girl knelt and prayed for help, an angel rekindled it. The story explains why the saint always is represented accompanied by an angel, who is lighting her lantern.

---

[1] Old-fashioned Belgian charcoal stoves have open grilles on top. The verse means that when father carelessly counted out the money over the grille, the coins fell through and were lost.

Many miracles are attributed to Saint Gudule who died at Nivelles (Nijvel) in 712.

SINT GREGORIUS or SAINT GRÉGOIRE (Saint Gregory)

March 12

Saint Gregory the Great, the sixth-century monk who became a pope, is patron of school children and scholars. On his feast day boys and girls take a holiday in honor of this pious saint to whom popular legend attributes many kind acts. One is that he freed frogs from the ice of early spring; another that he loved beggars, whom he deferentially called "Father" and fed at his own table with food served on golden plates.

School children rise early on March 12. Dressed as "little soldiers of Saint Gregory," they take a big basket for gifts and parade through the streets, singing an old song. A noisy drummer announces the approach of the little procession. Pope Gregory himself, in gaudy vestments and gold paper crown, is attended by standard-bearers and followers arrayed in colorful odds and ends of cotton, velvet or silk. The little girls of the procession wear big bright shoulder bows, which capricious March winds snatch at and billow out like butterfly wings.

A troop of angels is one of the procession's traditional features, possibly because of the legend that once, when Gregory was walking through the slave market at Rome, he saw for sale a group of comely heathen youths from Britain. Upon learning their nationality Gregory exclaimed, "Were they but Christians, they would truly be *angeli* [angels], not *Angli* [Anglo-Saxons]!"

The little procession makes neighborhood rounds. At each door the children pause hopefully, chanting this old song which suggests treats are welcome for their holiday feast:

> This is the school boy's holiday,
> Today we shall have crusty bread
> And red, red wine.
> Long live good Saint Gregory!

ONZE LIEVE VROUWEDAG (Annunciation)

March 25

Many folk-beliefs surround the Day of Annunciation, anniversary of the Angel Gabriel's announcement to the Virgin Mary of the Mystery of Incarnation. The Belgian peasant believes this holy time to be important in weather lore, and thinks that a fair eve predicts a plentiful harvest.

Legend says Our Lord bade even wild birds and animals to observe the Annunciation feast with quiet meditation. The cuckoo alone disobeyed the command and continued his usual raucous calling throughout wood and dale. As punishment for his disobedience God doomed the bird to eternal restless wandering, without a nest of his own.

*CARNAVAL (Carnival), in Binche, province of Hainaut

The Sunday, Monday and Tuesday preceding Ash Wednesday

Carnival, which falls on the Sunday, Monday and Tuesday before Ash Wednesday, is celebrated throughout Belgium with varying degrees of gaiety. Binche, Alost, Eupen and Malmédy are particularly famous for picturesque observances. Possibly the most remarkable celebration, however, is the Carnival of the Gilles, at Binche.

It is said that this spectacular event originated in 1549, when the Low Countries provinces which constitute modern Belgium were part of the empire ruled by Charles V. Charles sent his son, who was later to rule Spain and the Low Countries as Philip II, to visit the provinces, and Charles' sister, Marie of Hungary, who was regent under Charles for the area, gave a great entertainment to honor her visiting nephew and to celebrate recent Spanish conquests in Peru. Many think that the *gilles,* with their enormously tall,

---

* Stars indicate movable feasts that depend upon Easter. See Table of Easter Dates and Movable Festivals Dependent upon Easter, p. 246.

plumed headdresses, colorful Inca costumes, foot stamping and strange rhythms, started as a ballet to honor the *Conquistadores* who, under Pizarro's leadership, had subdued the Peruvian Indians eight years before.

The word *gille* means clown. It is the ambition of every male inhabitant of Binche to be a gille at least once in his lifetime. The costumes are costly and elaborate. The brightly-colored blouses are stuffed out with straw; the bell-bottomed long trousers trimmed with many rows of locally-made Binche lace. The deep, gold- and lace-trimmed collars are decorated with tinkling bells and the broad sashes adorned with symbols of the zodiac. The gilles wear heavy wooden shoes with which they clap out their rhythms as they dance tirelessly through the streets, by day and night. On their left arms the performers carry baskets of oranges, which they aim at friends and acquaintances during the dance through the town.

As Albert Marinus, one of Belgium's great folklorists, aptly says:

> The honor, the joy, the pride of a city: The Gilles.
> The honor, the joy, the pride of its inhabitants: The Gilles.

*VASTENAVOND (Shrove Tuesday)

The Tuesday preceding Ash Wednesday

The last day before Lent culminates a long series of joyous carnival events which vary in character from place to place. *Koekebakken,* or pancakes, and *wafelen,* or waffles, are *Vastenavond* delicacies in many households, for rich foods are indulged in everywhere before the rigors of fasting begin.

Walloon farmers have a superstition that cabbage eaten on this day will prevent flies and caterpillars from destroying the cabbages growing in gardens.

In some places boys and girls go about singing traditional ditties from door to door. In return, they receive such gifts as apples, nuts and strips of bacon. The children then go for a picnic, broiling their bacon on long willow spits and holding high holiday before Lent starts.

7

*ERSTE ZONDAG VAN DEN VASTEN (First Sunday of Lent)
First Sunday in Lent

In some parts of the Ardennes the first Sunday in Lent is called the "Sunday of the Great Fires," because bonfires are built on the hilltops. For days preceding, children of Grandhalleux go from house to house begging wood for fires. If people refuse to give fuel, the children chase them next day and try to smudge their faces with ashes.

When the fires are lighted, young people dance and sing about them. Later they leap over the embers with wishes for good crops, good luck in marriage and freedom from colic.

Seven Lenten fires seen on this night are said to be protection against witches. Sometimes parents tell the children they will receive as many eggs at Easter as they can count fires on the first Sunday in Lent. According to old peasant belief, neglect to kindle "the great fire" means God will kindle it himself—that is, He will set fire to the house.

*WITTE DONDERDAG (Holy Thursday)
The Thursday preceding Easter

On this day the chimes cease ringing in the church towers and people say, "The bells have flown to Rome."

The Ceremony of Foot Washing is observed in many cathedral churches and in parishes which are endowed for the purpose by rich families. Twelve old men from "God's House," as the almshouse is called, are selected on account of their piety to enact the role of the Twelve Apostles. The clergy bathe the feet of the men and bestow bread and alms, in memory of Jesus, who washed the disciples' feet at the Last Supper.

*GOEDE VRIJDAG (Good Friday)
The Friday preceding Easter

All churches are draped in black in memory of Jesus' Passion and a general air of gloom pervades the streets of towns and cities.

In the villages peasant women often wear mourning on this day. In the afternoon everybody attends the three-hour Passion service.

*ZATERDAG VOOR PASEN (Saturday before Easter)

The Saturday preceding Easter

The chimes that "flew to Rome" on Holy Thursday return the night before Easter. At the Saturday Glory Service they ring joyously throughout the land and parents tell the children that the bells "sow colored eggs in the gardens." In candy and pastry shops, also, one can plainly see the bells have paid a visit; for windows and show cases are filled with all kinds of beautiful bell creations in colored sugar, chocolate and marzipan—many of them decorated with artificial flowers or pretty ribbons—all of them delicious to eat.

In some places boys and girls rise early on Easter morning to search for eggs in the gardens; in other districts egg hunts are a feature of the Saturday festivities. Eggs are either dyed in bright solid colors or else decorated with bird and flower designs. Every garden overflows with eggs, which are hidden in tree crotches, behind shrubs, in the grass, behind piles of stones. The children fill little baskets with their treasures. After exhausting the resources of their own gardens, the youngsters visit grandparents, uncles and aunts. Everywhere they go there are more eggs to hunt, for Belgian chimes are no less generous with Easter eggs than with their joyous Resurrection music.

SPEL VAN SINT EVERMARUS (Game of Saint Evermaire), in Rutten (Russon), province of Limburg

May 1

On May 1 the villagers of Rutten reenact the legend of Saint Evermaire and his seven companions who were murdered in the year 699, when on pilgrimage to the Holy Land. The tale of horror—a twelve-hundred-year-old thriller—goes something like this:

9

The pious Evermaire and his friends sought lodging at nightfall at a hospitable farmhouse (according to some, a château) in the environs of Tongres. The woman who received them was deeply impressed by the obvious sanctity of the eight pilgrims. Consequently she warned them against Hacco, her bandit husband, who was temporarily absent on a raid, but might soon return.

The weary Evermaire and his comrades slept at the house, but rose at dawn and quietly slipped away on their journey. Hacco, meanwhile, had returned and learned, somehow or other, about his holy guests. He soon tracked them down in the forest nearby, killed the eight men and left their corpses on the ground where they fell.

The game of saints and bandits celebrated in Rutten today commemorates the evil Hacco's massacre of Saint Evermaire and the seven good men. For upwards of ten centuries (the play did not start until some two hundred years after the event, we are told) inhabitants of Rutten and their descendants have faithfully presented the drama in all its gory detail.

At about half past ten in the morning people gather for the religious procession at the Chapel of Saint Evermaire, and march about the casket with the saint's reputed bones. Then the statue of Saint Evermaire is borne aloft, followed by seven men representing the companions, and Saint Evermaire himself, carrying pilgrim staff and wearing knee breeches, white stockings and cockle-shell-embellished cape. A group of winged guardian angels follows protectingly.

Fifty "brigands" riding heavy farm horses are led by Hacco, master villain, who wears a bright jacket with gold buttons. His band of desperados is dressed in white knee-breeches, red jackets and hats with red plumes. In the chapel meadow, where the play is given, the bandits charge furiously upon the holy men. After a good deal of dialogue and hymn singing the saint finally falls dead from an arrow, among the bodies of his slain companions.

10

PROCESSIE VAN HET HEILIG BLOED (Procession of the Holy Blood),
in Bruges (Brugge), province of West Flanders

The first Monday after May 2

The city of Bruges annually holds an imposing procession in honor of the Sacred Blood. The ceremony originated in the year 1150, when Thierry d'Alsace, returning from the Second Crusade, brought to Bruges a phial said to contain a drop of Christ's blood.

The sacred relic, preserved in a marvelously wrought gold *châsse*, or reliquary, is carried in procession from the Chapelle du Saint Sang to the Cathedral of Saint Sauveur. There the châsse is placed upon the altar during the celebration of solemn Pontifical Mass. The bishop reverently lifts the relic for veneration by all before it is again returned to its chapel.

The procession is composed of many different floats, representing episodes of scriptural and historical interest. Marchers on foot and horseback accompany the tableaux which cover a wide variety of subjects, ranging all the way from Adam and Eve in the Garden to the crucifixion of Jesus. Both marchers and riders weave in and out among the scenes, while talking and singing as if acting parts on the stage.

In the procession there are also pilgrims, members of church societies and religious orders, trade guilds and representatives of the Brotherhood of Sacred Blood. All groups carry their own banners and insignia. Last of all come the priests and high church dignitaries dressed in elaborate feast day robes and bearing the golden casket with the Sacred Blood. A reverent hush falls over the vast crowd, as spectators sink to their knees. The relic passes. Again the street takes on festival appearance. Church bells ring, street banners flutter, bands play and all Bruges gives itself over to gaiety and joy.

SINT DYMPHNA or SAINTE DYMPHNE (Saint Dymphna), in Geel, province of Antwerp

May 15

Since the thirteenth century pilgrims have gone to Geel on May 15, to visit the tomb of Saint Dymphna, special guardian of the insane. During her Novena the saint's protection is sought against mental illness. Insane persons, or the friends or relatives who represent them, crawl nine times over Saint Dymphna's reputed sarcophagus, meanwhile invoking her blessing.

Legend says that Dymphna, daughter of a seventh-century Irish king fled to Geel to escape her pagan father's insane demand for an incestuous marriage. The king pursued his daughter to Geel, where he beheaded her.

Gradually people came to regard Dymphna as patroness of the mentally deranged. More and more sick patients were brought to the saint's tomb at Geel and were tenderly looked after by the townsfolk. Eventually a small infirmary was built next to the thirteenth-century Church of Saint Dymphna.

The fame of the community grew through the centuries until, about 1850, Geel was placed under state medical supervision. Today Colony Geel is noted throughout the world for its humane and remarkably successful "boarding out" system, which cares for two thousand or more harmless mental patients as "paying guests" in homes of the inhabitants of Geel, or of neighboring communities. Provision is made for both pauper and well-to-do cases. All patients enjoy home life, healthful occupation and freedom, under the kindly supervision of carefully selected householders.

DÉJEUNER MATRIMONIAL (Matrimonial Tea), in Écaussines-Lalaing, province of Hainaut

Whit Monday

On this day young unmarried women of Écaussines-Lalaing hold an amusing "matrimonial tea" in honor of "all the bachelors in the world." The gay event is supposed to have originated centuries ago when bachelors were scarce in the district.

At nine in the morning all visiting unmarried men are welcomed at the Town Hall and invited to write their names in a big official guest book. Then there are receptions, speeches of welcome by local officials and pretty *mesdemoiselles*, sightseeing tours, band music, general laughter and merrymaking. Just to walk through the streets is fun because they are gaily decorated with streamers, pennants, and humorous verses appropriate to the occasion.

At three in the afternoon the annual tea is announced. The affair is presided over by one of the young women who welcomes the bachelors in the name of her sisters—all the old maids of Écaussines-Lalaing. The speech, accompanied by much hilarity, is followed by the "tea," which consists of coffee, beer, and special regional sweets.

Of course, the affair does not end with the tea. Folk-dancing in the streets, band music and merrymaking far into the night, bring this popular festival of youth to a happy climax.

SINT MEDARDUS (Saint Medard) *June 8*

The anniversary of Saint Medard, sixth century Bishop of Vermand, is important in peasant weather lore. According to an old folk rhyme, rain on Saint Medard's Day means forty days of wet weather:

> *S'il pleut le jour de Saint Médard*
> *Il pleut quarante jours plus tard.*

SINT JANS VOORAVOND (Saint John's Eve) *June 23*

In some places young people dance and sing about bonfires which they light on Saint John's Eve, the longest night in the year.

Several days before the Eve groups of children go about from farm to farm, begging for firewood with this traditional song:

> Wood, wood, lumber wood,
> We come to get Saint John's wood.
> Give us a little and keep a little
> Until the Eve of Saint Peter's Day

It is an old folk belief that embers from the Saint John's fires will protect homes and barns from fire during the coming year, and jumping over the lighted bonfires is considered an antidote against diseases of the stomach.

13

SINT PIETER (Saint Peter)

June 29

In some rural areas peasants recall Saint Peter's martyrdom by building bonfires. Nowadays the custom is gradually disappearing, but some years ago children trundled wheelbarrows from farm to farm in the neighborhood and begged wood for Saint Peter's fires.

Old and young joined in building the fires, lighted in remembrance of the fire before which Saint Peter warmed himself when he denied Jesus. As flames leaped high, the children danced in a ring, singing:

> Saint Peter, come and join us
> In our circle of joy.

Often people light candles on this night and say the rosary in commemoration of Saint Peter.

Since Saint Peter is patron of fishermen the ceremony of Blessing the Sea is performed each year at Ostend, Blankenberge and other seaport towns, on the Sunday following the saint's day. All fishermen, mariners and others who are exposed to the dangers of water participate in the ceremonies. Following mass a procession of clergy, church dignitaries and seamen carry votive offerings, flowers and garlands to the shore. Then the priests enter the boats and go out to bless the waves.

BOETPROCESSIE VAN VEURNE (Procession of Penitence), in Furnes (Veurne), province of West Flanders

Last Sunday in July

It is said that the annual Procession of Penitence at Furnes originated in 1099, when the Crusader, Count Robert II of Flanders, returned from Jerusalem with a fragment of the True Cross.

Today's solemn procession features episodes from the Passion story. Some are dramatized by actors playing the parts of various Old and New Testament characters; others by carved wooden figures, mounted on platforms and carried on the shoulders of penitents.

Forty or more of the groups are introduced by angels or other characters who recite explanatory verses concerning scenes that are to follow.

Horse-drawn floats, decorated cars and the colorful banners and standards of the organizing committee all form a part of the impressive procession. But the most moving figures of the spectacle are the black-hooded penitents, many of them barefoot, who bend and stagger under the heavy burden of full-sized wooden crosses. Both men and women are among the penitents. All wear coarse woolen robes and hoods having only slits for eyes. These people are not actors. They are seeking expiation from sin through bearing their crosses, even as Jesus bore his to Calvary.

Last of all the Sacred Host appears, carried by several bishops. As the Sacrament passes, spectators kneel in adoration. A hush falls over the great crowd. Once the procession has returned to the Church of Saint Walburga from which it issued, however, all Furnes gives itself to the joy of a *kermess* (fair) in the market place.

MARIA-HEMELVAART DAG (Assumption of the Virgin Mary), in
    Hasselt, province of Limburg
                    Third and fourth Sundays in August

In Hasselt, capital of Limburg, the festival of *Virga Jesse,* Virgin of the Line of Jesse, is celebrated every seven years on the third and fourth Sundays in August. According to tradition, the image of the Virgin once stood in a forest tree, at the crossroads which mark the present site of Hasselt. Travelers left offerings at this shrine and prayed for a safe journey. Gradually reports of the image's miraculous powers spread until, by the fourteenth century, pilgrims from far and wide came to worship at the tree.

Today the people of Hasselt in solemn procession carry through the town an ancient, blackened image of the Virgin, which they claim once stood in the crossroads tree. The procession proceeds under a series of arches, commemorating various dramatic episodes in the town's history.

15

On Assumption Day (August 15) priests in some other parts of the province bless *kruidjes,* or bouquets made up of nine different kinds of flowers. Pious peasants preserve these bouquets throughout the year. At the approach of a bad storm they pull off a few flower petals and toss them into the fire, as everyone kneels and recites the opening lines of the Gospel according to Saint John.

Les Vêpres de Gouyasse (Marriage [2] of Goliath), in Ath, province of Hainaut

Practically every Belgian town and village has its giants,[3] which are paraded through the streets on special occasions during the year. The annual wedding of Goliath, at Ath, is one of the most spectacular of these affairs. Many of the towering figures, which measure upwards of twenty feet, represent various biblical, historical or legendary characters. A man walks inside the figure, a peephole in front allowing him to get air, as well as to look out and see where he is going.

Ath boasts many giants, which appear on different occasions. On the Saturday before the fourth Sunday in August the great event is the procession of Goliath, who, for centuries, has been the town's patron and protector. Goliath, wearing helmet and breastplate and carrying a mighty club, is accompanied to the Church of Saint Julien by Madame Goliath, who has long black tresses adorned with orange blossoms. The bride and bridegroom are escorted by other giants, including Samson bearing a broken column, a figure representing Mademoiselle Victoire, in gold crown and voluminous cape, and a hideous, mustachioed Ambiorix.

In 1461 in the procession known as that of Saint Julien, a giant figure was introduced for the first time. As the years went by other figures were added from time to time by various local guilds. Among other characters there was the symbolic one *Tiran,* or *Tyrant,* who may have represented Ambiorix, leader of a Gaulish tribe.

[2] Literally, vespers.

[3] Antwerp, Turnai, Lier, Veurne, and Binche are a few of the many places which are especially famed for their giants.

The procession of giants, accompanied by colorful floats representing symbolic and historical events, proceeds through the streets to the Church of Saint Julien. There Goliath and his bride remain standing on either side of the portals while the town officials enter the church for the singing of *les vêpres de Gouyasse.*

Following the religious ceremony the procession goes to the *Gran' Place* where the battle of David and Goliath is enacted by the recitation of traditional verses between David and Goliath. The play ends with this classic line spoken by Goliath:

Je n'sus nieu co mort! "I am not dead yet!"

ALLER-HEILIGEN DAG (All Saints' Day)

November 1

On this day prayers are said in memory of all the saints who are not mentioned in the calendar. Toward evening the All Souls' Eve services begin. People visit cemeteries, decorate the graves with flowers and wreaths and light candles in memory of the deceased.

The next day people eat special "All Souls'" cakes. According to one old superstition, "the more cakes you eat on this night, the more souls you can save from Purgatory."

SINT HUBERTUS VAN LUIK or SAINT HUBERT DE LIÉGE (Saint Hubert of Liége), in St.-Hubert, province of Luxemburg

November 3

Saint Hubert, patron of dogs, the chase, and victims of hydrophobia, is especially honored in the Ardennes, where he is said to have experienced a miraculous vision. On his feast day people throughout the forest area near the little town of St.-Hubert bring their dogs to thé Church of Saint Hubert for the priest to bless and sprinkle with holy water.

The custom originated in a seventh-century legend about Hubert, a pleasure-loving, profligate young nobleman who devoted himself to the chase, to complete neglect of all church festivals. One Good Friday, when hunting in the Ardennes, he suddenly saw a pure white stag, with an illumined crucifix gleaming between his antlers. The supposed spot of this vision (which affected Hubert so powerfully that he renounced the world, became a monk, and eventually Bishop of Liége) is marked by a chapel on the farm of "La Converserie," about five miles from St.-Hubert.

By the time of Hubert's death in 727, he was famed throughout the countryside for piety and good works. Saint Hubert's tomb (though not his bones, which once were hidden from enemy invaders and eventually lost) is in the Church of St.-Hubert. Annually thousands of devout pilgrims visit the shrine. In the church are reputed relics of the saint, including both hunting-horn and mantle. Even a shred of the latter, when placed on the head, is thought to cure sufferers from hydrophobia.

Throughout Belgium many churches are dedicated to the saint. Saint Hubert's Mass on November 3, officially opens the hunting season. In some places housewives prepare special loaves of bread which are blessed at the early morning mass. The bread is then carried home, the sign of the cross is made, and everyone breaks fast by eating a piece of the blessed loaf. People feed the bread to dogs, horses and other animals as a protection against rabies throughout the year. According to an old folk-jingle:

> I came all the way from Saint Hubert's grave,
> Without stick, without staff,
> Mad dogs stand still!
> This is Saint Hubert's will.

SINT MAARTENS DAG (Saint Martin's Day)

November 11

Saint Martin is a popular saint to whom over four hundred Belgian churches are dedicated. His day is greatly anticipated by Belgian boys and girls, who celebrate the festival with processions, bonfires and general merrymaking.

In some part of the country Saint Martin, like Saint Nicholas,[4] calls in person on the feast day Eve and brings gifts to the children.

---

[4] See *Sint Nikolaas Vooravond*, December 5.

If the boys and girls have been good he bestows apples and goodies; but if they have been bad he suggestively throws a whip on the floor.

On the saint's day handfuls of apples and nuts are often tossed into the room while the boys and girls stand with faces turned toward the wall. In Veurne, Bruges and some other towns children carrying lighted lanterns march through the streets at nightfall. The young people sing Saint Martin songs and ask for gifts of goodies. *Gauffres,* little waffle-like cakes, are particularly popular on Saint Martin's Day.

SINT NIKOLAAS VOORAVOND or LA VEILLE DE SAINT NICOLAS (Saint Nicholas' Eve)

December 5

Children write annual letters to Saint Nicholas, the invisible gift-giver, whose black Moorish servant slips down the chimney on this night and leaves toys in the empty shoes set by the fireplace. The child's father always promises to post the letters because he alone knows how to reach the saint.

Saint Nicholas rides a donkey and is attended by his assistant. The saint sees everything. He knows everything, but no child has ever seen or known him. The children leave carrots and pieces of bread in the chimney corner for Saint Nicholas' donkey who surely will be hungry from journeying across village housetops.

In the evening parents and children sit close to the fire and tell stories about the life and works of Saint Nicholas, fourth-century Bishop of Myra, who traditionally wears rich robes, gold miter, and an enormous bishop's ring on the left hand. The saint is the friend of all children, but special patron of little boys because of his legendary restoration to life of three small lads, whom a wicked inn-keeper killed, salted down in brine and then served for dinner.

The children sing charming little songs in their saint's honor. Suddenly a shower of sweets flies through the door. Boys and girls scurry around under tables and chairs to capture their share of

19

booty; but by the time the last bonbon is found, Saint Nicholas has vanished.

The following day youngsters rise early and run to the chimney to see what the saint has left for them during the night. The shoes contain special treats such as an orange, a piece of marzipan, flat hard cakes known as *klaasjes,* perhaps an almond-filled *letterbanket,* or initial of the child's name. *Speculaus,* a kind of hard spicy gingerbread molded in the form of Saint Nicholas, is a seasonal delicacy all children anticipate. Often there are useful gifts, besides, such as a hand-knit sweater, a pair of bright warm mittens, a gay woolen muffler, or even a suit or pretty frock.

KERSTDAG (Christmas)

December 25

Christmas is a religious season observed by attending special services in the churches and wishing friends and neighbors a Merry Christmas. After midnight mass, the whole family gathers about the Christmas log to celebrate *la veille de Noël* (Christmas Eve). Ghost stories and tales are told, old ballads sung, and gin freely passed. Someimes the gin is lighted as the log falls to ashes. Many popular superstitions exist regarding Christmas Eve when, according to peasant belief, water turns to wine and people can look into the future.

Children await Christmas morning eagerly. If they are good and have said their prayers faithfully throughout the year, the Angel Gabriel or, in some places, the Child Jesus, is thought to slip an *engelskoek* (angel's cake), a kind of a bun, under the pillows of sleeping boys and girls.

ALLERKINDERENDAG (Holy Innocents' Day)

December 28

December 28 is the traditional anniversary of the slaughter of Bethlehem's innocent children by Herod, who wished to be sure of killing the Infant Jesus. According to popular legend two of the unfortunate children were found buried in the Convent of Saint Gerard, in the province of Namur. In Belgium, as in some other countries, Holy Innocents' Day eventually became a time when children were allowed to play all sorts of tricks on their elders.

In some places children try to put adults under lock and key and make them buy themselves out of bondage. Early in the morning the "innocents" attempt to get possession of all keys in the house. Whenever an unsuspecting grown-up enters a closet or room, he may unexpectedly find himself a prisoner. His freedom is not restored until he pays the forfeit the boys or girls demand— an orange, a toy, spending money, a sweet—the ransom varying with his keeper's whim. The adult who is held for ransom is called the "sugar uncle" or "sugar aunt."

SINT SYLVESTER VOORAVOND or LA SAINT SYLVESTRE (New Year's Eve)

December 31

"Sylvester"[5] is the nickname popularly applied to the lazy boy or girl who rises last on the final day of the year. Since "Sylvesters" traditionally have to pay a forfeit to their brothers and sisters, each child tries to be first to bound out of bed on the morning of December 31.

Girls, especially, try to be industrious on this day because of the old saying that one who does not finish her handwork by sunset will remain an old maid throughout the year.

All over Belgium the *réveillon,* or New Year's Eve family party, is a gay event. At midnight everyone kisses, exchanges good wishes for a Happy New Year and drinks toasts to absent relatives and friends. In the cities, cafés and restaurants are crowded with pleasure-seekers who eat, drink, and bid a noisy farewell to the Old Year.

[5] In Belgium, Germany, Switzerland and a number of other European countries, Saint Sylvester's Day, anniversary of the death, in 335, of Pope Sylvester (or Silvester) I, is observed popularly with all kinds of traditional customs and ceremonies in anticipation of the coming year.

2

FESTIVALS OF DENMARK

NYTÅRSDAG (New Year's Day)

January 1

In towns and cities throughout Denmark the New Year marks the beginning of one of the most important social events in the calendar. Men and women attend church services and later call on relatives and friends to wish them a Happy New Year. The conventional call lasts for about a half hour and the customary refreshments consist of wine and small cookies. The exchange of visits is carried on for about a fortnight.

HELLIG-TRE-KONGERS-DAG (Day of the Three Holy Kings)

January 6

Hellig-Tre-Kongers-Dag, the twelfth day after Christmas, brings the festive season to an official end. The Christmas tree is dismantled, all greens are taken from the house and the Christmas ornaments packed away for another year.

This is the night when young girls traditionally play fortune-telling games. One time-honored method for a girl to decide her fate is to walk backward, throw a shoe over her left shoulder and pray the Holy Kings to reveal the future. The man who subsequently appears in her dreams will be her future husband.

FJORTENDE FEBRUAR (Fourteenth of February)

February 14

On this day school children exchange friendship tokens, which consist of pressed snowdrops accompanied by original verses. The sender signs the *gaekkebrev*, or joking letter, with a series of dots--

one dot standing for each letter in the name. When the boy who receives the gaekkebrev guesses the sender's name correctly, the girl is expected to reward him at Easter with a chocolate or sugar egg. If, on the contrary, the boy fails to decipher the name, he is expected to pay the forfeit.

* FASTELAVN (Shrovetide)

The Monday preceding Ash Wednesday

Fastelavn, the Monday preceding Ash Wednesday, is a general school holiday and one of the gayest times of year for boys and girls. Everybody celebrates the day by eating *Fastelavnsboller,* or Shrovetide buns, which are as important in youthful games and customs as in festive adult menus.

In some places children armed with "Lenten birches," or branches decorated with brightly colored paper flowers, rise at four or five in the morning, enter the rooms of parents or grandparents and waken them by beating the bedclothes with their switches. "Give buns, give buns, give buns," the children shout, meanwhile inflicting resounding smacks with their branches. From the mysterious depths of the covers the "sleeping" grown-ups always produce the traditional Fastelavnsboller (and sometimes even candy), with which the youthful tormentors customarily are rewarded. Possibly this custom survives from ancient times when the "Easter smacks," delivered in many lands at this season, were regarded as part of an early spring purification rite.

In both town and rural communities older children dress up in fancy costumes and fantastic masks and make neighborhood rounds, singing for buns and rattling collection boxes:

> Buns up, buns down,
> Buns for me to chew!
> If no buns you give
> I'll rattle till you do!

* Stars indicate movable feasts that depend upon Easter. See Table of Easter Dates and Movable Festivals Dependent upon Easter, p. 246.

chant the youngsters, jingling the boxes in which they collect coins for a Fastelavn feast.

At this season there are many parties at which children play different kinds of bun games. A favorite stunt is to suspend a bun from the chandelier by a string. Everybody takes turns at trying to get a bite of the tempting morsel when the string is set in motion. The one who succeeds gets the bun as prize.

An old Danish Shrovetide game which adults play extensively even in modern times, is called *Slå Katten af Tonden,* or "knocking the cat out of the barrel." Often an artificial cat (originally a live one) is enclosed in a suspended wooden barrel—decorated with paper flowers, painted with cat pictures. Each player, armed with a wooden stick, takes a mighty swing at the barrel. The one succeeding in smashing it is proclaimed "Cat King" and receives a prize.

In some Danish seaport towns the Fastelavn boat is a feature of the season's festivities. A great boat manned by twelve seamen is placed on a truck drawn by several horses and paraded through the streets. Horn players sit beside the driver. A seaman carrying the national flag announces the approach of the truck, which is followed by members of the Seamen's Guild.

The unique procession halts frequently during its progress through the town. "The ship is coming! The ship is coming!" shout the townsfolk. The musicians play and the men dance. Contributions are collected for sick and needy seamen.

*PÅSKE (Easter)

After the Easter morning services the day is spent quietly at home. For children Easter means eggs to eat and eggs for games. In South Jutland boys and girls rise early and hunt in the garden for "hare's nests." When found, the children shriek with joy since the hares have a way of leaving not only dyed hens' eggs but eggs of chocolate and sugar which sometimes are decorated with delectable pink and yellow frosting roses. In some places children have contests with dyed eggs, which they roll down hill. The boy or girl whose egg goes the longest distance without breaking wins his opponent's egg and retains his own.

*ANDEN PÅSKEDAG (Second Easter Day)

The day after Easter

This is a general holiday. Stores are closed and in the cities all places of amusement, such as theatres, concert halls, clubs and restaurants, are crowded to capacity.

VALBORGSAFTEN (Walpurgis Eve)

April 30

In Jutland, bonfires are built on the hilltops on Walpurgis Eve, for this is the time when superstitious folk say witches and demons ride broomsticks through the air to hold rendezvous with the Devil at the Brocken, in the Harz. According to old belief, the lighted fires prevent the evil spirits from stopping on their way and harming man and beast. Be this as it may, the bonfires make a happy excuse for merrymaking on May Day Eve. Old and young dance and sing about the fires which, incidentally, serve to dispose of a great deal of useless trash accumulated during the winter months.

Customs vary from parish to parish. In most places, Saint John's or Midsummer,* rather than Walpurgis Eve, is the traditional time for building bonfires.

STORE BEDEDAG (Great Prayer Day)

The fourth Friday after Easter

This day of prayer dates back to the time of Christian VII, when his worldly Prime Minister, Count Johann Friedrich von Struensee, decided upon one great day of prayer as a substitute for the many holy days which the Church observed.

---

* See *Sankt Hans Aften,* June 23.

FESTIVALS OF WESTERN EUROPE

Bells in every church announce the eve of *Store Bededag*. In olden days it was customary for Copenhagen burghers to greet the spring by putting on new clothes and strolling along the city ramparts. Then they went home and ate *varme hveder,* a kind of small square wheat bread, served piping hot. Today people still eat the traditional bread. They still dress in spring finery but, instead of walking along the ramparts, they promenade on the famous Langelinie, or boulevard which faces Copenhagen's water front.

On Store Bededag stores and places of business are closed and special church services held.

*PINSE (Pentecost, or Whitsun)

The fiftieth day after Easter

Pentecost or Whitsun is the great spring holiday. For weeks beforehand housewives are scrubbing, scouring and putting everything to rights. Tailors are busy, too, because Whitsun is the traditional time for new summer clothes. Since beech trees are beginning to bud at this season many Copenhagen residents go by bicycle to woods and forests and gather armfuls of tender young branches. These boughs are used to decorate the houses—in symbol of welcome to early spring.

According to an old folk saying, "the sun dances on *Pinse* morning." Townsfolk, as well as country people rise at dawn to witness this miracle. In Copenhagen it is customary to get up early and go to Frederiksberg hill to watch the sun rise and "see it dance." According to custom, coffee, which is served in the garden, must be on the table by six o'clock, although the sun is up long before that hour.

Anden Pinsedag, or Whit Monday, is a general holiday. People make excursions to the woods for picnics or go to rural restaurants for an outdoor party and a good country meal, followed by dancing and singing. Indeed, singing is an important feature of most celebrations, as this is the day when singing society members, accompanied by wives and children, make all kinds of rural expeditions.

26

DENMARK

SANKT HANS AFTEN (Saint John's Eve)

June 23

Midsummer Eve—the longest night in the year—is universally celebrated with merrymaking, rejoicing and building enormous fires on the hills. Folk dancing, speeches and singing make this night a memorable occasion for young and old.

Often bonfires are topped by old tar barrels or other inflammable materials. Sometimes, also, the effigy of a witch (doubtless a pagan symbol of Winter or Death) crowns the immense pile of wood and rubbish. As flames mount, lighting the sky for miles about, the pre-Christian drama of the conquest of darkness by light is unconsciously reenacted; for on Midsummer Day the sun reaches its highest point in the heavens.

In coast hamlets blazing fires are made along the shore, and people going out in boats to view the bonfires sing romantic songs in honor of the beautiful summer night.

MORTENSAFTEN (Saint Martin's Eve)

November 10

Saint Martin's Eve, coming at the season when crops are gathered and geese are fat, is celebrated in the homes with a family dinner. Harvest foods and roast goose, traditional to the occasion, are eaten in many homes.

As one informant explained, "Legend says Saint Martin was hiding in a barn when a stupid goose gave his presence away by cackling. *That's* why the bird lost her neck and we eat her on *Mortensaften!*"

JULEAFTEN (Christmas Eve)

December 24

Christmas, the season of good will and rejoicing, is the greatest holiday in the Danish calendar. For weeks in advance farmers' wives turn their houses upside down in a frenzy of floor scrubbing, brass polishing, laying in huge supplies and baking dozens of traditional cakes, cookies and fancy breads. On "Little Christmas Eve," December 23, it is customary in many places to make enough apple fritters to last over the next three days.

Farmers are busy, too, since they must tidy up everything outdoors as well as in the barns and stables. Horses, cows and sheep all receive extra food and care for, according to ancient folk belief, the manger animals stand at midnight in honor of Jesus' birth. A sheaf of grain, tied to a pole and erected in the garden, provides holiday fare for the wild birds. Even city apartment dwellers do not forget to tie bunches of grain to the balconies at this season.

In country places the farmer traditionally makes the sign of the cross over ploughs and harrows and places them under cover. Should the "Shoemaker of Jerusalem" or, as some say, the Wandering Jew, find any unblessed or uncovered implements lying about, he would sit down and rest, thus bringing bad luck to the farmer.

The explanation of this superstition is found in an old Danish legend which says that Jesus, when carrying his heavy cross to Calvary paused to rest at a shoemaker's door. "Go on faster, go on faster!" ordered the shoemaker, pointing to the road. "I shall go on," replied Jesus looking at the man, "but thou, thou shalt wander until I return."

Folk say that for more than twenty centuries now the Shoemaker of Jerusalem has wandered across Denmark's icy fields on Christmas Eve, searching in vain for an unblessed plough. Should he succeed in finding one he could stop and rest, his wanderings over forever; for then, according to peasant tradition, the shoemaker's curse would be transferred to the godless farmer.

Thus far no Danish farmer has forgotten to bless his plough, nor has he left it carelessly lying about. But on Christmas Eve as the church bells strike twelve, people say they can hear the Wandering Jew wailing across the heath before he disappears for another twelve months.

At four or five on Christmas Eve the village bells start ringing joyously and everyone goes to church. Later people return home to feast and make merry within the family circle. Houses are gaily ornamented with red and white candles, the *Dannebrog,* or Danish flag (with its white cross on a red background) and, of course, the Christmas tree—a young spruce with evergreen needles, the symbol of everlasting life. The tree is always a beautiful sight with its decorations of red and white wax papers, fancy cookies, shining stars and little colored bags of sweets. In addition, there are plenty of small Danish flags, bright tinsel and delightful homemade ornaments.

Christmas Eve Supper, usually served at six o'clock, is the high point of the holiday. Traditionally the meal starts with *risengrød,* or rice porridge, which has cinnamon on top and a big butter "eye" in the center. The exciting feature of the risengrød is the whole almond inside. Whoever finds this coveted morsel in his portion receives a prize, such as a marzipan fruit, or some other trifle. Of course, the merriment and suspense are increased when the finder does not disclose his luck until everyone else has consumed his last grain of rice.

The rice pudding is followed by a wonderful array of foods, chief of which is the roast goose, adorned with small Danish flags and stuffed with apples and prunes. Browned potatoes, red cabbage and currant jelly accompany the bird, while rich apple cake, fruits and nuts follow for dessert.

After dinner and a hearty *"Tak for mad,"* "Thanks for the meal" to the head of the family, old and young go to the adjoining room, take hands, and dance about the Christmas tree

"It's Christmas again, Christmas again," sing the merry dancers, "And Christmas lasts till Easter!" Then follows the rueful refrain, "It isn't true! It isn't true! Lent comes in between!"

Christmas carols follow. At last it is present time. Often the youngest child hands out the gifts, which are piled beneath the tree. After all gifts have been opened, admired and enjoyed, there are games played for spice-cake forfeits. Before bedtime there is more food—coffee, sandwiches and many different kinds of sweets.

In olden times people always remembered the *Jule-Nisse* at Christmas. He was the gnome said to dwell in attic or barn. He looked after the household's welfare and was responsible for its good—or bad—luck. The Jule Nisse always received a generous portion of risengrød, with an added helping of butter. Nowadays, alas, nobody seems to see Jule-Nisse. He lives on, nevertheless, in all true Danish hearts, and the brave little red-capped, grey-bearded gnome is always well represented in Christmas cards and holiday decorations.

JULEDAG (Christmas)

December 25

Christmas is spent quietly in the homes. All day, following morning church services, relatives and friends drop in to exchange greetings and good wishes.

Throughout the holiday season hospitality is offered—and accepted—in every household. According to an old superstition, whoever enters a house at Yuletide without partaking of the family's cheer will "carry away the Christmas."

Anden Juledag, Second Christmas Day, which follows Christmas is often celebrated by country dances at the village hall, a community Christmas tree gathering or, in towns and cities, by attendance at theatres and concerts.

NYTÅRSAFTEN (New Year's Eve)

December 31

Instead of "blowing in the New Year," as was customary in the past, young people now "smash it in" by bombarding people's doors, or "let it in" by setting off fireworks. Once these noisy demonstrations were intended to frighten away powers of darkness; now noise making is just part of the New Year's Eve fun.

For months ahead boys save up worthless earthenware. On New Year's Eve they break it against the house doors of friends and neighbors. The most popular man in the town or village is he who has the greatest number of old pots and bowls smashed against his door.

According to traditional etiquette, the master of the house rushes out and tries to catch his noisy guests, who run away after the attack. They do not run too quickly, however, because those who are caught are treated with cakes, cookies or doughnuts. The young people who explode fireworks outside the door are similarly welcomed and offered holiday cheer.

In many parts of West Jutland the last night of the year is considered the time for all sorts of pranks and practical jokes. The farmer does well, therefore, to put everything under cover and bolt the barn door; otherwise, cart wheels may mysteriously find their way to the well and pitchforks to the rafters!

Just at midnight church bells peal out the passing of the year. In towns and cities bands of gay masqueraders swarm through the streets. Banquets, dances, dinners and gala parties are features of the evening's entertainment. In homes throughout the land the traditional supper includes holiday boiled cod and mustard sauce, with *aquavit* to drink. The Christmas candles are lighted again. Laughter and merriment flow as freely as aquavit for the final night of the year is a time for relaxation and fun.

3

FESTIVALS OF FRANCE

Le Jour de l'an (New Year's Day)

January 1

The first day of the year is characterized by family reunions, visiting and the exchange of presents and greeting cards The name *Jour des Étrennes,* Day of New Year's Presents, is often given to January first because of the widespread custom of gift giving.

Early in the morning children give their fathers and mothers little handmade articles and wish them *"Bonne Année."* Tradesfolk send their errand boys or girls to patrons with the season's compliments and something characteristic of their trade. The fish merchant, for example, may offer oysters, the baker a *brioche,* the butcher a chicken, the dairyman a dozen eggs, and so on. It is customary to give wine and étrennes of money to those who bring the presents. Servants and clerks generally are allowed a double month's pay as a New Year's gift. *Bonbonnières* filled with chocolates or other sweets, flowers, and all kinds of *fruits confits et marrons glacés* (preserved fruit and candied chestnuts) are the customary gifts exchanged among family and friends.

The New Year's dinner is an elaborate affair, attended by relatives from far and near. In the afternoon men call on their women friends and younger people on their elders. The streets present a festive air, with their brilliantly-lighted shop windows and crowds of eager holiday folk—laughing, exchanging greetings and hurrying to meet friends.

In the evening a dinner party usually is held at the home of the "head of the house"—the eldest member of the family. As the French "family" means *all* the relatives, whether close or several times removed, these reunions are large affairs which are greatly enjoyed by both old and young.

FRANCE

Le Jour des Rois (Day of the Kings)

On *le Jour des Rois,* or sometimes on the Eve, it is customary to give to the parish poor. In Alsace children go about from door to door, begging for eggs, bacon and cakes. Three of the youngsters represent the Three Kings by dressing in long robes and wearing gold paper crowns; a fourth carries a pole topped by a paper star. In Normandy bands of boys and girls make neighborhood rounds with lighted lanterns and empty baskets. The children sing traditional verses in which they ask the rich to share bounty with the destitute. Householders give the young visitors gifts of food and drink, money, or clothes.

In some parts of Brittany a beggar leads through the streets a horse, gaily bedecked with mistletoe and ribbon. From the saddle hang empty baskets which soon bulge with donations of food and wearing apparel.

Le Jour des Rois is celebrated with parties for both children and adults. The *galette des rois,* or cake of the Kings, traditionally brings an elaborate feast to an exciting climax. The cake, which is round and flat, often is cut in the pantry, covered with a white napkin and carried into the dining room on a small table. The *galette* always is cut into one more piece than the number of guests. The extra portion, intended for the first poor person who comes to the door, is called *la part à Dieu,* God's share. The youngest member of the party, who sometimes hides under the table, is asked to name the person for whom the piece of cake is intended. Great suspense prevails during the distribution ceremony because a bean (in some places a tiny gift or a china doll) is baked in the cake.

The person finding the token becomes king or queen for the evening. The monarch chooses a consort and together they rule the party. Whenever they drink the guests shout, *"Le roi boit! La reine boit!"* "The king drinks! The queen drinks!" The entire company similarly comments upon and imitates with mock ceremony every move the royal couple makes.

FESTIVALS OF WESTERN EUROPE

*MARDI GRAS (Shrove Tuesday)

The Tuesday preceding Ash Wednesday

Mardi Gras is the last day of Carnival, the three-day-period of boisterous hilarity preceding Lent. Festivities are especially colorful in Nice, Cannes, Menton, Grasse and other southern cities, where people go out into the streets in costume and indulge in all sorts of noisy pranks, such as parading, tooting tin horns, singing and pelting passers-by with confetti and flowers. Each town has its own *bataille de fleurs* (battle of flowers) preceding Lent. Flower-decked cars and floats drive for hours along the streets and boulevards. As friends and acquaintances pass and repass they pelt one another with missiles of flowers.

In Nice, where festivities assume more picturesque proportions than elsewhere, an enormous effigy of His Majesty King Carnival, surrounded by a train of clowns and buffoons, is formally presented with the keys of the city. King Carnival is seated on a throne from which he rules the scene. On Shrove Tuesday night, following a brief but merry reign and a torchlight procession, King Carnival is burned at the stake.

In Paris and some other cities butchers observe the Carnival with the fête of the *Boeuf Gras,* or Fat Ox. An ox decked with garlands, flowers, ribbons and festoons of green, is led through the streets in procession. The beast is followed by a triumphal cart bearing a little boy known as the "King of the Butchers." The crowd pays tribute to the small king by blowing horns and throwing confetti, flowers and sweets.

Brilliant parties, balls and other festivities mark the end of the pre-Lenten gaieties.

LE PREMIER AVRIL (April First)

April 1

Poisson d'avril, April fish, is the name French people apply to one who is fooled or mocked on April first. Confectioners' windows

34

display chocolate fish on this day and many friends anonymously send each other humorous postcards imprinted with pictures of fish.

Nobody knows the real origin of the custom. Many think it dates back to the time when France adopted the reformed calendar in 1582 and with it the change of the beginning of the New Year from March 25 to January first. People began sending fake gifts on April first (which originally culminated the New Year feast), as a joke on those who previously had received their *étrennes*, or New Year's gifts, on that day. It is thought that, since the first of April falls within the zodiacal sign of Pisces, the fishes, the term *recevoir un poisson d'avril*, to be made an April fish, or fool, came into popular usage.

*MI-CARÊME (Mid-Lent)

The fourth Sunday in Lent

In many parts of France the gloom of the Lenten season is broken by the mid-Lent festivities.

In Paris the day is celebrated by the fête of the *blanchisseuses,* or laundresses. Washerwomen from each of the various metropolitan districts select a queen. Later a "queen of queens" is chosen and she elects a king, who sits beside her as she rides through the streets on a float. Then come the district queens, each with her own brilliant retinue of courtiers and ladies-in-waiting.

In the evening the laundresses attend a colorful ball, presided over by their queen of queens.

PÂQUES (Easter)

Church bells are silent from Good Friday until Easter in token of mourning for the crucified Christ. Mothers and nurses tell the children that "the bells have flown away to Rome."

Early on Easter morning the children rush into the garden to watch the bells "fly back from Rome." As the small folk scan the sky for a glimpse of the returning bells their elders hide chocolate

---

* Stars indicate movable feasts that depend upon Easter. See Table of Easter Dates and Movable Festivals Dependent upon Easter, p. 246.

eggs, Jordan almonds, almond-paste candies and all sorts of other good things where the boys and girls can find them. "You are too late to see the bells," declare the grown-ups. "See, they have already passed this way! They have dropped sweets under your very noses."

The tradition of the Easter bells is told in an old lullaby which goes something like this:

> Do-do-ding, ding dong sleep little man,
> Do-do-ding, ding dong,
> The bells have gone to Rome.
> It is time to sleep,
> The bells have flown away.

> They have gone to Rome,
> Down there, down there, far away, you see,
> To visit the Pope, a saintly man,
> An old man, dressed in white is he.
> The bell of each church
> To him secretly speaks
> Of all the good little ones,
> And he himself *le Bon Dieu* tells
> The name of each good child.

> Do-do-ding, ding dong, sleep little man.

Easter is probably the one Sunday in the year when almost everyone goes to church. Candles blessed at the Easter service are carried home and lighted only on special festivals, for an Easter taper must last until the following *Pâques.*

It is as traditional to eat omelet for Easter morning breakfast as for everyone to wear something new. Eggs play an important part in all festivities. Children receive gifts of candy eggs and, in parts of western France, it is customary for village choir boys to go from farm to farm the day before Easter, begging for eggs for their holiday cakes. As the boys make rounds they sing threatening ditties such as this:

> Madame has hidden her hen
> So she will not have to give us anything.
> Do you know what will happen?
> Alleluja!
> Her hen will die!

FRANCE

LE PREMIER MAI (The First of May)

May 1

In many places people rise at dawn and go to the woods to search for the first *muguets,* or lilies-of-the-valley. Sprays of the pressed flowers, accompanied by messages of love and affection, are sent to distant friends as *portes-bonheurs* (charms). Street corners resound with shrill cries of *muguets* vendors, who hawk their fragrant wares and urge passers-by to purchase lilies-of-the-valley for friends. Everywhere people declare the flowers are lucky; that any wish one makes while wearing lilies-of-the-valley is bound to come true; and that it is especially good fortune to receive them from one who loves you.

LA FÊTE DE SAINT GENS (Festival of Saint Gens), in Monteux, region of Provence

Sunday following May 15

Saint Gens, patron of the fever-afflicted and intercessor in time of drought, was born in Monteux where he is said to have averted a great drought in the twelfth century. He is honored twice annually in his native Provence—first, at Monteux on the Sunday following May 15, and again, at Beaucet, the first Saturday and Sunday in September. On both occasions ceremonies for the saint are similar, consisting of processions with his image at the hermitage of Saint Gens, prayers for the sick and supplications for rain.

Saint Gens is pictured as ploughing a furrow with an ox and a wolf. Legend says the holy man retired to a desert place near Mont Ventoux, where he worked the land with a team of stout oxen. One day a wolf attacked and ate one of the oxen. Saint Gens made the wolf do penance by hitching him with the remaining animal and ploughing in the place of the devoured beast.

37

LA FÊTE DES SAINTES MARIES (Festival of the Holy Maries), in Les Saintes-Maries-de-la-Mer, region of Provence

May 24, 25

Thousands of gypsies from all over the world annually pour into the little fishing town of Les Saintes-Maries-de-la-Mer to honor Sara, their patron saint, on May 24, and Saints Marie Jacobé and Marie Salomé, on May 25.

For days before the pilgrimage gypsies from France, Italy, Spain, Portugal and many other countries travel in steady procession across the marshy Camargue. On horseback and afoot they come, in thundering motor trucks and expensive trailers, in limousines and dilapidated cars. The dark-skinned pilgrims pitch camp on the outskirts of Les Saintes and soon a noisy, humming community arises. Horses are tethered to trees, pots set boiling. Washlines sag with colorful garments. Youngsters, wrapped in gaudy comfortables, nap on trailer roofs. Groups gather about to eat or sing, to dance or play haunting melodies on harmonica or guitar. All classes of gypsies are represented, all occupations.

Regardless of widely differing economic status and social position these nomads from every land have one common interest: all are pilgrims. All come to kneel at the shrine of black-faced Sara the Egyptian,[1] founder of their race. At least once in his lifetime every gypsy hopes to pray at her shrine, to burn an enormous candle before her image, to leave an offering for her to bless.

Throughout the centuries countless legends have sprung up concerning Sara and how she became the gypsies' guardian. Possibly the best known version is that Sara was the handmaid of Marie Jacobé, sister of the Blessed Virgin, and Marie Salomé, mother of the Apostles James and John. After the Crucifixion, in the attempt to destroy Jesus' followers, the two Maries were cast adrift in a frail bark, without rudder, sails, or provisions. The holy women were accompanied by Lazarus, who was raised from the dead, his sisters

---

[1] Gypsies are popularly and erroneously believed to be Egyptians.

Martha and Mary Magdalene, Joseph of Arimathea,[2] who eventually carried the Holy Grail to Glastonbury, Maximin and others.

Legend says that Sara, the Maries' devoted servant, was left behind on the Palestinian shore. An old Provençal song tells how:

> Sara, the pious handmaid
> Weeps and wants to follow
> And serve them even to death
> Upon the raging sea.

Marie Salomé, moved by Sara's entreaties, reputedly threw her mantle on the turbulent waters. Sara caught it and was drawn to her mistress' arms. The tiny craft, guided by an angel and Sara the gypsy, miraculously reached Provence, close to the spot where Les Saintes now stands. There the two Maries, served by Sara to the end, worked and preached, while other members of the company spread out over Provence—Martha [3] to Tarascon, Maximin to the town that bears his name, the Magdalene [4] to continued penance at La Sainte Baume.

The legend many gypsies prefer is that Sara was a tribal queen of the Camargue. Miraculously learning of the Maries' arrival in their little skiff, she welcomed the holy women, was baptized by them and then led them to the temple of the sun, where her tribe had assembled. Tradition affirms that the two Maries converted the gypsies and that their pagan altar became France's first Christian shrine.

Sara, the gypsy queen, worked with the saints and helped them. At their death she buried them. Above their tomb an oratory was built and later, the twelfth century fortress church of Notre Dame de la Mer, where thousands gather today for the annual festival. Sara's bones (since she is not a canonized Christian saint) lie in the crypt close to her pagan altar, while those of the Maries—in a blue

[2] Dorothy Gladys Spicer, *Yearbook of English Festivals* (New York, The H. W. Wilson Company, 1954) "Pilgrimage to the Holy Thorn," p. 11-15.
[3] *La Fête de la Tarasque*, p. 44.
[4] *La Fête de la Madeleine*, p. 45.

ark-like reliquary painted with scenes from their lives—rest in an upper chapel, above the church choir.

On May 24, the first day of the pilgrimage, the statue of Sara is brought up from the dark crypt, where she stays throughout the year, and placed in the church before the congregation. At morning mass the ark of the Maries is slowly lowered from the upper chapel window by means of creaking, flower decorated cables. *"Vivent les Saintes Maries! Vive Sainte Sara!"* shout the frenzied gypsies. Hundreds of dark hands reach up eagerly to touch the descending reliquary. Parents hold children up to implant resounding kisses on the battered box. The old and infirm pass their hands over it "for health."

At last the casket, is settled into place on a trestle before the altar and the traditional canticles to *"Nos Saintes Marie et Jacobé"* echo sonorously through the ancient church.

After Mass the gypsies carry the image of their patron in colorful procession for the ceremony of blessing the sea. By night Saint Sara is back in the crypt, but no longer alone, because her tribespeople keep vigil with her. Hundreds of tapers burn before the image, the brow crowned with pale roses, the black painted face worn by kisses of the faithful. Each year the gypsies give Sara a new robe, which is put on over the worn garments of previous years. Beside her hangs a clothesline filled with handkerchiefs, neckties, head scarves, and socks, left by the gypsies who seek their patron's special blessing. There are photographs, also, and an offering box, bursting with gold earrings, chains, bracelets and other valuables— all left with thanks for past favors and petitions for future benefits.

On May 25, the second day of the festival, the gypsies bear the images of the two Maries from the church to the sea, just as they took out Sara on the previous day. Preceding the gypsies and the Maries, comes a group of local girls, dressed in traditional *Arlésienne* costume. The long silk dresses of gray, blue, orange, yellow and rose, have ruffled lace fichus crossed over the ample bosoms. Little embroidered ribbon caps perch like trembling butterflies on the graceful dark heads, with hair parted behind and swept up on either side. No fête in this part of France is complete without a procession of girls in these regional costumes, many of which have been handed down from mother to daughter for generations.

Following the *Arlésiennes* the gypsies proudly carry the heavy platform with the images of the Saints, standing erect in a little blue, tinsel-trimmed boat. The Maries—one in pink satin mantle, the other in blue—wear chaplets of flowers. A mounted honor escort of *gardiens,* or cowboys, riding the evil-eyed wild ponies of the Camargue and carrying the iron-tipped tridents used for prodding bulls, attend the Maries.

The Archbishop of Aix, with miter and staff and a silver arm-shaped reliquary, follows. Then come clergy with crosses and banners, and a throng of chanting gypsies and visitors. The procession is more gay than solemn, for the singing is noisy, the colors bright, and the Maries' pink and blue satin robes billow mischievously in the brisk sea breeze.

Through the long straggling village and out across the sands the procession advances. The *gardiens,* raising their tridents in salute, ride swiftly into the sea. Then the horsemen turn, forming a semicircle about the Saints as the gypsies carry them into the waves. The Archbishop, meanwhile, enters a boat decorated with multicolored pennants. Raising the silver arm so all can see, he solemnly blesses the waters which traditionally brought the Maries to these shores nineteen centuries ago.

At afternoon vespers in the church the gypsy pilgrims chant a final petition:

> Great *Saintes Maries,* we are about to leave you.
> Intercede for us before God
> So He will preserve our souls and bodies,
> So He will help us to be better.

Two swarthy men, standing in the upper chapel window pull on the creaking cables and slowly elevate the reliquary of the Maries. As on the previous day, hysterical shouts of *"Vivent les Saintes Maries! Vive Sainte Sara! Vivent les Saintes Maries! Vive Sainte*

Sara!" resound through the sanctuary. Gypsies with outstretched arms vie with each other to be last in touching the ascending casket. Finally the ark reaches the chapel window, where it remains suspended until the festival ends.

At the conclusion of religious ceremonies the congregation rapidly disperses for the horse races or bull ring. Some pilgrims, however, linger about the well in the center of the church and start lowering empty wine bottles by strings into the waters below. Centuries ago, when parishioners fled to this fortress church at sight of enemy ships, the same well enabled them to resist siege for indefinite periods. Today the waters are thought to possess miraculous curative powers. "They will cure the headache," according to one gypsy informant who was corking up his bottle, "but only," he amended, "if drawn on *le jour de fête.*"

*La Pentecôte (Pentecost) (Whitsun)
The fortieth day after Easter

All city people try to spend this two-day spring holiday in the country. Picnics, excursions and outings of all kinds are planned at this time.

*La Fête-Dieu (Corpus Christi)
The Thursday following Trinity Sunday

This great church festival, celebrated in honor of the Blessed Sacrament, is observed throughout France. Gorgeously robed priests, followed by choir and laymen, carry the Eucharist through the streets under canopies that are richly embroidered in gold.

In some towns and villages the path of the Eucharist procession is covered with a thick carpet of rose petals. Prizes are offered for the most beautifully decorated houses. Often people pin flowers to sheets which they hang against walls or the sides of buildings. One of the most picturesque aspects of the festival are the *reposoirs,* or small altars, which villagers set up out-of-doors—often at the crossroads. These shrines are covered with hand-embroidered or lace-trimmed altar cloths and decorated with candles, images, flowers, or garlands of green. Canopies of interwoven green branches give the altars the appearance of woodland chapels. The priest gives his benediction to these places of worship as he makes the village rounds.

La Veille de la Saint Jean (Saint John's Eve)

June 3

The widespread custom of lighting bonfires on the *Veille de la Saint Jean* originated with the ancient Druids who built fires at the summer solstice in honor of the sun god.

In many larger places midsummer festivities begin with a dinner at the *hôtel de ville* (town hall) for distinguished guests. Later visitors and townsfolk gather with fanfare and music about the bonfire to which everyone—from the oldest man or woman to the youngest child—has contributed fuel—a log, a stout branch, perhaps only a bundle of slender faggots or a single twig.

In many parts of Brittany the bonfire ceremony is observed with religious solemnity. In Finistère, people try to build their bonfires near chapels dedicated to Saint Jean and the priest kindles the pile at the close of vespers. After singing hymns and chanting prayers the young folk dance about the fires.

La Saint Jean is also the night of love. According to one favorite song:

> This is Saint John's,
> The beautiful day
> When lovers walk together.
> Let's go, pretty heart,
> The moon has risen!

It is usual to sing old folk songs and dance traditional rounds as the flames blaze toward the sky. As they die down young couples frequently leap over the embers. In some places the wish is made that crops will grow as high as the young people jump. In Béarn, vaulting nine times across the fire is said to ensure a prosperous year, while in Berry the act is thought to prevent illness during the next twelve months. People gather up the ashes from the Saint John's fires and strew them over the fields with prayers for a good harvest.

Customs vary from region to region. In Upper Brittany it is usual to build fires about tall poles erected on hilltops. A boy named Jean or a girl named Jeanne provides a bouquet or garland for the pole and kindles the bonfire. The young people of the village dance and sing about the great fire as it burns.

In the sheep-raising Jura district La Saint Jean is a shepherds' feast. Shepherds drive flower-crowned animals in procession and later nail the wreaths to stable doors, as a protection against the forces of evil.

LA FÊTE DE LA TARASQUE (Festival of the *Tarasque*), in Tarascon, region of Provence

Last Sunday in June

In 1469 King René instituted two colorful annual processions to commemorate Saint Martha's capture of *la Tarasque,* a voracious man-eating monster whose lair was on the wooded banks of the Rhône. The first procession occurs on the last Sunday in June (approximately Whitsuntide); the second on July 29, Saint Martha's Day. Although the processions differ widely in character, both celebrate the same event. *La fête de la Tarasque* lapsed a few years ago. It is described, nevertheless, because local groups are hoping to revive it.

Provençal tradition tells how a monster with a lion's head and dragon's tail periodically appeared, ravaging the entire countryside and feeding on both flocks and men. Tarascon's citizens lived in fear. One day sixteen of the town's armed youths went out to slay the beast. Eight returned unharmed; eight the monster grabbed and crunched to death as the victims' legs dangled from bloody jaws.

At this point the saintly Martha (sister of Lazarus and the Magdalene and one of the holy pilgrims to reach Provence with

Les Saintes Maries) set forth alone for the monster's den. The creature was noisily devouring its meal as the saint approached, armed only with holy water and a cross. She quickly sprinkled the monster with the sacred water, knotted the end of her girdle about its neck, and led it, subdued and docile into Tarascon. There the townsfolk stoned the monster to death and, impressed by their miraculous deliverance, adopted the Christian faith.

In the first procession of *la Tarasque* eight men, representing the eight devoured youths, walk inside the hideous-looking spiked body and manipulate the slashing tail and snapping jaws. Eight other men—the lucky ones who escaped—walk as guards beside the monster, which charges into the crowd and snaps furiously at spectators.

On July 29 *la Tarasque,* tamed by Saint Martha's power, trots along behind a young girl who represents the saint. She is dressed in white and leads the fearful creature leashed on her slender crimson ribbon belt.

LA FÊTE DE LA MADELEINE (Festival of the Magdalene), in Sainte Baume, region of Provence

July 22

> *À la Madeleine*
> *Les noix sont pleines,*

"on Saint Magdalene's Day the walnuts are full grown," is an old folk saying which refers to the day when young girls visit the reputed grotto of the Magdalene in the forest of Sainte Baume.

Mary Magdalene, the sister of Lazarus and Martha of Bethany, was one of the little company to set out from Palestine in a frail boat and miraculously to arrive on the shores of Provence. Legend says she wandered eastward from Les Saintes-Maries-de-la-Mer until she came to *la fôret de la Baume,* the forest of the Cave. There she resolved to do further penance for her sins. Angels took her to a grotto high in the rocks. Clothed only by her long reddish tresses, with psalm book and crucifix in hand, the Magdalene reputedly spent thirty-three years [5] living on wild roots and berries and suffering from torturing thirst. Local artists have pictured her lying alone in the cave, angels hovering above her head and wild animals coming near. Sometimes her tearful eyes look upon a vision of the Virgin. The saint's usual attributes are a staff, a skull and a jar of ointment. After long years of fasting, prayer and meditation, it was time for the Magdalene to die. Her friends, the angels, tenderly transported her to the oratory of Saint Maximin, who administered the last rites. And when the Magdalene died people said that her purified soul, in the form of a dove, flew straight to Heaven's gates.

Ever since the thirteenth century thousands of pilgrims have visited *la Sainte Baume,* the holy cave. The grotto is hewn out of the solid rock on the rugged wooded hillside. Although the favorite pilgrimage comes on July 22, the saint's reputed death day, the shrine is visited at all times of year. Formerly, a journey to the grotto was especially important to betrothed couples, who sought the saint's help and built up little piles of stones at the wayside to ensure fruitful unions. Today hundreds of young girls scramble up the rocky ascent to the grotto to pay honor to the Magdalene and implore her to furnish husbands.

LE PARDON DE SAINTE ANNE D'AURAY (Pardon of Saint Anne d'Auray), in Auray, region of Brittany

July 25, 26

Auray's famous Pardon is celebrated in honor of Saint Anne, mother of the Virgin Mary. Legend claims that Saint Anne appeared in 1623 in a vision to a peasant, Yves Nicolazie, and commanded him to interest the faithful in rebuilding her ruined chapel. The peasant reported what he had seen to the bishop, who believed him. Soon afterward, a mutilated wooden image of the saint was unearthed in a neighboring field. This event attracted worshippers from far and near, who brought offerings so the effigy might be

[5] Seven years, "twice seven years," often thirty years, are also given as the length of the wilderness sojourn.

46

enshrined. The church of Auray was built. Later it became a place of pilgrimage for pious believers from many parts of France.

Annually thousands of devout Christians fast and ascend on their knees the *scala santa,* or sacred stairway, which leads to the chapel enclosing Saint Anne's statue. Breton peasants believe that if they burn their candles at the shrine, Saint Anne will bless their homes, crops, and ships at sea.

The Pardon of Saint Anne is one of the most picturesque of all French religious festivals, since Breton peasants—both men and women—attend in the rich and beautiful costumes for which their region is famed. The procession of male pilgrims, on the second day of the Pardon, is particularly colorful. The clergy, in striking embroidered vestments, lead the group with gleaming crosses and magnificent church standards. Bands and banners, acolytes swinging censers, choir boys in feast day robes, and earnest-faced peasants carrying their village emblems—all give contrast and variety to the festival that blesses homes, crops, and ships at sea.

L'Assomption (Assumption)

August 15

This church festival commemorates the Virgin's ascent into heaven. The holiday serves as an occasion for going to the country for picnics, outings and all sorts of excursions.

La Toussaint and Le Jour des Morts (All Saints' Day and All Souls' Day)

November 1, 2

These two legal, as well as church holidays are widely observed. On *La Toussaint,* All Saints' Day, there are joyous services in memory of all the saints who are glorified. *Le Jour des Morts,* or All Souls' Day, is dedicated to prayers for the dead who are not yet glorified. During the week before, women in mourning visit the cemeteries to clean the family graves and decorate them with artificial flowers and wreaths of immortelles. On the day of the festival there are church services, followed by visits to the churchyard. Relatives gather to hold family reunions and pay honor to the dead.

In Brittany, where many folktales warn of evils likely to befall those who tamper with the bones of the dead, children delight in playing gruesome practical jokes in the cemeteries. They frighten visitors, for example, by rattling bones in empty pails, or by putting lighted candles inside skulls and setting them up in dark corners of the graveyard.

LA SAINT MARTIN (Saint Martin's Day)

November 11

Foire de la Saint Martin, "Saint Martin's fair," is the term the French gives to feasting at this season, while *mal de Saint Martin,* "Saint Martin's sickness," is what they call the upset stomachs that result from over indulgence. November 11 honors Saint Martin of Tours, fourth-century patron of the city and special guardian of vine growers, tavern keepers and beggars. Saint Martin is the presiding genius of harvest foods and festivities. He is a gay and jovial saint, popularly associated with robust autumn fare such as roast goose and the first new wine.

Saint Martin's Day, which marks the anniversary of the translation of the saint's relics, is observed with impressive ceremonies at his shrine in Tours Cathedral. Many legends about the saint have come down through the centuries. The one which associates him with beggars is possibly the best known. Once, when a soldier —for Martin was first a soldier, then a saint—he saw a naked beggar shivering at the gates of Amiens. Without hesitation the young man divided his cape with his sword, gave half the garment to the beggar and kept half for himself.

LA SAINTE CATHERINE (Saint Catherine's Day), in Paris

November 25

The *midinettes,* girls of the Parisian fashion industry who still are unmarried at twenty-five, *coiffent la Sainte Catherine*—don amusing little white paper caps called *Catherinettes*—in honor of Saint Catherine, and pay gay tribute to the patroness of old maids.

Employers give the girls the afternoon off, often allowing them to use their workrooms for celebrating the occasion with a buffet supper and dancing. The girls choose a queen who, like her followers, also wears a cap, and escort her through the streets of Paris. Often a group of girls will mischievously surround and kiss some handsome young man.

Coiffer la Sainte Catherine, "to don Saint Catherine's bonnet," is an expression used to warn girls they are likely to become spinsters.

La Sainte Barbe (Saint Barbara's Day)

December 4

In some parts of France Saint Barbara's Day marks the opening of the Christmas season. On Saint Barbara's Eve in southern France, especially in Provence, wheat grains are soaked in water, placed in dishes and set to germinate in a warm chimney corner or sunny window.

According to old folk belief, if the Saint Barbara's grain grows fast, crops will do well in the coming year. If, on the contrary, it withers and dies, crops will be ruined. The "Barbara's grain" is carefully tended by the children, who on Christmas Eve place it— a living symbol of the coming harvest—beside the *crèche,* or miniature representation of the manger scene.

La Saint Nicolas (Saint Nicholas' Day)

December 6

According to ancient French tradition the Virgin once gave Lorraine to Saint Nicholas as a reward. Consequently, the good saint became the special patron of that region, which he visits each year. Of course, Saint Nicholas does not confine his activities to Lorraine alone, for with his feast day, on December 6, children's Christmas festivities really begin.

In Lorraine, where *la Saint Nicolas* is very important, representatives of the saint, dressed in bishop's regalia, walk through the streets followed by *le Père Fouettard*, with a bundle of switches. Then comes a cart containing a salt barrel and figures of three young lads. According to legend the saint miraculously resuscitated three boys after an avaricious inn keeper murdered them and put their bodies in a keg of brine, intending to serve the flesh to hungry customers.

On Saint Nicholas' Eve children place their shoes near the fireplace and retire with a prayer that the saint will remember them.

> *Saint Nicolas, mon bon patron,*
> *Envoyez-moi quelqu'chose de bon,*

is an old French rhyme. The good things children anticipate are sweets and candies; the bad they fear, especially if they have been naughty during the year, are whippings from *le Père Fouettard*, Saint Nicholas' companion. He is a stern disciplinarian, and he remembers how children have behaved during the past twelve months. As a reminder of his watchfulness, small ribbon-tied bunches of birch twigs accompany even the gifts Saint Nicholas leaves for good boys and girls.

La Veille de Noël (Christmas Eve)

December 24

French families prepare for Christmas Eve with the *crèche*, or miniature nativity scene, which is made with small figures representing the Christ Child, Joseph and Mary, the Magi, the animals and shepherds, set against a charming background of moss, stones, and small branches. The crèche, which exists in a great variety of forms—simple in many homes and elaborate in the churches—survives from medieval times, when miracle plays were enacted from small stages set up in the street or market place.

In Provence the crèche is characterized by little gaily-colored clay figures called *santons*. These small figures represent not only the Holy Family, but all sorts of familiar village characters—the butcher, the baker, the spinner, basket maker and flute player, all of whom, like the Magi and shepherds, come to adore the Infant Jesus and present him with their simple gifts. Sometimes tricolored candles, symbols of the Trinity, light the nativity scene. Shortly before Christmas, Marseilles holds a santons fair which is attended by people from all over Provence. Here they purchase the traditional figures which are made by a score of families living between Nice and Marseilles. The molds for the santons, which depict with loving accuracy the costumes and occupations of the Provençal peasant, have been handed down in these families from father to son for approximately three hundred years.

At midnight the church bells joyously anounce the birth of Christ and the hour of Christmas Mass. In Paris cathedrals the service is magnificent, while in rural districts the ceremony is observed more simply. The beautiful church crèche, dramatically lighted with burning tapers, the singing of old provincial carols, incense, the pealing of many bells—all combine to make this service the most colorful of the year.

At Les Baux, in Provence, a celebrated Christmas Mass called the *Fête des Bergers,* Festival of the Shepherds, is annually performed. Shepherds and shepherdesses, dressed in regional costume, make symbolic offering of a new-born lamb to the Christ Child on the anniversary of his birth.

The shepherds place a lamb in a small two-wheeled wagon, which is drawn by a ram and elaborately decorated with flowers, lighted candles, and tinkling bells. The spokes of the wheels are wound with flowers, while the cart's bent-twig canopy is gay as a Christmas tree with lighted tapers, garlands, and pretty ornaments. The lamb is drawn about the church in joyous procession. The shepherds, carrying burning candles and offerings of fruit, sing ancient Provençal carols to the traditional accompaniment of flute and drum. The procession stops at the altar where a young shepherd lifts up the lamb and presents it to the officiating priest. Later shepherds and shepherdesses take communion.

Similar shepherds' Masses are held elsewhere in Provence, one of the most beautiful being at the Abbaye de Saint-Michel de Frigolet, not far from Les Baux.

After attending Midnight Mass it is customary throughout France to hold family parties at which the *réveillon,* or late supper is served. Traditional foods for this repast vary from place to place. In Paris and the Ile-de-France, for example, there are oysters, *pâté de foie gras,* blood sausage, pancakes, many varieties of sweets and white wine. The following day the newspapers always report the number of kilometers of blood sausage people have eaten at réveillon!

Goose is served in many areas. In Provence people say that the reason for eating this favorite food is that the goose welcomed the Wise Men with its cackling as they approached the Christ Child's stable. Snails and mullets are as traditional to the Provençal réveillon as oysters to the Parisian. Pike, celery, and chard are essential in the main course, which custom dictates should be followed by eleven different desserts. These include such delicacies as roast chestnuts, hazelnuts, figs, dates, raisins, apples, pears and nougat.

After supper the grandfather or oldest member of the household, surrounded by the family and farm servants, always used to pour a little wine on the Yule log while uttering a traditional toast:

> Be happy! Be happy!
> May *le bon Dieu* make us happy.
> Even though we are gone next year,
> Let us be happy today!

Among the Bretons buckwheat cakes and sour cream are important Christmas Eve fare, while roasted chestnuts with milk are eaten in some parts of Auvergne. In other places the chestnuts must always be served with wine. Pancakes are traditional to Franche-Comté, turkey and chestnuts to Burgundy. In other words, each region boasts its own réveillon specialty, prepared and served in its own special way.

FRANCE

On Christmas Eve children carefully set out their shoes near the fireplace since they believe that *le Père Noël,* Father Christmas, or, in Alsace, *le petit Jésus,* will stop before dawn and fill them with nuts and sweets, sometimes even with coveted toys.

In some places carol singers with lighted tapers and a small crèche, go from house to house singing old carols of Jesus' birth and receiving small money gifts in return. In southern France, there are charming puppet shows of the Christmas story, as well as village processions representing Joseph, with Mary and the Child on a donkey. A chorus accompanies the little group and sings songs of the Holy Birth.

NOËL (Christmas)

December 25

Christmas is a time for family dinners, reunions and parties, rather than merrymaking and exchanging gifts. Oysters, roast goose, or turkey with chestnut and pork filling, *bombe glacée,* and an abundance of fine wine are a few of the delicacies which characterize the Christmas feast in many city homes.

4

FESTIVALS OF GERMANY

NEUJAHR (New Year's Day)

January 1

The first day of the year must be lived as you would live during the next twelve months, according to German folk tradition; for New Year's Day is the time of new beginnings. The housewife takes care that her home is in order. Everyone puts on at least one new garment. People try not to spend money, but jingle coins in their pockets "for luck." No unpleasant tasks are undertaken. Of course, both doctor and chemist are avoided. Everybody settles down to having a good time with family, friends, and neighbors.

At the beginning of the year people universally exchange greeting cards, but the giving of gifts is confined largely to money remembrances for the postman, janitor, cleaning woman and others who have served the family faithfully during the year.

DREIKÖNIGSFEST (Festival of the Three Kings)

January 6

The Festival of the Three Kings marks the end of the Yuletide season. On this day the Christmas tree is lighted for the last time.

Boys and men dressed as the Three Kings wander about towns and villages of the Kinzig River area and elsewhere, singing old folk songs of the Wise Men and begging for alms. The Kings wear gold paper crowns and carry large cardboard stars. One of their favorite songs says that:

> The Three Holy Kings
> Carrying their star
> Like to eat and drink;
> But they don't like to pay
> For the goodies they get!

In many parts of the country, particularly in western and southern Germany, salt and chalk are consecrated in church on this day. The salt is given the animals to lick, while the Three Kings' traditional

54

initials, C.M.B., for Caspar (also, Gaspar, Kaspar), Melchior, Balthasar (or. Balthazar), are chalked above house and stable doors. This is thought to keep evil from entering and harming man or beast. In the Bavarian Forest peasants write above the lintel the legend, "Caspar, Melchior and Balthasar, protect us this day from all danger of fire and flood."

Epiphany parties are frequent, with the traditional cake as a special feature of the celebration. A bean, or sometimes a coin, is hidden in the cake. Whoever finds the symbol in his portion becomes king of the feast.

In Upper Bavaria peasants wearing horrible-looking wooden masks go about cracking long whips and symbolically driving out Frau Perchta (also known as Berchta, or Bertha), nature goddess of ancient Germanic mythology and custodian of the dead. According to folk belief the mysterious witch wanders about and harms mortals on the Twelve Days between Christmas and Epiphany. On *Perchtennacht*, or Epiphany, Perchta and her cohorts, symbolizing powers of both good and evil, are thought to fructify the fields and to frighten naughty children.

The Perchta masks which are handed down from one generation to another, are terrifying in their fantastic ugliness. Some have protruding fangs for teeth, bulging eyes, sinister wrinkles and hairy faces. Those who wear the masks dress in slovenly kerchiefs and dirty aprons, and march through the streets with brooms, chains, and hatchets, fully looking the part of the relentless furies they are intended to represent.

*Fastnacht (Shrove Tuesday)

The Tuesday preceding Ash Wednesday

Fastnacht, as Shrove Tuesday is called, is celebrated throughout Germany with masquerades, carnival processions and ceremonials that vary in character according to locality and folk custom. In the Rhine district where many of the carnivals originate in religious rites, there is strict adherence to the sacred pattern. In Mainz, on the other hand, companies of guards pitch camp along city thoroughfares—

especially in the cathedral area—and form a bodyguard to Prince Carnival. In Cologne, Prince Carnival presides over a Fool's Court. He is surrounded by councilors wearing high peaked hats and the badge of the Order of Fools. The Sparks, as Prince Carnival's bodyguard is called, wear the uniforms of old Cologne's·City Guards and carry wooden muskets over their shoulders.

In Munich Shrovetide observances are marked by much of the pageantry and splendor of the Middle Ages. Actors dressed in court costumes of former days perform ancient guild dances, while historical floats and ceremonies portray much of the picturesqueness of Munich's past.

Eastern Saxony boasts some of the most charming carnival celebrations of all Germany. In this region a symbolic battle is fought between representatives of Winter and Spring. Winter always is vanquished and Spring welcomed with laughter, merrymaking, and song. In some localities this kind of carnival celebration occurs somewhat later than Fastnacht. The character of the spring drama varies from district to district. In Eisenach, for example, where the battle of the seasons has been observed since 1286, "Summer is won" by burning Winter in effigy after his defeat by Dame Sun.

People of Baden-Württemberg call Fastnacht *"Fastnet"* in local dialect. For over five hundred years Rottweil on the Neckar has celebrated a Fastnet parade with all kinds of traditional figures such as three huge cocks, known respectively as *Guller, Federhannes,* or Feathery John, and *Biss,* or Bite. Another feature of the parade are groups of Fools, wearing costumes decorated with ball-shaped bells, who dance about and recite verses of "fools' wisdom" to the crowd.

*KOPENFAHRT (Kope Procession), in Lüneburg, State of Lower
    Saxony

Shrove Tuesday

The Kope Festival, observed at Carnival time by Lüneburg's salt miners, dates back to the Middle Ages. According to a chronicle of

---

* Stars indicate movable feasts that depend upon Easter. See Table of Easter Dates and Movable Festivals Dependent upon Easter, p. 246.

1471, an early duke of Lüneburg granted journeymen salters—the sons of master salters—the privilege of holding the annual celebration which has been observed for almost five hundred years.

The *Kope,* a stone-filled wooden barrel, originally was dragged through the town's narrow byways by strong horses which were mounted by *Salzjunker,* or young journeymen salters. Horses and riders were followed by festively-garbed local officials such as aldermen, councilors, and scribes. Then came a long line of salt mine laborers, townsfolk, and trumpeters. Through the centuries the *Kopenfahrt,* or Kope procession, has become a folk, rather than a historical, event. Today, as in the beginning, the trumpeters still blast loudly on their instruments in an attempt to unnerve the spirited horses. Great skill is therefore required on the riders' part in order to guide the animals safely through the streets and bring them to the mouth of the salt mine. There the Kope is ceremoniously dumped on a huge pile of wood and set on fire.

Following the bonfire the procession returns to the market place and with solemn rites enacts the ceremony of initiation of the Salzjunker into the Guild of Master Salters. For a thousand years Lüneburg, famed for its salt-mining industry—the source of the town's prosperity—has paid high tribute to this important Guild. Following initiation ceremonies there is a great banquet.

According to some authorities the Kopenfährt originated in pagan, rather than medieval times. Consequently the flames of the great bonfire are thought to symbolize the Sun God's triumph over forces of darkness, while the rolling of the Kope through the streets represents the relentless passage of time. Quite aside from such speculation, the ancient festival was revived in 1950 following a period of interruption, and once more the event is a characteristic feature of the old salt town's annual carnival merrymaking.

*Brauteln (Wooing a Bride), in Sigmaringen, State of Baden-Württemberg

Shrove Tuesday

Brauteln is the name Sigmaringen gives to a Carnival custom which started in 1648, at the close of the Thirty Years' War. In that year bachelors who dared to become engaged were honored with a peculiar ceremony. According to local tradition Sigmaringen's young men were hesitant about assuming the responsibilities of marriage and family life, due to widespread hunger and pestilence following in the wake of the war. Accordingly, the town's population diminished so rapidly that the *Schultheiss,* or Mayor, decided to take drastic steps.

Finally the Schultheiss conceived a unique plan: He would honor the first young man who was courageous enough to become engaged with the *Brauteln,* or "Wooing a Bride" ceremony. This meant that the bachelor would be carried at the head of a brilliant procession about the pump in the market square. No pains would be spared to make the event a memorable affair. The man would be accorded so much prominence that other bachelors would be encouraged to take wives.

The mayor's plan must have worked since the ceremony still continues. Annually on Shrove Tuesday every man is *brautelt* who has married within the last twelve months, has moved to town for the first time, or celebrated his twenty-fifth or fiftieth wedding anniversary.

The yearly two-day carnival ceremony is impressive. Heralds dressed in three-cornered hats, black breeches, and white shirts and stockings, go about the town with the Sigmaringen standard. Accompanied by drummers and pipers, the heralds stop at the house of each eligible bachelor on their list and invite him to be brautelt, by dancing before the door. Woe to the man who refuses to participate in the ceremony, for he must pay a ransom!

To the accompaniment of a lively tune the heralds briskly carry eligible candidates about the town pump, while their victims treat the jubilant spectators with apples, pretzels, and sausages.

> And thus it always will be
> As long as laughing and kissing go on;
> As long as the Danube flows;
> As long as the girl gets her man,

according to one old *brautel* song.

Yet another Sigmaringen song has come down through the centuries. The words, which doubtless were applicable in 1648 when husbands were scarce, are hardly appropriate for the modern young woman. The song is jolly, however, and therefore worth repeating:

> Let's live long and be merry.
> Semmering [1] girls set caps for the lads.
> But all, alas, is useless!
> Not a single girl gets a sweetheart!

*PALMSONNTAG (Palm Sunday)

The Sunday before Easter

In most parts of Germany Easter festivities start on Palm Sunday. Customs vary widely from place to place, but everywhere they symbolize resurgence of life and joy in the budding spring.

In the Black Forest, for example, people decorate tall poles with pussy-willows, heart or cross motifs, and long multicolored ribbon streamers. These gay Eastertide emblems are set up before village houses and later carried in procession to church, where they are consecrated by the priest.

In Bavaria on the other hand, the poles are transformed into glittering trees, with branches cut from twelve different kinds of wood. The branches are bent and fastened to the poles in semicircular shape, then gaudily decorated with colored glass beads. Villagers carry the trees in joyous procession to the church. After the blessing the peasants set up the trees in the farm fields to ensure fertility to crops, protection from hail and drought, and preservation from all other disasters.

Most unusual of all Palm Sunday customs, perhaps, is the *Palm Esel,* or wooden Palm Donkey, symbolic of the animal upon which Jesus entered Jerusalem two thousand years ago. The Palm Donkey, survival of a rare folk custom, is reverently carried to the village church. Devout parishioners believe that by touching the wooden

---

[1] Semmering in local dialect means Sigmaringen.

59

image they, too, may share the same mystic blessing which people doubtless thought emanated from the humble ass when it carried the King of Israel.

*GRÜNDONNERSTAG (Green Thursday) (Holy, or Maundy Thursday)

The Thursday preceding Easter

Anyone refusing to eat green salad on *Gründonnerstag,* or Green Thursday, is in danger of "becoming a donkey," according to old Saxon tradition. To be on the safe side children eat an entire green vegetable dinner on this day. Often the meal is supplemented by a special dish prepared from cottage cheese.

Many interesting egg superstitions are associated with the Thursday preceding Easter. One saying is that an *Antlassei,* or Holy Thursday egg, stays fresh for the entire year. Another claim is that such an egg, when ploughed into the first furrow, ensures a plentiful harvest. It is also believed that an Antlassei is just the thing to prevent ruptures. And to keep one on hand in the house will safeguard the premises from lightning during the next twelve months.

*KARSAMSTAG (Holy Saturday), in South Germany, Hesse, and the Rhineland; KARSONNABEND, in Berlin and North Germany

The Saturday preceding Easter

On Holy Saturday housewives dressed in their most elaborate peasant costumes carry the Easter foods to church for consecration by the parish priest. It is customary for each woman to line a large basket with snowy linen and decorate it with gay ribbon streamers. She then fills the basket with a variety of Easter foods—the long braided loaf of holiday bread, the colored eggs, a portion of bacon or ham and, most important of all, butter molded into the form of a lamb—the Lamb of God—with a ribbon tied around the neck and a banner on a long stick inserted into the flank.

After the food has been blessed housewives take their baskets home and start preparing the feast day dinner.

GERMANY

*OSTERN (Easter)

Eastertide customs, many of which originated in early Germanic pagan rites, are largely concerned with eggs, fire, and water.

Eggs, the ancient heathen fertility symbol and the early Christian emblem of the Resurrection, inspire all kinds of games and customs for both children and adults. Modern children generally accept the idea that the Easter Hare brings their holiday eggs and hides them in many out-of-the-way nooks and corners. In the past the stork, the fox and the cuckoo, rather than the Hare, were credited with dispensing eggs.

In many places, especially in Swabian villages, pretty little "rabbit gardens" are made ready for the Hare. In the Deister mountains, near Hannover, he finds carefully prepared nests of moss awaiting his visit. Of course, the Hare prefers to hide his eggs in gardens and out-of-door nooks; but in stormy weather he manages, somehow, to find curious indoor places for boys and girls to search for his offerings. The Hare brings not only dyed hens' eggs of purple, green, and yellow; sometimes there are toothsome chocolate eggs with wonderful little pictures inside, which may be viewed through openings in one end. Sometimes the Easter visitor even leaves elaborate little pink or blue satin eggs, containing exciting presents of sweets, perfume or tiny lace trimmed handkerchiefs.

Eggs are not only presented to friends but are important in all the Easter games. Friends give each other beautifully hand-painted eggs which are made according to distinctive traditional designs. The exquisite patterns are passed down from one generation to another in certain towns and villages. Often a special legend or verse accompanies the decoration. In many places, on the other hand, it is customary for village girls to present their suitors with red eggs. Should the girls fail to have their gifts ready, however, the boys spank them with canes!

Eggs play an important role in the Easter sports. In northwestern Germany, for example, peasants have formal contests to see who can devour the greatest number of eggs. Egg duels, known as *Eier-Spacken,* or *Eier-Doppen* always are immensely popular. Contestants face each other, holding hard boiled eggs by the round ends. Each stabs his adversary's egg with the pointed end. The player who succeeds in cracking the greatest number of his opponent's eggs wins, and receives all the damaged eggs as prize.

Eierlesen, or egg gathering, and *Eierschieben,* or egg rolling, are two of the season's most popular sports. The egg gathering contests, particularly, require great agility and skill. Eggs are placed at intervals along a racing track. Running down the track at a starting signal, the boys try to see who can gather up the most eggs in the allotted time. The game is even more exciting when, as in the Black Forest and some other areas, contestants ride down the line on horseback or bicycles.

In Germany as in the United States, egg rolling contests are confined chiefly to children. This sport usually comes on Easter Monday. Boys and girls play their game on a hillside. The child whose egg rolls the greatest distance wins. In some villages the girls play *Caningeln,* a game in which an egg is rolled through a ring. This feat requires great agility and skill.

By far the most ancient and dramatic of all German Easter customs are the bonfires and fiery wheels which are common to sections of the Harz, the Rhineland, Oldenburg and Westphalia.

The fires, built on mountain tops and ridges, are survivals of pagan sacrificial rites, while the flaming wheels, symbolic of the sun, are reminiscent of early Germanic fire worship. In some neighborhoods young people go about singing traditional rhymes and asking for contributions of fuel or money for the Easter fires. Generally these fires take the form of huge piles of tar-soaked barrel staves, tree limbs and roots.

In the vicinity of Luegde, a Westphalian village, the usual bonfire consists of huge seven-foot oak wheels with straw-packed spokes. Each family in the village contributes straw to the gigantic wheels which weigh approximately eight hundred pounds. The wheels, poised at the top of a hill, are set afire. Thousands of spectators gathered about Easter bonfires on adjoining hills watch and cheer as the tremendous wheels start on their course down the hillside into the valley below. Each time a wheel reaches the bottom of the hill ablaze, a shout of joy rises from the breathless villagers who regard this as portending special blessing to the land and a rich harvest to the farmer.

Water no less than fire is important in Easter rites, especially among young girls of the Harz, Thuringia, and many other regions. The girls, rising at dawn stealthily go out to the river bank and dip up "Easter water." If they do not utter a single word and then bathe in the water, they will be rewarded with beauty throughout the year. For those who cannot go to the river bank there is, of course, the Easter morning dew which, when used for bathing the face, is sure to make it look fresh and charming.

Spring flowers and grasses are important in Easter ceremonies, especially in the Black Forest. There blossoms and leaves are fashioned into symbolic crosses and hearts and taken to church for blessing. The Easter sunrise is considered important, too; for if the sun dances and you can see it, you will be blessed with good luck throughout the year.

Easter brings special joys to shop and factory workers who don knapsacks and go out into the country; and to young and old of towns and villages, who put on new spring finery and join the ranks of Sunday afternoon participants in the traditional Easter parades.

GEORGIRITT (Saint George's Parade), in Traunstein, Upper Bavaria
April 23

Saint George, the great soldier saint of the Middle Ages who reputedly was martyred on April 23 about the year 300, is honored annually at Traunstein and some other Bavarian villages by the *Georgiritt,* or Saint George's Parade. For George, who represented the flower of knighthood, became protector of horses and their riders. On his day the parish priest blesses both beasts and men and sprinkles them with holy water.

According to Jacobus de Voragine, thirteenth-century compiler of *The Golden Legend,* Saint George arrived at Lybia's pagan city of Sylene just as a dragon which demanded human tribute was terrifying the entire countryside. Saint George, finding Sylene's citizens in deepest mourning, soon discovered that it was the turn of the King's daughter to be sacrificed to the demon's appetite. Dressed in wedding garments of purest white, the young girl calmly sat down by a stagnant pool outside the city. Fortunately the story had a happy ending. Saint George came upon the Princess and awaited the monster's arrival at her side. At last the charging dragon appeared. Saint George stuck his sword down the fiery throat. The Princess then tethered the beast to her girdle and triumphantly led him into Sylene. There the saint promptly slew the dragon—once Sylene's fifteen thousand citizens had agreed to be baptized into the Christian faith.

Throughout the centuries the story of Saint George has symbolized the victory of good over evil. Many claim that the legend, which finds its counterpart in the Siegfried cycle and other mythological stories, represents renewal of life in early spring and the conquest of Summer over Winter.

Today the ancient victory of the saint on horseback is commemorated when Traunstein farmers mount their gaily garlanded horses and ride them across the fields and three times around the parish church. After receiving the priest's blessing on the horses, as well as other farm animals, and on crops and gardens, the procession, accompanied by drums and trumpets, turns toward the village. The festival finally ends with ritualistic sword dances which, like the Saint George legend, have come down from medieval to modern times.

*HIMMELFAHRTSTAG or HIMMELFAHRT (Ascension Day)
The fortieth day after Easter

Many picturesque local customs mark the celebration of Ascension Day which is the holiday when everyone tries to get into the country for picnics and outdoor festivities. In the villages of Fienstedt, Gödewitz, Salzmünde, Zörnitz, Gorsleben, and Krimpe, in the Mansfeld district of the State of Saxony-Anhalt, the drinking of "Ascension beer" is traditional to the day.

According to thirteenth-century documents of these hamlets, villagers are commanded to drink beer on this day in memory of the Countess Elizabeth; for it was she, in olden times, who relieved the inhabitants of the payment of tithes.

Himmelfahrtstag (which always falls on a Thursday) is the accepted time for men to get together with other men on excursions to the country. According to one informant, this custom started in Berlin. In the nineteenth century the male merrymakers hired a horse-drawn *Kremser,* or charabanc, to take them out of town. Later, buses, trucks, motor launches, and little steamers—all decorated with festive streamers, garlands, and pennants—were chartered for the men's day of freedom. Often clubs hike part of the way to some point of scenic interest.

Hearty refreshments of food, beer, and wine are features of the excursions; and even if hubands return home at night a little the worse for wear, wives are not expected to complain.

*PFINGSTEN (Pentecost or Whitsun)
The fiftieth day after Easter

Pentecost, even more than Ascension Day, is a great spring holiday which everyone tries to spend in the country. In both urban and rural communities houses and doorways are decorated with birch branches in honor of spring. Characteristic *Pfingsten* ceremonies and customs take place in many different parts of the country.

Near Schramberg in the Black Forest, for example, shepherds assemble on the Fohrenbühl Hill to do a brisk business in buying and selling cowbells. Bells of varying sizes and tones are tried out, both singly and together, for every shepherd wants to acquire a harmonious set of bells.

Once the day's business is transacted, the shepherds choose partners and dance the *Hammeltanz,* a traditional country dance which is performed around a sheep. The dancers hand a staff back and forth between them. Suddenly a bell rings. The shepherd who happens to be holding the staff at the moment receives the sheep as prize.

In parts of the Harz Mountains, noted for the breeding of song birds, members of the local *Finkenklubs,* or Finch Clubs, enter their birds in singing contests. The winning bird's cage is decorated with flowers. Later in the day the villagers assemble to sing the old folk songs of the district.

A Pentecost Bride and Bridegroom are features of the celebration at Kötzting, in Franconia, which is noted for the colorful procession of some two hundred horsemen, who perform the annual *Pfingstritt,* or Pentecostal Ride. The horsemen, led by the priests carrying church banners and crosses, make a pilgrimage to the Steinbühl church in the Zeller valley.

Deidesheim in the Rhenish Palatinate, is famed for its annual auction of a buck goat at Pentecost. This custom dates back to the early fifteenth century. According to tradition Kaiser Rupprecht commanded, in 1404, that the city of Lambrecht should each year provide a buck as tribute for use of the Deidesheim forest and pasture lands. The ancient custom has been observed for over five hundred years.

*Der Meistertrunk (The Master Draught), in Rothenburg-ob-der-Tauber, State of Bavaria

Whitsuntide

Each Whitsuntide the ancient city of Rothenburg honors the memory of Georg Nusch, the man who, in 1631, took one of the most famous drinks in history and so saved the town's councilmen from death and her inhabitants from humiliation. The celebration takes the form of a historical pageant in which over a thousand of Rothenburg's citizens reenact, in colorful period costume, the drama of the siege of their city in the Thirty Years' War.

According to legend General Tilly's victorious army stood within Rothenburg's walls and declared that all members of the town council were to be hanged. Moved at last by the entreaties of the councilmen's wives and daughters, the enemy general finally changed the sentence and declared that only four councilmen, chosen by lot, would be put to death.

The whole history of Rothenburg might have been changed had not the *Pokal,* the huge state beaker, which was filled to the brim with the town's best wine, been brought in at this moment. The drinking vessel, which held three quarts, was quaffed again and again by Tilly and his aides, who passed it from hand to hand around the table. Some of the liquid still remained, even after repeated draughts.

Then Tilly suddenly had an idea: If there was a Rothenburg man, he declared, who could drink the contents of the goblet at a single draught, and who would be willing to do so, knowing that the wine was poisoned, that man could save the council members from hanging!

A deep hush fell over the room. Finally the silence was broken by Georg Nusch, an ex-burgomaster, who volunteered to accept the challenge.

The story goes that Georg Nusch, in the presence of the amazed General Tilly and his companions as well as his fellow Rothen-burgers, drained the three-quart Pokal and then fainted. According to recently discovered documents, the wine was not really poisoned; but the brave Nusch, willing to sacrifice his life for the councilmen, believed that it was.

It was the ex-burgomaster's heroic exploit which saved four men from hanging and Rothenburg from occupation. The historic event, which now has become almost a folk legend, is reenacted each Whitsuntide, and once or twice during the summer, in the ancient town of Rothenburg.

*Fronleichnams-Fest (Corpus Christi Day)
The Thursday following Trinity Sunday

Corpus Christi Day is celebrated throughout Catholic Germany with picturesque processions through streets that are charmingly decorated with flowers and garlands of green. Crucifixes and pictures of Christ are prominently displayed from window ledges and the steps of cottages and village fountains. In many places people display bright hangings and spread carpets before their houses in honor of the Sacrament and the large crucifix that are carried through the parish. One of the most beautiful features of the processions is the group of children, dressed in white with flower chaplets on their heads and nosegays of fragrant blossoms in their hands. Girls and women in magnificent regional costume add further distinction to the joyous event.

Probably the most dramatic of all Corpus Christi processions are those of Lakes Staffelsee and Chiemsee, in Upper Bavaria, which take place on the water, rather than in the streets.

Boats adorned with flowers and garlands and carrying church banners and holy symbols, glide across the lakes and are reflected in the crystal clear waters. Devout worshippers following in other boats chant liturgies which fill the still air with music and echo solemnly across the lakes.

SOMMERSONNENWENDE (Summer Solstice)

June 23

Bands of young people march singing to hills and open places to build enormous bonfires in honor of the summer solstice. First comes a picnic supper, which is eaten in the early summer twilight. Then the *Johannisfeuer,* or Saint John's fire, is lighted. Boys and girls dance and sing old folk ballads about the huge bonfire. The more hardy lads leap through the flames, while young lovers join hands and try to jump over the fire together. If they succeed, they never will be parted, according to current folk belief.

LINDENFEST (Linden Tree Festival), in Geisenheim, region of the Rhineland)

Three day festival, second weekend in July

Geisenheim boasts a six-hundred-year-old linden tree which is the center of the annual celebration for sampling new wine. Geisenheim is the oldest town in Rheingau County which, for over a thousand years, has been renowned for flourishing vineyards and precious wines.

GERMANY

During three days of festivities the ancient linden is illumined and folk dances in costume are held beneath its spreading branches. The town fairly bursts with laughter and merrymaking, since visitors from all over the world come to taste Geisenheim's wine and participate in her annual orgy of feasting, visiting the vineyards and making pilgrimages to Marienthal, a picturesque Franciscan shrine, which is hidden in a nearby wooded valley.

High above the sounds of festivity and merrymaking the chimes of the old Rheingau Cathedral chime out melodiously:

> What bells are those, that ring so slow,
> So mellow, musical, and low?
> They are the bells of Geisenheim,
> That with their melancholy chime
> Ring out the curfew of the sun.
> —LONGFELLOW. *Christus.* Part Two. VI

SCHÄFERLAUF (Shepherds' Race), in Markgröningen, region of
   Swabia
   Saint Bartholomew-tide, about August 23, 24, 25

Markgröningen and other Swabian towns honor Saint Bartholomew, patron of herdsmen, with a three-day festival which includes a barefoot Shepherd's Race.

The celebration begins with a church service, which is followed by a colorful procession through the town, a welcome to guests and a program of sports and contests. Chief among the latter is the race which barefoot shepherds and shepherdesses run in pairs across the stubble fields.

The victors are honored by a shepherds' dance, a water carriers' race and other events. These features are followed by a historical play known as *Faithful Bartel.* Period costumes, processions, pageants and general merrymaking all are features of the celebration.

Later in the day toasts are drunk to the winners in the season's first new wine, and both shepherds and shepherdesses are entertained by a sumptuous rural feast.

69

PFERDEWEIHE (Blessing of Horses), in St. Märgen, region of the
Black Forest

Day of the Nativity of the Virgin, September 8

On the Day of the Nativity of the Virgin, Black Forest farmers
and their wives bring their horses to St. Märgen to receive the priest's
benediction. St. Märgen, long known as the center of a famous horse
breeding area, is especially noted for the sturdy horses which work
the neighboring farms.

The horses, which are brought to town from outlying hamlets,
are festively decked with well-polished traditional brasses. Nosegays
adorn the harnesses while ribbon streamers, interwoven in manes
and tails, flutter gaily as the horses trot. Both men and women,
dressed in picturesque costumes of the Black Forest valley, add
brilliant splashes of color to the handsome procession of horses.

ALMABTRIEB (Return from Mountain Pasture), in the German Alps

Some time in September

The day that the flower-decked cattle are driven down from the
mountains to winter in their valley homes is the occasion for merrymaking and rejoicing throughout the German Alps. All summer
long the animals, under the watchful eye of rosy-cheeked *Sennerinnen,* or herd-girls, have roamed at large and grazed in lush mountain
pastures.

Now the cattle are sleek and fat. There is a frosty nip in the
September air. It is high time to take the animals back to winter
shelter. The entire village turns out to celebrate the homecoming
and to welcome both girls and beasts; for as the animals prosper,
so thrives the farm. The village band is on hand to greet the picturesque procession. There are, also, the priest, the school master,
the farmer and his wife and, of course, the herd girl's sweetheart,
family, and friends. Last, but by no means least, there is a host of
village children dressed in gay regional costumes.

The air throbs with suppressed excitement, for long before the
slow moving animals swing into sight, the rhythmic clanging of deep-
toned bells echoes melodiously from the distant mountain passes.

Almabtrieb is indeed a gala event. The adornment of the cattle, like the costume of the herd-girl, differs considerably from place to place, but always is picturesque. In the Berchtesgaden area, for example, around the beautiful Alpine lake known as Königssee, the herd leader wears a distinctive traditional head-dress which is a most elaborate creation. It resembles a two-tiered crown, which the herd-girl's clever fingers fashion from thinly-shaved colored wood. The shavings are woven into stars, bows, or other intricate designs and fastened to the lower tier, while the upper is surmounted by a small, gaily decorated fir, which looks like a miniature Christmas tree.

Skillfully, the Sennerinnen drive the cattle down from their Watzmann Mountain summer quarters, making sure to guide them safely along rocky paths and treacherous ledges. The final stage of the journey comes when their charges reach Königssee at the foot of the mountain, and broad-bottomed flower-decked boats ferry them across the lake. A triumphant shout rises from the impatient reception committee waiting on the opposite shore.

Once the cattle are safely driven to winter shelter the real festivities begin. Each farm couple prepares a sumptuous welcome home supper, which is followed by music, dancing, and singing lasting far into the crisp autumn night.

TURA MICHELE MARKT (Tura Michele Fair) in Augsburg, state of Bavaria

September 29

On September 29, Saint Michael's Day, the city of Augsburg holds an annual autumn fair to which hundreds of peasants from far and near come for trade and pleasure. Chief among the day's attractions is the hourly appearance of figures representing the Archangel and the Devil. The figures are built in the foundation of Perlach Turm, or Tower, called *Tura* in local dialect. This slender structure, which rises to a height of two-hundred-and-twenty-five-feet and stands next to the Peter's Kirche, north of the Rathaus, originally was a watch tower. In 1615 the watch tower was heightened and converted into a belfry.

Almost a hundred years earlier the group depicting the saint and the devil had been installed in the tower's understructure. Annually on his feast day the archangel's armor-clad figure, holding a pointed spear, appeared whenever the tower bell struck, and stabbed at the devil writhing at his feet.

During World War II the historic figures—the delight of generations of fair-goers—were destroyed. Since then a new group has been made and installed. Today, as for over four centuries, spectators continue to gather about the Tura and to watch breathlessly the symbolic drama of Michael, head of the Church Triumphant, dealing death blows to the dragon which brings evil and destruction to the world of men.

MÜNCHENER OKTOBERFEST (Munich October Festival), in Munich, state of Bavaria

Usually the third Sunday in September; when there are five Sundays in the month, from the fourth Sunday in September to the first Sunday in October

In Munich the *Oktoberfest* celebrates the annual season of drinking huge quantities of new *Münchener* beer, feasting on *Steckerlfisch*, or stick-fried fish, tasty sausages of all sizes and shapes, plump chickens and whole oxen, spit-roasted over pan fires.

The Oktoberfest, with its drinking, feasting, and general jollification, is the anniversary of the marriage of King Ludwig I and his bride, Theresa, on October 17, 1810. The Theresienwiese, or Theresa Meadow, where festivities are held, was named in honor of Ludwig's queen. Today hundreds of Bavarian peasants crowd into this huge area to carry on the tradition of merrymaking on a royal scale.

The festival opens as the burgomaster taps the first keg of beer. The beer, which is drawn from barrels, is served by buxom *Fräuleins* in native costume and is drunk from enormous steins.

Powerful brewery horses decorated with gleaming brasses and colored ribbon streamers, clatter noisily through the narrow streets, dragging heavily-loaded beer trucks. Festivity is in the air. Everywhere one sees bright costumes. and hears folk singing and the tireless rhythm of dancing feet.

Munich's Oktoberfest, which annually is attended by millions of visitors from Germany and foreign countries, is noted for all kinds of amusements besides eating and drinking, although food consumption is an important part of the annual celebration. Merchandise is bought and sold from cleverly-decorated booths which feature household articles, clothing, foodstuffs, and sweets. Burly farmers enjoy an agricultural show, while carnival features such as merry-go-rounds, side shows, and sports events, furnish entertainment for the general public. In addition to historical pageants and a magnificent parade which shows costumes from all parts of the country, there is the traditional *Schäfflertanz,* or Coopers' Dance. The dance is a five-hundred-year-old custom. It is performed every seven years during carnival season in Munich, a city in which beer coopers have always been much respected. Twenty-five coopers, in colorful costume and the leather aprons of their trade, execute the steps of the dance, slowly swinging hoops of fir branches and beating time with their tools on barrels. The dance was last performed at the Oktoberfest in 1956.

GRENZUMGANG (Boundary Walk), in Springe Deister, Lower Saxony

1961, and every ten years thereafter

Springe Deister observes its Boundary Walk once every decade. The celebration was revived in 1951, following a twenty-three-year lapse.

Boundary Walk festivals, held in many German towns, differ from place to place according to local tradition. The custom dates back to the Middle Ages when surveying in the modern sense was unknown. In those days land-owners and churchmen, accompanied by stalwart armed men, periodically reviewed the boundaries to see that marking stones were in place and hunting or fishing rights observed. In later times woodsmen and soldiers walked town and village boundaries and, when all was in order, ended the ceremony with a huge feast.

In Springe Deister Boundary Walk celebrations start with morning reveille and a Fire Department band concert. The burgomaster then reads a proclamation concerning the day's activities.

Generally the local band leads off a group of marchers who carry the town's treasure chest at their head. At the first boundary a delegation from an adjoining town meets Springe's citizens. An appropriate ceremony is held, drinks are exchanged. The group then continues to the next boundary point, and the next. Each time the marchers are joined by more neighbors, each time they indulge in further cheer. By the time final rounds are completed the marchers are hilarious. Their ranks have so greatly increased, moreover, that the group divides and proceeds in different columns to various points, where festivities are continued.

SCHÜTZENFESTE (Marksmen's Festivals), all over Germany
At various times during the year

Throughout Germany, from small cities to large ones, the *Schützenfest,* or Marksmen's Festival, is one of the most important annual events. These festivals originated five or six hundred years ago with the decline of the knights' feudal power. Archery contests by citizen marksmen superseded medieval tournaments of the knights. Marksmen, rather than knights, became responsible for the protection of towns and villages against enemy attack.

At regular intervals contests were held to keep these guardians of the peace in top form. People gathered from far and near to witness their feats of skill. Gradually, the marksmen's contests became gala events, lasting for several days. Throughout the centuries popular elements were introduced, such as processions in costume, folk dance exhibitions, special foods and various amusements. In this way the marksmen's festivals finally developed into folk festivals in which everyone participated. Today they are observed with an enthusiasm which is rivaled only by the holiday spirit prevalent at Christmas, the New Year, and Carnival.

Each town and hamlet celebrates its Schützenfest at its own time and in its own way. In Biberach, for example, the festival occurs on the first Monday and Tuesday of July. For centuries the town has featured a procession of children dressed in period costume who are accompanied by local bands and colorfully attired heralds. In places like Düsseldorf and Neuss, on the other hand, the event occurs in late August, while Hannover celebrates on the first Sunday in July. Some forty or fifty marksmen's societies participate in these events. The man who scores highest in the contests is crowned *Schützenkönig*, or King of the Marksmen, and is escorted through the streets to the accompaniment of blaring trumpets and beating drums. Colorful banners, stretched across the streets, flutter in the breeze. Spectators shout themselves hoarse as the King proceeds triumphantly to his coronation and receives homage from his thousands of admiring subjects.

LEONHARDIRITT (Saint Leonard's Ride), in Bad Tölz, State of Bavaria

November 6

November 6 is the namesday of Saint Leonard, the sixth-century hermit-abbott, who was reared by his godfather, the pious Saint Rémy, Archbishop of Rheims. Saint Leonard is patron of prisoners and farm animals, especially horses and cattle. This saint, who won many tourneys before giving himself to God, is especially revered in Bavaria and Austria, where numerous chapels are dedicated to his name. These small shrines, which usually are situated in mountain places outside the villages, are covered with votive offerings consisting of horseshoes, pliers, pails, and other objects associated with horses and cattle raising. Iron chains, also, are often present, for Saint Leonard reputedly had power to break chains and set all prisoners free.

Saint Leonard is honored throughout Bavaria but nowhere, perhaps, more picturesquely than at Bad Tölz, where peasants in native costume celebrate his namesday by riding to church in *Truhenwagen,* chest wagons, which are gaily painted with incidents from the saint's life. Religious ceremonies are held in a chapel on top of Kalvarien, Calvary Mountain, which overlooks the river Isar. The small edifice was built in 1772, on a spot once occupied by a huge old tree.

From homesteads and farms high up in the mountain festival wagons—possibly sixty in all—come drawn by spirited horses wearing gleaming brass-studded harnesses. The animals proudly toss manes and flip their long tails, which are decorated with flowers, ribbons, and sprays of green. An outrider, carrying a colorful banner, accompanies each conveyance. Great white horses draw a wagon in which members of the clergy and the Tölz councilmen ride in state.

The procession, led by a handsome horseback rider and accompanied by the local rifleman's band, assembles at the foot of Calvary Mountain and makes its way up the steep ascent to the Chapel. There the worshipers walk three times about the sanctuary and, following open air Mass, receive the priest's blessing on both horses and wagons.

Later the procession returns to town where the group disbands to the accompaniment of lively music. The "Riders of Saint Leonard," as the mounted escort is called, then participate in a whip cracking contest—an ancient and honored sport in this part of Bavaria.

In many hamlets cattle, rather than horses, participate in the Saint Leonard's Ride, for they, also, fall under the saint's special protection. Hundreds of miniature iron votive churches are consecrated and then purchased by faithful worshipers, in the hope that Saint Leonard's intercession will preserve the animals from sickness and disease throughout the year.

GERMANY

MARTINSFEST (Saint Martin's Festival)

Saint Martin's Eve, November 10,
Saint Martin's Day, November 11

Martinsfest is a festival of significance to both Catholic and Protestant Germany. The occasion honors Saint Martin, jovial fourth-century friend of children and patron of the poor, and also Martin Luther, leader of the Reformation in Germany, born November 10, 1483. German Catholic communities along the Rhine and elsewhere, but especially in Düsseldorf, pay annual tribute to Saint Martin; while Protestant groups, notably in Thuringia, long have celebrated Martin Luther's birthday in picturesque fashion. In prewar Erfurt, where Martin Luther attended the university, it was customary for thousands of children, carrying lighted lanterns, to form in procession and march up to the Plaza before the Cathedral and the Severi Church. There the young people with their lanterns traditionally formed the "Luther rose," or the escutcheon of Martin Luther.

In many Black Forest areas Saint Martin's Day is celebrated by a village fair. Along the Upper Rhine, however, where Frankish missionaries first introduced the Christian faith and venerated Saint Martin as their patron, the Eve is characterized by children's lantern processions and the Day by feasting on roast goose. Rural inhabitants of Black Forest and Lake Constance districts usually plan their feast to coincide with the slaughter of the family pig. Friends and neighbors, the school master and the priest are invited to dinner and village youngsters come around from door to door. They chant traditional ditties and demand "a sausage so long you can wind it three times around the oven, across the room and out to the singing boys!"

Legends abound to explain the eating of goose on this day. One is that the saint died after eating a whole goose at a single meal. Many claim that the custom of eating goose originated in pagan times when, according to German mythology, the bird was sacrificed to Wotan, father of the gods. Others say that Martinmass feasting began with thanksgiving ceremonies for Freya, goddess of plenty.

77

Saint Martin in Germany, as elsewhere in Europe, is regarded as patron of the harvest and friend of the poor. On his anniversary people invite others to share their bounty, to make merry, feast on autumn foods and drink the new red wines. Saint Martin himself set the pattern for sharing when, as a dashing young soldier at the gates of Amiens, he divided his cloak with a beggar.

Saint Martin's Day is for family, friends, and the needy, but Saint Martin's Eve is for children.

> Let's be happy, let's be gay,
> Let's be children all today,

is the ancient song which resounds through Düsseldorf's streets at nightfall, as hundreds of jubilant boys and girls scurry hither and yon, swinging fantastic lanterns from long poles and gathering for their famous procession. An adult, representing Saint Martin, heads the long line. Then come the children, bobbing homemade lanterns of every conceivable size and shape. Some of the simpler goblin lanterns are made from hollowed-out pumpkins or beets, illumined by lighted candles. There are also wooden lanterns with elaborately colored windows, strange animals, and cunningly fashioned windmills. Among the more ambitious creations are lanterns representing Lambertus Church with its leaning tower.

Through the streets the children advance, singing, holding their lanterns, which rise and fall like the waves of the sea. Against the background of the city's ancient gabled façades; through the cobbled streets of the *Altstadt* or old town, on into the broad avenues of the town's newer parts the procession steadily moves, the children's lighted lanterns casting fantastic shadows against the dark walls of silent buildings.

From every quarter the Saint Martin's Eve theme song,

> Let's be happy, let's be gay,
> Let's be children all today,

rises like a mighty chant from the throats of hundreds of clear-voiced boys and girls. The words are caught up by thousands of spectators and repeated in the cracked voices of aged men and women on the sidelines who, on this one night in the year, relive their lost youth.

GERMANY

HAMBURGER DOM (*Dom* Fair) in Hamburg
November until Christmas

Hamburg's ancient *Dom* probably is one of the most unique Christmas fairs not only in Germany, but in the world. The fair gets its name from the fact that, in olden days, it was held in the open square before the Dom, or cathedral. Today the fair occupies the Heiligengeistfeld, or Holy Ghost Field, in the center of town.

There are booths filled with all kinds of exciting toys, sugared gingerbreads, and myriads of useless knicknacks which attract the eye and lure the last pfennig from pockets of holiday shoppers.

The Dom opens in November and continues until shortly before Christmas.

ADVENT (Advent)
The four weeks preceding Christmas

Advent customs vary from place to place, but everywhere in Germany the four weeks before Christmas are looked upon as a preparation period for the greatest festival of the Christian year.

In towns and villages of northern Germany every household has a "Star of Seven," a seven-branch candlestick. On Christmas Eve the candles are lighted. At midnight each family carries its glowing pointed "star" across meadows, through dark crooked lanes, along snowy streets to service in the village church. There, amid a blaze of lighted stars, parishioners reverently kneel and welcome the *Christkind* to their hearts and homes.

Many families make Advent wreaths of fir which are decorated with gold or silver ribbons or just scarlet woolen threads. Sometimes the wreaths hang from the ceiling beams; sometimes they adorn the tables. On each of the four Saturdays or Sundays in Advent a candle is lighted—one on the first day,[2] two on the second, three on the third, and so on. Members of the family or groups of friends customarily sit about the lighted wreath, singing seasonal carols and preparing handmade Christmas gifts.

[2] The Advent candles are lighted on Saturday in Catholic areas; on Sunday in Protestant sections.

CHRISTKINDLSMARKT or CHRISTKINDLESMARKT (Kriss Kringle's [3] Fair), in Nuremberg, State of Bavaria

Early December until Christmas

Nuremberg's *Christkindlsmarkt,* one of the most traditional of Germany's many holiday fairs, starts about December 4 in the old town's marketplace and continues until Christmas. The fair is so ancient that nobody remembers just when it began. In 1697 the historian Wagenseil, himself a native Nuremberger, described the event much as it is celebrated today. Many think that the fair originated in the Middle Ages and that it was associated with Twelfth Day ceremonials.

The mayor of the town opens the event with a speech. Then, to the accompaniment of Christmas music, a child dressed like Nuremberg's "gold angel" makes a dramatic appearance and welcomes visitors in verse.

The gold angel is reminiscent of an ancient event. In medieval times people who came to the fair saw in church a replica of the Christ Child in the manger. In those days it was customary to "give the Christ Child away" to the children in the form of a doll. After the Reformation, the original significance of the custom was lost and the Christ Child doll gradually became a Christmas angel. Today the angel is dressed in gold-colored robes of eighteenth-century style.

As Christmas approaches native toy-makers make thousands of reproductions of Nuremberg's golden angel. An angel graces every home and hovers as guardian over fair-time festivities. Quite aside from golden angels, however, the fair is distinguished by its rows and rows of colorful booths, each filled with such holiday delights as glittering Christmas tree decorations, clever toys such as only the fingers of Nuremberg craftsmen can fashion, marvelous *Lebkuchen* and pungent gingerbreads to make a child's nostrils tingle and mouth water. Then there are cunningly wrought figures of the baby Jesus in his crib, surrounded by Mary, Joseph, and adoring shepherds. There are small painted sheep, cows, asses, chickens and dogs—all so life-

---

[3] Christkindl, the Bavarian diminutive form for *Christkind,* or Christ child, has been corrupted to Kriss Kringle, the giver of Christmas gifts.

like and enticing that parents scarcely can drag their offspring past the tempting wares.

Even more attractive to youthful imagination, perhaps, are the numberless booths filled with such specialties as savory-smelling roasted sausages or delicately grilled herrings. There are sweets, of course, all kinds of traditional candies, hard spicy peppernuts, and little pink-frosted cookies, adorned with delightful sugar scrolls or, possibly, a brightly colored picture or bit of shiny mirror.

Yes, the Nuremberg Christkindlsmarkt is full of wonderful sights, sounds and smells. It symbolizes for grown-ups unforgettably beautiful childhood memories; for small boys and girls it is little short of paradise.

SANKT NIKOLAUS-ABEND and SANKT NIKOLAUS-TAG (Saint Nicholast Eve and Saint Nicholas Day)
December 5, 6

The Yuletide season opens officially on December 5, Saint Nicholas Eve, or on the morning of December 6, when the good saint appears in person in many towns and villages and calls on the children. Saint Nicholas (or, in some places, his assistant, Knecht Rupprecht, or Christkindle or Kriss Kringle) usually is regarded as a pre-Christmas messenger who examines the youngsters' behavior. He promises gifts of toys and sweets if the children are good. If they are bad, however, he flourishes bundles of birch rods and threatens punishment unless naughty ways are mended. Sometimes he reminds children of their waywardness by presenting little bundles of twigs, either real or of candy.

In some places children place a shoe or a large stocking beside the bed or outside the door. Saint Nicholas then leaves a small gift or a bundle of rods, to remind the little ones of their behavior— good or bad.

On Saint Nicholas Eve, in the Rhineland and in northern Germany, the holiday *Spekulatius* makes its first appearance. Spekulatius is traditional hard gingerbread which is made in molds to represent Saint Nicholas, little men, or animals. Sometimes, also, it comes in thin, yard-long loaves.

HEILIGABEND (Christmas Eve)

December 24

Christmas is the gayest holiday of the German calendar and the *Weihnachtsbaum,* or Christmas tree, with its lighted candles, gilded nuts, multicolored paper garlands, shining red apples and dancing, raisin-eyed gingerbread men, is the symbol of the German Yuletide. The real holiday begins with Christmas Eve church services, which are followed by home festivities and family gatherings.

In most parts of Germany the trimming of the Christmas tree is done on the twenty-fourth, although in some places people do it whenever convenient on the days preceding. Usually the rite is performed in greatest secrecy by the heads of the household, who are the only persons having access to the room in which the tree is kept. Presents for each member of the household, including the domestics, and *bunte Teller,* plates filled with apples, nuts, *Pfefferkuchen,* marzipan and other goodies, as well as presents, are grouped under and about the tree.

At last the white candles on the Christmas tree are lighted and all other lights extinguished. A bell rings and the children are allowed to enter the room and look at the tree in all its glory. After singing Christmas carols, which usually include such old time favorites as *O Tannenbaum* and *Stille Nacht,* the moment for the *Bescherung,* or distribution of presents arrives. The children are told that their gifts have been left under the tree by the *Weinachtsmann* (the Christmas Man, Santa Claus or his helper, Knecht Rupprecht), or by *Christkind,* the Christ Child.

The rest of the evening is spent in opening gifts, singing and merrymaking.

GERMANY

SCHÄFER-WALZER (Shepherds' Waltz), in Assinghausen, region of
  Westphalia

December 24

For over a hundred years the gay rhythms of the "Shepherds'
Waltz" have characterized the Christmas Eve service of Assinghausen's little church. At midnight the bells ring out joyously and
devout villagers from throughout the parish hasten through heavily
drifted snows to the tiny church, where candles blaze and the pungent
smell of melted wax mingles with the spicy scent of pine.

Worshipers bend their heads reverently as the priest offers the
Christmas prayer and reads the Gospel story of the manger birth.
Suddenly, the merry strains of the Shepherds' Waltz flow through the
sanctuary and scores of heavily shod feet begin to beat time to the
gay dance music which issues from the organ loft.

The birth of the Son of God is welcomed in Assinghausen with
secular music, as a result of a century-old tradition. According to
church records Herr F. W. Grimme, local poet and church organist,
was playing a hymn on Christmas Eve, when word came that he had
just become father of a seventh child. On the anniversary of this
night two thousand years ago, reasoned Herr Grimme, shepherds
had brought glad tidings of Jesus' birth. Quickly the organist broke
off the stately hymn he was playing and started improvising a joyous
waltz such as he imagined the shepherds might have played on their
pipes, in honor of the arrival of Bethlehem's Child.

WEIHNACHTEN (Christmas)

December 25 and 26

Both December 25 and 26 are public holidays. In many homes
Christmas Day, *Der Erste Feiertag,* is strictly a family day which is
spent quietly in enjoyment of the Christmas tree, the new books, and
appropriate seasonal music. *Der Zweite Feiertag,* Second Christmas,
often is spent in more worldly fashion as a time for visiting friends,
attending dances, and indulging in all kinds of merrymaking.

83

Of course, food is important in all the holiday festivities. Roast goose and *Christstollen,* long loaves of bread bursting with nuts, raisins, citron and dried fruits, *Lebkuchen, Pfefferkuchen,* marzipan, and scores of other tempting dainties are important among the holiday foods. Berliners eat carp at Christmas. Whoever finds roe with his fish is happy, for the superstition is that he will find money in the coming year.

There are many old folk superstitions regarding the "Twelve Nights" between Christmas and Epiphany. Peasants often forecast weather for the twelve months by the "onion calendar." They cut an onion into twelve slices and sprinkle each portion with salt. The wetness or dryness of the coming months is predicted according to the degree of moisture found on each of the twelve slices.

ALLERKINDERTAG (Holy Innocents' Day)

December 28

Boys and girls of Thuringia celebrate the anniversary of King Herod's slaughter of Bethlehem's children with a custom sometimes called "whipping with fresh greens." Armed with switches and green branches the children go out into the streets and spank passers-by with their rods, demanding at the same time small money gifts.

The custom doubtless originated in pagan times when whipping was regarded as an early spring purification rite intended to drive out demons and disperse powers of darkness.

SILVESTERABEND [4] (New Year's Eve)

December 31

This is a merry night throughout Germany. Traditional foods, ancient customs, old fashioned games and beloved folk songs all play an important role in colorful celebrations that take place in various areas.

[4] See note p. 21.

GERMANY

People in different localities think it "lucky" to eat certain foods on this last night of the old year. For example, there is the traditional carp, which is served not only in the homes but in fashionable metropolitan restaurants. In northern Germany many people, especially those of the older generation, not only eat the fish but slip a few of the shining scales into their purses as a New Year's charm to ensure plenty of money in the next twelve months! Then there is the traditional *Silvesterabend* punch, a fine hot potent toddy made of cinnamon-and-sugar-flavored red wine, which is served with *Pfannkuchen,* or doughnuts.

Just as carp is thought by some to bring good luck, so Baden folk insist that their special dried pea soup is auspicious for all partakers.

Along the lower Rhine there are many delightful New Year's Eve foods including *Nöujoer,* or "little New Year" yeast cookies, baked in spiral wreath forms or in pretzel or circle shapes. In Bergisch-Land and Wuppertal the favorite pastry is *Ballbäuschen,* a toothsome fried cake stuffed with raisins and currants.

Regardless of locality, however, or the special fare enjoyed on Silvesterabend, everybody agrees that to secure a well-stocked larder for the coming year one must leave on one's plate a bit of every kind of food—at least, until after the clock strikes midnight!

According to ancient Germanic folk belief prowling demons, devils and other spirits of darkness must be routed on the last night of the year by mummery and noise. For the most part the superstition has been forgotten, but shooting parties still are popular at Berchtesgaden, in the Bavarian Alps, and elsewhere, and *Buttenmandl,* or Little Button Men, still run through streets of towns and villages. The Buttenmandl are peasants dressed in straw clothing who wear deerskin animal masks. They hold clanging bells and drag clanking chains in an effort to drive out evil spirits! Members of the shooting societies, on the other hand, do their part in routing demons by scaling the Berchtesgaden heights and shooting in unison five hundred or more old mortars.

In Schiltach on the Kinzig a four-hundred-year-old ceremony annually is reenacted with the midnight ringing of the church bells. Old and young, carrying lighted lanterns, assemble in the town square and pledge to protect their town under all circumstances. After a hymn of thanksgiving the lantern bearers visit the parsonage, where the pastor greets them and gives his blessing.

The procession then returns to the square where the Burgomaster of Schiltach delivers a New Year message in which he reviews events of the past year and extends best wishes for the one to come. The official greeting is accepted and congratulations returned by one of the town's leading citizens.

The last night of the year is regarded as a propitious occasion for looking into the future. "Lead pouring" parties are popular among young people who drop a little melted lead into a bowl of cold water and read fortunes for the coming year from the shapes the metal assumes. Thus a ship may mean a voyage to distant shores, a pig, food and plenty on the farm, a ring, a wedding, and so on.

In lower Rhine areas card games are the most popular pastime of the season. Everyone plays until midnight; but as soon as church bells begin to peal and sirens to blow, everyone throws down the cards and shouts the ancient greeting, *"Prosit Neujahr!"*

In some places bands of children go from house to house singing carols. Sometimes the songs are addressed especially to godfathers and godmothers. The children are welcomed by householders who give them presents of nuts, apples, *Pfefferkuchen* and coins.

In certain communities the night watchman still goes about at midnight on New Year's Eve and recites this traditional verse:

> In the name of the Lord
> The Old Year goes out the door.
> This is my wish for each of you:
> Peace forever, and
> Praise to God, our Lord.

5

FESTIVALS OF ITALY

Capo D'Anno (New Year's Day)

January 1

New Year's Day is celebrated with services in the churches, parties, visits, and all kinds of festivities. Children receive *strenna,* or money gifts, from their parents, while friends and relatives send each other flowers and bunches of mistletoe. Since early times Italians have attributed to mistletoe such miraculous properties as healing sickness, curing sterility in women and animals, and quenching fire. Today a piece of mistletoe is hung over the door to "bring luck" to all the household.

La Vigilia Dell' Epifania (Epiphany Eve)

January 5

Children receive gifts at Epiphany, in memory of the presents the Wise Men offered the Christ Child; but, unlike the tradition in Spain and some other countries, it is not the Magi who bring the gifts, but *la Befana,* the little old fairy witch woman. The name *befana* is probably a popular corruption of *Epifania,* or Epiphany, the feast that commemorates the visit of the Three Kings to Bethlehem's manger.

According to the legend current in Italy, Sicily and Sardinia, the Befana was sweeping her house when the Kings came by with offerings for *Bambino Gesù.* When the old woman was invited to accompany them, she tartly replied that she was too busy with her work. Later, however, when her sweeping was done, she took her broom and started out toward Bethlehem. She lost her way and could not find the Bambino, for whom she still searches.

FESTIVALS OF WESTERN EUROPE

Each year la Befana goes through Italy. Boys and girls write letters to her, asking for the presents they want, just as American children write to Santa Claus. The spry old witch slides down chimneys on her broom and always stuffs good children's stockings or shoes with pretty toys, but leaves pebbles, charcoal, or bags of ashes for those who are naughty.

In Rome preparations for Epifania start early in December with the famous toy fair in the Piazzo Navona. Fascinating toys dangle invitingly from the hundreds of gaily decorated stalls that are erected about the fountains. There are all sorts of holiday sweets, gay balloons and charming little painted figures for the Christmas *presepi,* or mangers.

The Piazza is thronged with children, young laughing mothers, bent old men and withered grandmothers who move from booth to booth—gossiping, bargaining, exchanging greetings and buying toys for the Befana to leave on Epiphany Eve.

The fair continues until January 5, when everyone buys at least one tin horn or trumpet, or perhaps a brightly-painted little clay figure that disguises a shrill whistle. The crowd surges back and forth through the Piazza, laughing, jostling, whistling and blowing, until all Rome seems mad and the air shrieks with deafening sound. To add to the general pandemonium processions of youths march about, blowing on large cardboard trumpets.

Epiphany Eve customs vary from place to place. In Adriatic coast towns and villages bands of men and boys go about from house to house, singing traditional Epiphany songs, and receiving small gifts in return. At Varenna, on Lake Como, men dressed like the Three Kings and their retinue go through the countryside with torches, bestowing gifts on the needy. In some other parts of the country people build bonfires. Dancing about the fires, they predict good or bad weather for the coming months, according to the direction from which the smoke blows.

ITALY

EPIFANIA (Epiphany), in Niscemi, Caltanissetta province, Sicily
January 6

"Clothing the Child Jesus" is the name of an old Epiphany custom which is observed at Niscemi. A poor parish child is borne naked to the church, where he is dressed to represent the Infant Jesus. After special religious services, a procession of priests and worshipers, carrying all kinds of gifts, take the child home to the joyous accompaniment of native bagpipes.

*CARNEVALE (Carnival)

January 17 to Ash Wednesday

Carnevale always begins on January 17 and continues until Ash Wednesday. The ceremonies of the last three days of the carnival are the gayest, especially those of *Martedì Grasso,* or Shrove Tuesday. Throughout Italy the occasion is celebrated with colorful pageants, masquerades, dancing, music and all kinds of merrymaking.

Every Italian town and village has its own special celebrations. In some places a Parade of the Months is a. carnival event. Allegorical figures representing the twelve months, pay homage to the "King," who is attended by four harlequins. The Months sing traditional verses to the King and later, as the procession moves about from place to place, the harlequins are crowned as members of the King's retinue.

Martedì Grasso, in Venice, is celebrated by the appearance of King Carnival who is greeted with traditional ceremony. As always, King Carnival is represented as a fat man, for eating and drinking are characteristic of pre-Lenten revelry. His straw body is filled with firecrackers and explosives and his reign, although merry, is brief, since his body is burned at midnight in the Piazza San Marco.

* Stars indicate movable feasts that depend upon Easter. See Table of Easter Dates and Movable Festivals Dependent upon Easter, p. 246.

FESTIVALS OF WESTERN EUROPE

SANT' AGATA (Saint Agatha), in Catania, Sicily

February 3, 4, 5

Saint Agatha, the rich and beatiful young Sicilian virgin whom a Roman prefect put to death in 251 because she refused to yield to him, is one of Sicily's most beloved martyrs. She is patroness of nursing mothers and women suffering from diseases of the breast, because her own breasts were amputated during the tortures she endured. In all her trials she remained steadfast in the faith, and Saint Peter himself is said to have ministered to her wounds.

Every Italian loves the Palermo-born Saint Agatha, but she is shown special reverence at Catania, where her relics are preserved in a silver-sculptured casket. Her *festa* begins on February 3, and ends on February 5, anniversary of her death. On each of the three successive days, a silver bust of the saint wearing a jewel-studded crown is carried in procession from the Cathedral to the city's various churches.

The unique feature of the procession is the display of the *ceri,* or immense wooden replicas of candlesticks, which are painted, gilded, and carved with episodes from the saint's harrowing martyrdom. Tumultuous shouts of *"Evviva Sant' Agata!"* ring out every time the ceri bearers halt along the line of march. The streets through which the procession passes are gay with paper pennants and streamers, flowers, and colorful festa hangings attached to balconies and windows.

Strings of many-colored electric lights enliven the scene at night. People buy all kinds of sweets and holiday foods from temptingly arrayed street stalls. Later they throng to the piazza to see the wonderful firework displays without which no saint's day celebration is complete.

SAN GIUSEPPE (Saint Joseph)

March 19

The anniversary of San Giuseppe, husband of the Virgin and patron of carpenters and cartmakers, and also of unwed mothers and orphans, is characterized in many places by feasting, merry-making, most of all, by sharing with the needy. For was not St. Joseph himself a humble carpenter of Nazareth, a pious and generous protector, "a just man," in the words of the Bible?

The day of San Giuseppe is celebrated differently in different places but nowhere more picturesquely, perhaps, than in Sicily. Villagers often prepare a feast table, the *tavola di San Giuseppe,* at which those portraying the Holy Family are guests of honor. The Family consists of an aged carpenter, representing Joseph, a poor local girl who is the Madonna, and an orphan boy, the *Bambino Gesù.* Other guests include orphans, widows, and beggars.

Everyone in the village contributes a share to the *banchetto,* or banquet, according to his means—food, money, candles or flowers. The women prepare all kinds of regional dishes, which vary from place to place. In some localities, for example, there is hearty *minestrone,* made with dried beans and vegetables. Neapolitans serve *zeppole,* or cream fritters. The Sienese have *frittelle di San Giuseppe,* Saint Joseph's fritters, which are sold from stalls outside the church that is dedicated to the saint. In Bologna there is *ravioli di San Giuseppe,* a delicious fried sweet, made with short crust instead of the usual ravioli dough, and filled with jam or almond paste.

In many places little cream puffs called *Sfingi di San Giuseppe,* are a favorite dessert. The puff shells, flavored with grated lemon and orange rinds, are filled with *ricotta,* Italian pot cheese, which is combined with chocolate and other tempting ingredients.

The feast is preceded by solemn morning mass. Then the priest and villagers lead the Holy Family in procession to the outdoor *banchetto,* where the food is blessed. Cheers of *"Viva la tavola di San Giuseppe,"* go up, as the viands, which are first blessed by the Bambino, are distributed.

A procession follows the banquet. The Holy Family, mounted on mules, is hailed by the villagers and given gifts of food and money as they ride through the streets. The celebration continues with singing, merrymaking, and rejoicing as the inhabitants dance about bonfires in honor of their beloved San Giuseppe.

*MEZZA QUARESIMA (Mid-Lent)

The fourth Sunday in Lent

At *Mezza Quaresima,* or Mid-Lent, *feste,* parties, dances and all kinds of gay street celebrations provide a single day's respite from the severity and monotony of Lenten gloom.

Just as *Carnevale* is represented as a fat man, so *Quaresima,* or Lent, is a lean, witch-like old hag. In Venice young people dance hilariously about her rag-stuffed effigy, because Lent is half gone. In parts of the Abruzzi, Quaresima appears as a tow figure pierced with seven feathers. The effigy is suspended from a rope stretched from side to side of the street. On each Saturday in Lent villagers pluck out one feather with great rejoicing, since each represents one of the seven weeks of Lent.

Children often receive toys in the guise of a lean old woman with seven legs. At *Mezza Quaresima* boys and girls cut their figures in two, throwing half away and keeping half until the end of Lent.

*DOMENICA DELLE PALME (Palm Sunday)

The Sunday preceding Easter

Palm Sunday ceremonies, like all Holy Week observances, vary widely from one place to another. Usually the piazzas in front of small village churches and great cathedrals are filled with worshipers in gay spring clothes, and picturesque vendors of olive branches and palms. The olive branches are gilded or silvered while palms, cleverly plaited into crosses with charming decorative detail, often are adorned with roses, lilies, or other flowers.

After olive branches and palms are blessed at morning mass, an impressive service follows in commemoration of opening the gates of Jerusalem, when Jesus went into the city as "King of Israel."

For this ceremony the priests leave the church in procession and knock at a closed door—the "gate" of Jerusalem. The portals are flung open in welcome and the clergy make the symbolic triumphal entry amid waving palms and joyous music.

*Giovedì Santo (Holy Thursday)
The Thursday preceding Easter

In some places in Sicily *Giovedì Santo* is observed with night processions of local guild members, who carry platforms with life-sized figures, representing various episodes in the Passion of Christ. Each guild is preceded by a band and followed by a group of men who stop now and then to explain in local dialect the story of the Last Supper, the Agony in the Garden, the Scourging, or whatever the scene depicts.

Both in Italy and in Italian communities of the United States, many churches reenact the ceremony of foot washing at the altar. Twelve poor men of the parish are chosen to represent the Twelve Disciples. The priest performs the symbolic act of bathing the disciples' feet. Following the ceremony each of the men receives a loaf of bread and a gift of money.

On Holy Thursday the Easter Sepulcher, or "Sepulcher of Christ" is prepared for the Good Friday services. In some churches the sepulcher, which is a recess in the north wall of the chancel, is covered with flowers in symbol of the tomb of Jesus. At Saint Peter's, in Rome, the Host is ceremoniously placed on the altar of a side chapel, which on the following day represents the sepulcher.

*Venerdì Santo (Holy Friday)
The Friday preceding Easter

In towns and villages throughout Italy dramatic processions go through the streets on Good Friday night with realistic figures of Jesus displayed on platforms. Sometimes the platforms, surrounded by flowers and candles, are borne on the shoulders of hooded and robed penitents. Sometimes young boys hold aloft large candles on long spiked poles, and men carry the cross, spear, crown of thorns and other Passion symbols. Lugubrious music, figures of angels displaying stained graveclothes and the sorrowing Virgin with clasped hands and agonized face, all add realism and pathos to these folk processions.

A deeply moving ceremony is held at Rapallo, near Genoa. A bier with the figure of the dead Jesus, the crown of thorns and nails of the cross, is carried from church to church through the town's dark winding streets. The only illumination comes from hundreds of tapers, burning in windows along the line of march. For hours the procession moves along its sorrowful route, accompanied by mourning men and women, uttering laments and singing penitential chants. After stopping at the Cathedral for the final mass, townsfolk carry their dead Christ to the nearby Baptistry and place the bier on the floor. Large white candles burning at the four corners of the bier cast flickering shadows across the figure of the inert blood-stained body. The melting wax sputters and falls in little pools on the floor. Devout worshipers come and go, kneeling before the image and praying.

*SABATO SANTO (Holy Saturday), in Florence, province of Tuscany
The Saturday preceding Easter

The Mass of Glory ending at noon on Holy Saturday announces the beginning of the Resurrection *festa.* The church bells which, in memory of Jesus' sufferings, have not rung since Holy Thursday, now peal out joyously. The churches, shrouded in gloom throughout the week, suddenly come to life. The black draperies drop from the altars, revealing figures of the risen Lord. Tapers are lighted. Joy and gladness succeed darkness and sorrow.

Customs vary from place to place. Florentines observe the ceremony of the *Scoppio del Carro,* the Explosion of the Car, which probably is one of the country's most picturesque Holy Saturday observances.

94

The ancient Florentine family of de'Pazzi inaugurated the Scoppio del Carro by contributing a splendid exposive-filled car to the religious procession which carried a flaming torch from the altar of one church to another. The torch was lighted from a spark made by rubbing a flint against a fragment of stone, reputedly a piece of the Holy Sepulcher, which was brought to Florence during the Crusades.

Thousands assemble every year in the Piazza del Duomo before the Cathedral of Santa Maria del Fiore, to watch the spectacular explosion.

The modern *Carro,* an immense, colorfully-decorated wooden car with fireworks attached, is drawn into the piazza by white oxen and placed before the cathedral doors. A wire runs from the high altar inside the cathedral to the Car in the piazza. A dove-shaped rocket, ignited at the altar as mass terminates with the singing of the *Gloria,* shoots out along the wire through the open doors and sets fire to the explosives. The Carro bursts with tremendous noise and splendor.

Tuscan farmers watch the ceremony with fascination and dread. They believe that if the dove rocket performs adequately, harvests will prosper in the coming year; if anything goes wrong, however, crops will be bad and the season poor.

*La Pasqua (Easter)

Easter is a joyous day. After morning mass people generally eat, drink, visit and rejoice in the passing of Lenten gloom and the glory of the risen Christ.

Food plays an important part in the day's festivities and traditional specialties are as numerous as the country's towns and villages. *Agnellino,* roasted baby lamb, is universally popular for the Easter dinner, especially when served with *carciofi arrostiti,* roasted artichokes, with pepper, salt, and slivers of garlic discreetly hidden between the leaves. *Brodetto Pasquale,* a delicious Easter broth, delicately herb-flavored, often starts off the feast, while holiday breads, pastries, and small cakes abound in every region. One seasonal treat that children in many places enjoy is a rich bread shaped like a crown and studded with colored Easter egg candies.

SAN NICOLA (Saint Nicholas), in Bari, province of Apulia

May 7, 8

Italians celebrate the *festa* of San Nicola, prototype of the modern Santa Claus, on May 7 and 8, anniversary of the transfer of the saint's relics to Bari, rather than on December 6, his calendar day. *La Befana,*[1] not San Nicola, is the children's gift bearer, but the good saint is deeply loved and revered as protector of virgins, orphans, schoolboys, seamen, pawnbrokers, pirates, robbers, and many others.

In the eleventh century sailors brought the saint's relics to Bari from Myra, Asia Minor, where he died as Archbishop in 326. Today his bones rest in the crypt of the Romanesque Church of San Nicola, which was begun in 1087 in the saint's honor. Thousands of pilgrims come from far and near to worship at the tomb of the wonder-working saint and to ask his help for the sick, for children, for those at sea, for all who sin.

Legends abound concerning the saint who gives protection to hardened sinners no less than to the young and innocent. One of the best known stories tells how the saint learned of the plight of three girls, daughters of an impoverished noble, who had no dowries. To save them from becoming prostitues, San Nicola, who had inherited a fortune, secretly went at night to the nobleman's house and tossed through the window a bag of gold as a dowry for the eldest daughter. The next night he repeated the act in behalf of the second daughter. On his third visit, however, the nobleman, who was awaiting the appearance of the unseen benefactor, caught at the saint's robe and tried to thank him. San Nicola made the grateful father promise never to reveal his identity, and slipped away.

[1] See *La Vigilia dell' Epifania,* January 5.

This story explains how San Nicola came to be regarded as the protector of young girls of marriagable age, as well as the patron of pawnbrokers, who adopted three gold balls as their symbol.

San Nicola is not an Italian saint. He was born in Asia Minor and there he died; but when infidels threatened desecration of his tomb at Myra, brave Barese mariners risked their lives, in answer to a vision, to carry his body by sea to their city. This is why, each year, sailors of Bari take San Nicola's image to the water in solemn procession. The saint's statue, robed in gorgeous gold and red vestments, with jewelled miter and archbishop's staff, is surrounded by flowers and carried aloft, accompanied by chanting and bands, high-ranking churchmen, seamen, and pilgrims with lighted candles.

At the wharf the statue is placed on a vessel decorated with flowers and banners and taken out to sea. Hundreds of small craft, crowded with pilgrims and fishermen follow the image, to pay their respects and seek the saint's blessing. At night the image is returned to its place of honor on the silver-embossed altar of San Nicola's crypt, and the great festa ends with spectacular displays of fireworks.

*FESTA DEL GRILLO (Cricket Festival), in Florence, province of Tuscany

The fortieth day after Easter

In most European countries Ascension Day, the fortieth after Easter, is the early spring holiday when families go to the country to picnic and spend the day out of doors. Many Florentines do not go to the country, but spend the day out-of-doors enjoying the spring in their own unique fashion. Parents pack generous lunch baskets, gather up the children, and flock to Cascine Park to celebrate with them the *Festa del Grillo,* or Festival of the Cricket, for the chirping cricket is a symbol of spring.

Hundreds of brightly-painted wicker or wire cages imprisoning hundreds of crickets caught in the Park, dangle from vendors' stalls. Each child must have his caged grillo, for tradition says it brings good luck if it still sings, when carried home.

In the past children hunted their own *grilli* on this day, but now the insects are sold in cages. Food stalls with sweets, ices, and soft drinks; balloon stalls with hundreds of red, blue, orange, and green balloons, hundreds of youngsters scurrying hither and yon with little painted cages—all make this festa one of the happiest and gayest spring events for everyone—except the grilli!

*Corpus Domini (Corpus Christi)
The Thursday following Trinity Sunday

Corpus Christi, the festival honoring the institution of the Eucharist, is celebrated with splendor throughout the country. Each town and hamlet observes the day in its own fashion, but everywhere flowers, music, church banners, and colorful processions give beauty and picturesqueness to the event.

The fragrant mosaic flower carpets of Genzano, on Lake Nemi, are among the most beautiful of all Corpus Christi decorations. For blocks the brilliant flower petal tapestries mark the route over which priests in embroidered vestments carry the Blessed Sacrament. Often the petals are made in geometrical patterns, armorial designs, the Angel of Peace, or other elaborate motifs.

At Brindisi the outstanding feature of the procession is a richly-caparisoned white horse which the Archbishop rides at the head of the procession.

In Perugia the Corpus Christi procession, which starts from the Gothic Cathedral, is elegant and splendid, with rich banners, lighted candles and flowers. Balconies and windows are draped with brilliant hangings, and bystanders toss flowers in the path of the Sacrament as it is reverently carried through the streets.

Corso Del Palio (Race for the *Palio*),[2] in Siena, province of Siena
July 2

The *Corso del Palio,* Race for the *Palio,* is the name of the spectacular horse race which the Sienese hold twice a year in the

---

[2] The word *palio* is applied to both the race and to the silken banner which is the prize of the victorious city ward.

Virgin's honor. The first race, on July 2, is for the armless *Madonna di Provenzano;* the second, on August 16 (the day following Assumption) honors the *Madonna del Voto,* protectress of Siena. The *Palio,* one of Italy's most colorful events, originated in the thirteenth century and has retained its medieval character throughout the years.

The treacherous race track is the narrow cobbled road surrounding the shell-shaped Piazza del Campo, a magnificent natural amphitheatre which is dominated on one side by the beautiful Gothic Palazzo Pubblico.

Siena is divided into seventeen *contrade,* or wards, each of which goes by the name of the symbol painted on its silk banner. Nobody seems to know the origin of these contrade symbols, which include such colorful names as Unicorn, She-Wolf, Snail, Dragon, and Tortoise.

Ten of the contrade are contestants in the race, and they are selected by lot from the total number, since the race course is too narrow to accomodate all seventeen. A *barbero,* or race horse is assigned by lot to each *contrada,* which chooses its own jockey. The prize—one of glory, not of money—is a magnificent black and gold fringed banner. This standard is awarded to the winning contrada and is kept at its headquarters as a proud sumbol of prowess in winning the race for the Virgin.

On the morning of the race the Palio is blessed in church, and before the event riders and their barberos, decorated with the colors of their ward, are blessed at the altars of the churches in the respective contrade.

Before the race a gorgeous medieval procession parades around the race course. First come the mace bearers, then the contrade with their officials, pages, horsemen, drummers and trumpeters, all dressed in colorful costumes of the Middle Ages. Among the most picturesque figures in the procession are the standard bearers who toss and twirl the heavy silk contrada banners with a grace and skill possible only after generations of practicing the ancient art of flag throwing.

The stately procession moves about the Piazza del Campo amid the wild cheers and deafening plaudits of the crowd. Last of all, a pair of white oxen with gold and black trappings, draw the cart with the Palio, the trophy for the winning contrada.

Just before the race begins each jockey is given his *nerbo,* a stinging ox-sinew whip which Palio rules permit him to use in trying to unseat his opponent or to incapacitate his opponent's horse if, by so doing, he can press his own mount on to victory.

The winning jockey is raised on the shoulders of the crowd. His horse is showered with caresses. After a brief prayer of thanksgiving at the race course, both rider and horse return to the church in the contrada to offer further expressions of gratitude for victory.

Revelry, music and merrymaking, a victory banquet and toasts to the winning jockey and horse continue far into the night as the victorious contrada celebrates the glorious race in honor of the Virgin.

Il Giorno Dei Morti (The Day of the Dead)

November 2

Throughout Italy people decorate the graves of the dead with flowers and candles on *Il Giorno dei Morti.* At five o'clock in the morning solemn masses are announced by the church bells tolling as for the passing of the dead.

In spite of the day's somber beginning Il Giorno dei Morti is not entirely a period of gloom; for like all other Italian *feste,* it has its own traditional foods and picturesque customs. *Fave dei Morti,* beans of the dead, is the name given to delectable little bean shaped cakes, made of ground almonds and sugar, combined with egg, butter, flour, and flavoring. These small cakes are white, or are tinted pink or chocolate. In the vicinity of Rome young people often announce engagements on the Day of the Dead. The man sends the engagement ring to his fiancée in the conventional little white box, but this is traditionally packed in an oval container filled with fave dei morti.

In Sicily where the ancient cult of the dead is possibly strongest, children look forward to November 2 with great anticipation. If they are "good," mind their elders, and pray for the departed during the year, the *morti,* or souls of the family dead will return on this night with presents of sweets and toys.

Gaudily colored, tinsel-trimmed, candy dolls are among the children's most coveted gifts in the Palermo area. Large and small figures of historical characters, dancing girls, fair ladies, and plumed knights are some of the many candy doll favorites which make Il Giorno dei Morti a real *festa* to boys and girls.

San Martino (Saint Martin)

November 11

From Venice in the north to Sicily in the south, it is traditional to taste the new wine on the day of San Martino. According to legend San Martino shared his cloak with a poor drunkard who stumbled and fell. Consequently his *festa* is celebrated freely by all lovers of wine.

Customs vary from village to village, but in many places people sample the new wine on this day, feast and carry San Martino's statue in colorful procession through all the town's byways and alleys.

Santa Lucia (Saint Lucy), in Syracuse, Sicily

December 13

Tradition says that Santa Lucia, patroness of Syracuse, was born about 283, of noble family. She had her eyes removed because their beauty had attracted a heathen nobleman. Her rejection of her suitor led first, to her torture, and eventually to her death by the sword.

Santa Lucia, one of Italy's most beloved saints, is patroness of all who suffer from diseases of the eye. Her image in the Duomo, at Syracuse, represents the young Christian martyr holding her eyes in a vessel. Throughout Italy and Sicily her *festa* of December 13 (she has another on May first) is celebrated with bonfires, torchlight processions, and illuminations. This "feast of lights" is appropriate, since people say that Lucia became blind on the shortest day of the year.

In Syracuse the day of Lucia's martyrdom is observed with a magnificent procession in which her bier is carried through the streets by torchlight. The festa of May 1 commemorates the miracle of food which came to Syracuse during a great famine, when the desperate inhabitants went to the Duomo to implore Santa Lucia's help. While the people were praying, a ship laden with life-giving wheat entered the harbor and saved the city from starvation. This is why Italians always eat *cuccidata,* cooked wheat, on both of Santa Lucia's festival days.

La Vigilia (Christmas Eve)

December 24

Christmas in Italy is a religious festival which begins with a Novena of devotional preparation and a twenty-four hour fast, from sunset of December 23 to sunset of December 24. In most homes the first day of the Novena is observed by making ready the *presepio,* or miniature Bethlehem manger, which represents the essence of Christmas to most Italians. On each morning throughout the *Novena* many families gather before the presepio to light the candles and offer prayers. The presepio, with its charming clay or wooden figures of the Holy Family, the angels, shepherds, and kings, are said to have originated over seven hundred years ago with Saint Francis of Assisi.

In many families the Bethlehem mangers are precious heirlooms, handed down and added to, from one generation to the next. For weeks before Christmas small manger figures are on sale in every market and village fair. The settings usually are fashioned in the homes from cardboard, moss, and bits of twig, or from more professional properties. Sometimes backgrounds are very elaborate, showing the sacred grotto, the tavern, shepherds' huts, and shining pools, all set in a charming Italian landscape. The figures of the

Magi journey across the countryside with their camels and precious gifts. Angels, suspended from invisible wires, seem to sing joyous halleluiahs and ragged shepherds kneel before the tiny pink-cheeked Babe, with their offerings of flowers, fruits, and new-born lambs.

In parts of Calabria and the Abruzzi *zampognari,* or itinerant bagpipers come down from the mountains and go about from house to house playing pastoral hymns before the *Bambino Gesù* of the little homemade mangers at village shrines. The musicians receive gifts of food or money at the various homes.

Christmas Eve is strictly a family gathering. When the candles are lighted before the presepi, the children "surprise" their elders by reciting little verses learned weeks in advance. At last the *cenone,* or festa supper is served. This is a meatless meal with many regional variations. *Capitoni,* a variety of large eel, is vastly popular among the well-to-do. Fish of all kinds and fowl are also typical seasonal foods, while *cardoni,* or artichokes cooked with eggs, often accompany eel dishes. Of course, there are all kinds of fancy holiday breads, including *panettone,* the famous currant loaf, and such sweets as *cannoli,* a cheese-filled pastry, *torrone,* or nougat, and many other delicacies.

The Yule log, rather than the Christmas tree, is important to Italian boys and girls. Sometimes they tap it with little sticks, asking for the gifts they want. In certain places the children assemble about the log and are blindfolded. Starting with the youngest, each one recites a little verse to the Bambino Gesù. When their bandages are removed, the children see before them little presents the Bambino has left. Few presents are given on Christmas Eve, and then only simple things for small children and old people. *Epifania,* as already seen, is the time for gift giving.

Family parties continue until almost midnight when everyone attends church services and worships before life-sized figures of the Holy Family. In some rustic areas peasants lay modest gifts of nuts, flowers, and vegetables at the Christ Child's feet; in other places processions for the Bambino are accompanied by shepherds from the hills who play on bagpipes and flutes.

Christmas Day is generally a sacred holiday, celebrated with religious services in the churches and quiet family gatherings in the homes.

SANTO STEFANO (Saint Stephen), in Baiano, province of Avellino
December 26

People of Baiano celebrate the festival of Santo Stefano, the first Christian martyr, whom the Bible describes as "full of faith and the Holy Spirit," by chopping down a fine strong chestnut tree, called the *maio,* and setting it up in the church piazza. Woodcutters and young men hew down the tree, which they load on a specially constructed bullock cart and take to the piazza.

Amid music, rejoicing, and the blessing of the priests, the men set the martyr's tree in a deep hole and surround it with wood supplied by the townsfolk. Then, to the dramatic firing of rifles, the maio finally is ignited. After the fire has died down the ashes are sold for charitable purposes.

Boiled or roasted chestnuts are eaten on this day in honor of the martyr saint.

6

FESTIVALS OF LUXEMBOURG

NEITJORSDÂG (New Year's Day)

January 1

New Year's Day is a time for exchanging greetings and congratulations and visiting family and friends. Parents and relatives customarily give children gifts of money on the first day of the year.

LÎCHTMESDÂG (Candlemas), in Luxembourg-Ville, canton Luxembourg

February 2

Candlemas, the festival commemorating the Purification of the Virgin Mary on the fortieth day after Jesus' birth and the Presentation of her Son at the Temple, gets its name from the custom of blessing candles in the churches. In Luxembourg-Ville school children carry blessed candles to the homes of shut-ins and persons too old or infirm to take their own candles to church for the customary benediction.

The boys and girls go from house to house with lighted candles attached to small spiked batons. Holding their torches high, the youthful visitors knock at doors and sing this Song of Lights:

> Open, open, we come with your candle.
> The wax we hold is blessed.
> None of us will be naughty today,
> For each child brings sacred vows.
>
> We hope that all your life
> You will see the light of sun.
> Open, open, here is the light
> With each child's sacred vows.

105

We hope that in this life
Neither mind nor soul will darken,
And that for you in heaven above
There will be everlasting light.

In return for their song the children receive such gifts as coins, nuts, apples, candies and buns.

*FETTEN DONNESCHDEG (Shrove Thursday)
The Thursday before the beginning of Lent

This is a great day for village children who, dressed in all sorts of fantastic costumes, go about in little bands to neighboring farms. The boys and girls sing a traditional song in which they ask for contributions.

Almost everyone prepares for the children's visit by making pancakes, waffles, and other good things. Farmers' wives usually listen to the song, distribute their gifts, and then gaily pack the children off on their rounds. Occasionally, however, a stingy householder refuses to treat. In the second verse of their ditty the children warn that such unsympathetic persons will be "like a sack of nuts": [1]

Here come the Good Lord's little singers.
Give us some bacon and peas,
A book, maybe two.

Then you'll have good health throughout the year.
If you don't give anything, you'll slip on the ice;
If you don't give anything at all,
You'll be like a sack of nuts!

BRETZELSONNDEG (Pretzel Sunday)
Fourth Sunday in Lent

On *Bretzelsonndeg,* or Pretzel Sunday, it is customary for boys to give their sweethearts beautifully decorated cakes in pretzel form.

* Stars indicate movable feasts that depend upon Easter. See Table of Easter Dates and Movable Festivals Dependent upon Easter, p. 246.
[1] The children mean they will pound stingy people with their fists, just as they pound nuts in a sack!

106

If a girl likes the boy and wishes to encourage his attentions she gives him a decorated egg on Easter Sunday and walks with him in the park. When the pretzel cake is big, the girl reciprocates with a large egg, possibly a beautifully adorned chocolate creation, filled with bonbons. If the cake is small, the egg, also, is small.

At Leap Year the pretzel custom is reversed, the girls giving cakes to the boys on *Bretzelsonndeg* and the boys giving the girls eggs at Easter. Not only boys and girls, but married couples as well, participate in the exchange of cakes and eggs.

*PELLEMSONNDEG (Palm Sunday)

The Sunday preceding Easter

Children carry "palms" [2] to church to be blessed by the priest. Following their consecration, the children, with palms aloft, form in a procession commemorating the joyous multitude which accompanied Jesus on his triumphal entrance into Jerusalem.

Boys and girls precede a group of priests, church dignitaries and choir boys who hold up a large crucifix, decorated with blessed palms. The procession goes about the church, first inside, then without, chanting in Latin the following hymn:

> Glory, praise, honor to Thee,
> Christ our King and Savior,
> To whom this child chorus sings reverent hosannahs.

> Thou art King of Israel,
> Glorious offspring of David,
> O blessed King, who cometh in the name of the Lord.

*CHARFREUDEG (Good Friday)

The Friday preceding Easter

Charfreudeg, or Good Friday, commemorates Christ's crucifixion and is a day of gloom. "The bells have flown to Rome for confession," is a popular saying which explains why all church bells are silent from Good Friday until Easter. School boys, taking over the

---

[2] In Luxembourg, the Netherlands and some other European countries, "palms" are branches of boxwood, which remain green and fragrant throughout the year.

function of the bells, go through the streets calling people to worship by shaking wooden rattles which make a melancholy sound.

On Good Friday all churches are draped in black and the prevalent atmosphere is one of sadness and solemnity.

*CHARSAMSDEG (Holy Saturday)

The Saturday preceding Easter

The ceremony of blessing water and fire precedes Midnight Mass. In the evening priests and parishioners, holding unlighted wax candles, gather before the darkened church. There the priest blesses the water to be used for baptism. He also blesses an altar fire from which he lights his candle. The second candle is lighted from the first, the third from the second and so on, until every candle is kindled. Then the entire congregation enters the church, which suddenly is illuminated with hundreds of lights.

The service continues with the singing of the *Gloria* at midnight, the traditional hour of Our Lord's resurrection. The organ rolls forth, church bells peal joyously and Easter is announced in every town and village.

On Holy Saturday it is customary for choir boys to visit from house to house. Everyone receives them warmly and gives presents of eggs and coins. The boys eat the eggs during the Easter holiday. The money is pooled and used to defray the expenses for an excursion with the priest to some place of special beauty or historic interest.

*O'SCHTERSONNDEG (Easter Sunday)

Easter Sunday is a happy occasion for everyone, but particularly for small children. They rise at dawn and search the gardens for the beautiful eggs which, parents say, are left at night by the Easter Bunny. The boys and girls, little baskets on arms, look behind stones, beneath bushes, among the tall grasses. The children's efforts are usually richly rewarded, for the empty baskets soon are filled with gaily colored dyed eggs, as well as with many of the marvelously decorated sugar and chocolate eggs for which Luxembourg is famous.

For the young girls who received *bretzelen,* or pretzel cakes, from admirers on *Bretzelsonndeg,* [3] Easter is no less exciting than for their younger brothers and sisters. Even the girl who was afraid of expressing her real sentiments earlier, now quite properly may give the boy of her choice an elaborately decorated egg shaped container, which is filled with all kinds of delectable sweets.

Dessert for the family Easter dinner usually is a cake, or sometimes an ice, made in a Pascal lamb mold.

*OCTAVE (Octave of Our Lady, Consoler of the Afflicted), in Luxembourg-Ville, canton Luxembourg
                    Fifth Sunday after Easter, for 8 to 15 days

The Octave of *Notre Dame la Consolatrice des Affligés,* observed in Luxembourg the fifth Sunday after Easter and from eight to fifteen days following, is the nation's most outstanding religious festival. Pilgrims from all parts of the Grand Duchy pour into the capital to honor Mary, the Consolatrice, to thank her for past protection and to pray for her help in the future. On September 26, 1666, Luxembourg-Ville's Municipal Council proclaimed the Blessed Virgin patroness of the capital. Twelve years later the entire nation was placed under her benign care.

"There are many, many legends about our Virgin," declared one informant, referring to the ancient image which annually is taken from the cathedral and carried through the streets in solemn procession.

According to one tradition several Jesuit students discovered the image in 1624, in the hollow of an oak, outside the then walled city. The statue was reverently taken to the Jesuit college church (which later became the cathedral) and placed on the altar. The same night the figure vanished mysteriously through locked doors and later was discovered in the oak. A second time the same thing occured. Only then did the Church Fathers realize the Virgin wished to remain outside the fortress walls.

[3] p. 106.

In 1625, a tiny chapel was built for the image. During the following year when pestilence claimed victims throughout the countryside, people thought many remarkable cures were wrought by the Consolatrice whose shrine became a pilgrimage center.

With the French Revolution the chapel [4] was destroyed; but the Virgin's image, believed to have been miraculously saved from destruction, was eventually installed in its present position of honor on the cathedral's main altar.

In 1666, when Luxembourg-Ville was dedicated to the patronage of Mary the Consolatrice, the keys of the city were entrusted to the statue. Tradition says that when Napoleon I made his triumphal entrance into the fortress after the Revolution, a little white-frocked girl officially presented him with the keys on a crimson cushion. "Take them back," Napoleon commanded. "They are in good hands." Since then, according to the Letzebuerger, or inhabitants of Luxembourg, the keys never have left the Consolatrice's hands.

"Some people wonder why our Virgin does not perform miracles such as curing a sick arm or head," confided a woman in attempting to explain the deep veneration everyone feels toward the patroness. "She does not do *outward* healing. She performs miracles *within*. The Consolatrice heals the spirit!"

"The great procession in Our Lady's honor will be Sunday," she continued. "Rain or shine, it will be then. Myself, I think it will rain," she said, gloomily scrutinizing the sky, "but the procession will go on just the same. The whole city will be decorated with young fir trees and flowers. The Grand Duchess and her family will be there. All the people will come with banners, whether it rains or not. It will be a great sight, Madame,—much better, of course, if it does not rain.

"There is a story that one year it rained and nobody attended. The rain was so bad nobody ventured out. But people said our Virgin went out alone. She went through all the city streets by herself. Everybody knows this is the truth. Next day they found raindrops on her robe."

---

[4] The modern Chapelle le Glacis, on the ancient boundaries of Luxembourg-Ville marks the reputed site of the destroyed shrine.

LUXEMBOURG

Sunday was bright and clear, despite predictions to the contrary. Luxembourg-Ville presented an enchanting appearance, with pots of blooming flowers at every window and colorful religious banners hung across streets. Fir trees marked the procession route. Four outdoor altars, decorated with flowers, candles and banners awaited administration of the Sacrament.

Each altar was unique. One displayed a white-robed image of the Consolatrice, against a background of palms and firs. White hydrangeas were massed at the feet. Overhead fluttered long graceful pennants of yellow, blue, and white.

By three o'clock the procession was forming before the closed cathedral doors. The various counties all had their own brass bands and handsome standards. Boy Scouts, Girl Guides, schools and seminaries, religious orders, men's and women's church groups and societies marched past in endless succession. Then, all at once, the cathedral doors swung open. Out tripped a bewitching procession of very small children, costumed as priests and bishops, scarlet-robed cardinals, and choir boys in red gowns and lace-edged surplices. One little boy, representing John the Baptist, wore knitted imitation fur over one shoulder, and clutched a plump toy lamb.

Many little girls had pale pink or blue frocks and matching eiderdown wings attached at the shoulders. "They represent angels of heaven in their innocence," said one informant. Some of the children, in long white satin or tulle gowns, wore gold circlets and carried sprays of gilded flowers.

The costumed children, scattering rose petals as they marched, preceded the first communicants. The little eight-year-old girls looked like brides, in long white dresses and filmy veils. The small boys wore black suits with fringed white satin arm bows.

In the hush that followed the appearance of the "Children of Mary," as the first communicants are called, the image of the Consolatrice des Affligés was carried out from the cathedral beneath a sumptuous canopy. The image of the Virgin was arrayed in dark blue velvet, embroidered with gold and jewels. A priceless lace veil fell from the crowned head to the hem of the gown. In one arm was the Infant; in the other a sceptre. From the wrist hung a rosary, a golden heart, and the symbolic key of Luxembourg-Ville.

Following the Consolatrice walked high ranking church dignitaries in gorgeous vestments of blue, white, crimson and gold; the Grand Duchess of Luxembourg, accompanied by the Prince and members of the Grand Ducal family; representatives of the Chamber of Deputies and other government officials. Last of all the Blessed Sacrament, displayed in a sun-rayed monstrance of gleaming gold, was borne from the cathedral under a richly embroidered canopy.

*SPRANGPROZESSIO'N (Dancing Procession), in Echternach, canton Echternach

Whit Tuesday or Pentecost Tuesday

Thousands of pilgrims from many parts of the world annually visit Echternach on Whit Tuesday, for the *Sprangprozessio'n,* or Dancing Procession of Saint Willibrord, patron of the town and founder of its abbey. Tradition says that for over six hundred years people have danced the same strange rhythm—three steps forward, two steps back—toward the shrine of the seventh-century Northumbrian saint who reputedly Christianized Luxembourg.

On Whit Tuesday I hurried toward the abbey courtyard before the basilica bells struck nine. In the cobble-stoned marketplace the *Friture Henriette* was heaping up piles of sausages and mountains of round white rolls. Already the air was heavy with the aroma of frying fish and potatoes. Managers of recently installed merry-go-rounds, dodgem cars and shooting galleries were busily polishing brass and adding last minute touches, for the *kermesse,* or fair, following the procession, would last far into the night. Close to the basilica vendors were arranging religious souvenirs and votive candles on little stands and chatting with arriving tourists.

The courtyard was rapidly filling. Autobuses discharged orderly crowds of pilgrims. There were youth groups, proudly carrying their banners; tall, bearded *Pères Blancs* from Marienthal Monastery, with gracefully draped white robes and long black rosaries; white-bloused girls; and boys in white shirts with handkerchiefs knotted about heads, who were ready to dance in the procession. Frequently priests and villagers from widely separated parishes stopped for handclasps and greetings, for the annual *Sprangprozessio'n* always unites friends from distant places.

As the crowd thickened, I squeezed in near the foot of the graceful stairway which leads, on either side, to the iron grilled tribune overlooking the abbey yard. There the aged Bishop of Luxembourg sat—a benevolent and commanding figure in tall miter and magnificent vestments. Beside me an old man in broad-brimmed black hat, adorned with a peacock feather, grasped a stout cane in tremulous, knotted fingers. A young priest, pale and gentle faced, stood reading from a breviary with purple, green and red markers. He and his little band, which included both aged and infirm, had come far, people said. The Sunday before they had started on foot from Prüm, "a village eighty kilometers away that once was Luxembourg territory, but now is German." Some of the women sat on little stools, heads bowed, lips moving, as they slipped rosary beads through calloused, toil-worn fingers.

Overhead swallows screamed and circled against the blue May sky. In the courtyard below a deep hush fell as *gendarmes* made way for the approaching religious procession. Archbishops, abbots and other churchmen, in vestments of blue, orange, and scarlet, slowly mounted the stairs and ranged themselves near the bishop. White-robed acolytes carried Saint Willibrord's reliquary, surmounted by a blue and white enamel cross. A cerise-robed priest stood motionless on the steps, holding a red-and-orange pagoda-shaped canopy.

The Luxembourg Bishop spoke clearly and movingly. He welcomed pilgrims and visitors and reminded them of the life and deeds of the Anglo-Saxon Willibrord, who came to Echternach thirteen centuries ago, bringing Christianity for the country and help for the sick.

The brief, impressive sermon ended, the crowd rapidly shifted. Thousands of procession participants took their places in the abbey grounds; thousands of spectators lined the streets and market place, or stationed themselves at windows and balconies facing the line of march.

Slowly the procession began to move. Heavy church banners, worked in gold thread and rich silks, swayed as the bearers marched. Upheld crosses glinted in the bright sunlight. A churchman in tall miter and gold lined cope raised his hand in benediction. Priests in black cassocks and pleated surplices, edged with precious lace, chanted in deep melodious voices the Litany of Saint Willibrord, "founder of churches, . . . destroyer of idols, . . . father of the poor." Hundreds of voices along the line caught up the words, which were almost drowned at times by the raucous brass bands and rasping violins preceding the different pilgrim groups. For hours the same tune was repeated until Echternach's narrow winding streets echoed and throbbed with the monotonous rhythm.

Eight or ten abreast the perspiring dancers came—jumping, singing—either holding hands or knotted handkerchief ends, in order to keep their lines. First came the weary pilgrims from Prüm and Eifel, led by their priests in short black jackets; then delegations from Aachen followed by some twenty-five groups from Beaufort, Berdorf, Wasserbillig, Ettelbruck and other communities throughout the country. Each parish had its own priests, standards, bands, and organized youth, church, or welfare groups.

Among the participants were elderly black-clad women and old men, such as one I saw, in suspenders and blue cotton shirt, who resolutely jumped in solo performance. Mothers danced with babies in arms, or sometimes alone, for children too ill to attend; old women danced for ailing husbands. There were plenty of rosy-cheeked boys and girls who had learned the traditional steps in school and danced with joy and precision. There were also sick children who sought miraculous help. For centuries the people of Echternach have danced thus to Saint Willibrord to invoke their patron's blessing in cures of epilepsy, "the falling sickness," and other ills.

The *Sprangprozessio'n* is deeply moving. As one man said, "Here you see rich and poor, young and old, Letzebuerger, French, Germans, Belgians. Today they are one. All come for the same purpose."

By one o'clock the procession had danced its slow tortuous way through the market place, past the Denzelt, or Town Hall, on to the basilica, for the Pontifical Mass and *Te Deum*. Finally the pilgrims knelt in the crypt before Saint Willibrord's marble sarcophagus, more beautiful than usual today, with hundreds of lighted candles and massed pink and white hydrangeas. Suppliants handed up worn breviaries and votive tapers to be blessed at the tomb, and drew water from the Saint's well nearby; for faith is strong that Willibrord, "consoler of the afflicted," will ever heed his people's prayers.

The origin of the *Sprangprozessio'n* is the subject of much speculation. The dance melody, according to one Echternach scholar, probably dates back to the fourteenth century, although the tune was not mentioned in writing until about 1420, by a monk of Treves. The music, which is known in the Moselle and Rhine valleys, as well as in the Eifel, once accompanied these old words:

> Adam had seven sons,
> Seven sons had Adam;
> Seven daughters he must have
> If he would marry them!

Echternach people whimsically explain the origin of the Dancing Procession by the legend of a Crusader, who set out from their town for the Holy Land. The man was accompanied by his wife, who died during the arduous journey. Several years later the Crusader returned to Echternach, to find that his wife's greedy relations had appropriated his lands and branded him a murderer.

The execution date was set for a Whit Tuesday. The condemned man was led to the gallows outside the town, accompanied by the executioner, town officials and taunting, jeering citizens. Under his arm the Crusader carried his beloved violin. Standing

115

on the scaffold above the scoffing crowd, he asked permission to play one final tune on his instrument.

Tucking the violin beneath his chin, the Crusader played a simple polka melody. Over and over he played it until the haunting rhythm hypnotized the bloodthirsty mob. The executioner began to dance; then the mayor and town councilmen. The priest joined in; finally all the people. Nothing could stop their frenzied steps. Even stray cats and dogs started to jump up and down in mad abandon.

The exhausted crowd begged for mercy, but the condemned man played on. Finally he descended the scaffold steps. Nobody tried to stop him. Still playing the same hypnotic air, he walked through the dancing crowd and disappeared in the adjoining forest. The citizens of Echternach continued to dance, unable to stop.

The tale has many variations. One is that the accused man was pardoned. Another is that Willibrord interceded for his people, thus saving them from dancing to death. Still another tradition is that, throughout the centuries, Echternach's citizens have held the annual Dancing Procession as penance for unjust condemnation of an innocent man.

The curious movements of the dance suggest a theory that they indicate either epilepsy, "the falling sickness," or Saint Vitus' dance, —both diseases Saint Willibrord was thought to miraculously heal. Yet another belief is that the dance commemorates Saint Willibrord's cure of cattle which, in the eighth century, were dying by hundreds of a mysterious distemper. The people beseeched their patron's help. When they finally combined their prayers with ritualistic dancing to the saint's tomb, the epidemic ceased and the cattle became well.

MUTTERGOTTESPROZESSIO'N OP D' BILDCHEN (Procession to Our Lady of Bildchen), in Vianden, Canton Vianden
The Sunday following the Feast of Assumption

Each year on the Sunday following August 15, the Feast of Assumption, a pilgrimage is made to the little white spired chapel of

Bildchen. The small sanctuary stands high above the river Our on a densely tree-covered hillside, midway between Bievels and Vianden. The Chapelle du Bildchen, as it is called, is a shrine for a statue of the Virgin which, legend says, two little goatherds discovered nearly a thousand years ago in these same wooded hills.

Annually the statue is removed from the chapel and carried in stately procession along the forest path, to Vianden's parish church. There the image remains until the Sunday after the Octave, when it is again returned to the woodland sanctuary.

The story of the Virgin of Bildchen has been recounted with many variations during the centuries, but probably the most current version is this:

On the first of May, in the year 994, two goatherds were gathering firewood on the hillside where the chapel now stands. While searching for fuel one of the boys found a little wooden statue óf the Virgin in the crotch of an old oak tree. He tossed the statue on the fire. Instead of burning, the wood became blindingly bright. Thoroughly frightened, the boys ran back to Vianden and related what they had seen.

Next day they returned to the scene of their adventure, accompanied by a priest. The Virgin, no longer in the firebed, was back in the tree. Awed, and convinced that the image possessed miraculous powers, the priest and children took it to the Vianden parish church. Next day the statue had disappeared and, as before, was found in the tree. After the same thing had occured several times, people realized that the Virgin wished her statue to remain where found. Before long it became the object of veneration by pilgrims throughout the land.

Years passed and the old oak died. The image was placed in the rocks until 1848, when the present shrine was built on the supposed site of the tree. The small white chapel is simple in the extreme. The Virgin's statue and a few fresh flowers stand on an altar from Vianden's parish church. Votive candles burn brightly beside the altar rail, for pilgrims seek the shrine not only in August, but at all times of the year.

A tablet above the chapel door bears the inscription: *Profer lumen caecis, pelle mala nostra.* "Give light to the blind; banish our ills." For centuries the blind and those afflicted with eye diseases and illness have sought aid of Our Lady of Bildchen. Along the woodland path from Viaden to the shrine are seven altars, depicting seven episodes in the life of Christ. At these altars the faithful pray and refresh the spirit with birdsong and sylvan beauty. A spring gushes from rocks close to the chapel. Here many pause to bathe their eyes in the clear waters, which are thought to possess curative powers.

Saint Haupert (Saint Hubert)

November 3

Many Luxembourg churches are dedicated to Saint Hubert, eighth-century "Apostle of the Ardennes" and patron of hunters and the chase. On the saint's anniversary huntsmen attend High Mass in honor of their protector. When leaving church they sound a blast on their horns, to indicate a minute of silent prayer. People say that even the dogs, which are kept outside during Mass, heed the silent moment when their masters pray for preservation from harm.

The religious service over, hunters and dogs joyously start for the chase. The traditional Saint Hubert's day outdoor meal is hot green pea soup, garnished with sausages and lean bacon.

Neklosdag (Saint Nicholas' Day)

December 6

The Festival of Saint Nicholas, patron of children, is anticipated by boys and girls for months and weeks ahead. The Sunday preceding the festival Saint Nicholas makes official entry into towns and villages throughout Luxembourg.

At Echternach, where the ceremony is typical of other places, Saint Nicholas arrives by boat on the river Sûre. The saint wears a red silk robe and tall miter and in white-gloved hands he carries a golden cross. He has a long gray beard and his bright eyes twinkle mischievously at boys and girls from behind gleaming spectacles. The genial bishop is accompanied by *Hoësecker,* a character children regard with some apprehension, since he carries on his back a large bundle of willow switches.

The mayor, aldermen, and other officials meet Saint Nicholas and *Hoësecker* at the quay, with a horse-drawn carriage, decorated with firs. The distinguished guests are escorted through the town in gay procession, followed by hundreds of excited school children. The boys and girls sing traditional songs to their beloved patron, to musical accompaniment by the town's brass band. One favorite song implores Saint Nicholas to leave plenty of bonbons:

> O, good Saint Nicholas, patron of school children,
> Bring me bonbons to put in my little basket.
> I want to be as good as a little lamb,
> To learn my lessons, so I shall receive bonbons!
> O, good Saint Nicholas, O, good, O, good Saint Nicholas.

At last the procession enters the marketplace. Saint Nicholas, with Hoësecker at his side, stations himself beneath the arched Gothic portico of the picturesque Denzelt, or Town Hall, which juts out into the cobbled square. Behind the saint are big boxes of gifts for the children, who are now excitedly hopping and jumping in anticipation of the moment of distribution.

The affair is perfectly organized. There is no confusion, no hitch in plans. The band plays joyous Christmas airs. The children start filing past Saint Nicholas and his assistants. First come mothers with infants in arms, then the larger children, up to twelve years old. Each child receives a generous-sized paper bag containing apples, nuts, delicious little cakes and sugar confections. The boys and girls squeal with delight; from time to time, however, they shrink back in fear as Hoësecker advances threateningly and brandishes a willow switch, to warn of the punishment awaiting disobedient and slothful children.

Excitement is far from over when Saint Nicholas and Hoësecker finally return to their boat on the Sûre and depart for another town. At dawn of December 6, the saint's real anniversary, youngsters in every home rush into the dining room, to discover the toys and toothsome sweets left for them by their beloved patron.

CHRESHDAGÔVEND (Christmas Eve)

December 24

Christmas Eve home ceremonies center about the tree, decorated with glittering colored balls and wax candles, which usually is displayed in the "best" room. Even more important than the tree is the traditional Nativity, which is placed beneath the branches. These miniature representations of the crib, with the Infant Jesus, Joseph, Mary, the shepherds and Wise Men, often have very old carved wooden figures which have been handed down from generation to generation and added to from year to year.

About seven in the evening the Christmas tree candles are lighted and the family enters the room singing carols. An elaborate cold buffet supper, served with tea, wine or liqueurs, follows the enjoyment of tree and Nativity and the distribution of gifts. Children play with their presents and adults amuse themselves with songs and conversation until time for Midnight Mass.

After Mass the family returns to a traditional supper of black pudding and roasted sausages, served with white cabbage and boiled potatoes and accompanied by wine or beer. Christmas Day festivities, aside from church services, rarely begin until noon.

7

FESTIVALS OF THE NETHERLANDS

NIEUWJAARSDAG (New Year's Day)

January 1

The first day of the year is set aside as a time for calling on friends, feasting on all kinds of exciting foods (including holiday cakes, breads and waffles), and drinking *slemp* (or *slem*), an old fashioned New Year's beverage, made with milk.

Among the season's baked specialties are *knijpertjes,* meaning, literally, "clothespins." This delicacy, a favorite in northern provinces, has been popular since the Middle Ages. *Duivekater,* another New Year favorite, is a long decorative loaf that is familiar to many through Jan Steen's famous Saint Nicholas Eve painting. This bread, made nowadays by a few professional bakers, is still eaten with as much relish as in seventeenth-century Holland. There are also numberless small holiday cakes and pastries, including such delicacies as *appelbeignets,* or apple dumplings, *oliebollen,* fried cakes, and *sneeuwballen,* or snowballs. In some places *soesjes,* a regional cake, traditionally accompanies the slemp. Once this steaming milk drink was sold to skaters from stalls on the ice-covered canals. The beverage was not only hot and refreshing; it cost but a few cents a cup.

A popular poet of former days who signed himself "The School-master," once wrote this satiric rhyme:

> Stop here! Stop here!
> Life is but a slippery skating rink.
> Bitter draughts, or milk and saffron.

"Bitter draughts" referred to alcoholic beverages, while "milk and saffron" meant slemp, a New Year's drink once as traditional to Netherlands as eggnog to Americans.

Here is a modified recipe:

Slemp

2 cups milk
2 teaspoons tea
2½ tablespoons sugar
1 stick cinnamon
Pinch of salt
Lemon-peel twist
Pinch of saffron
2 whole cloves ⎫ tied together
¼ teaspoon mace ⎭ in cheesecloth bag

Place all the ingredients, except tea and sugar, in the top of a double boiler. Occasionally press spice bag against side of pan. When milk is thoroughly flavored, remove peel and spices. Stir in tea and sugar. Strain into cups and serve hot with holiday cakes.

New Year's Day is as jolly for boys and girls as for their elders. Children scramble out of bed early and try to be first in shouting "Happy New Year" as relatives and friends enter the room. Parents, bachelor uncles and grandfathers reward the youngsters with shining new gulders for their savings banks.

On New Year's Day boys of Zeeland, Overijssel, and some other places go about from house to house ringing bells and wishing people a Happy New Year. Sometimes they make hideous noises on a home-made drum-like contrivance, called *rommelpot,* or rumble pot, and beg for pennies. The rommelpot is a large kettle with a piece of hide tightly stretched across the top. The boys work a stick up and down through a hole in the center of the skin, thus producing a loud rumbling sound which, when multiplied many times, makes an ear-splitting din. Possibly the rommelpot was originally intended to frighten away evil spirits from the homes, at the beginning of the year.

In cities householders receive calls from the newspaper man, the laundry man, the milkman and others, who are given gifts of money in return for their holiday greetings.

THE NETHERLANDS

DRIEKONINGENAVOND (Three Kings' Eve)

We are the Three Kings.
We sing and we dance,
Carrying the star
Which leads us from afar.
Kind Master and Mistress,
Please give us cakes
For this is Three Kings' Eve.

In many places groups of boys chant songs like this as they make the neighborhood rounds on this day and demand their share of *Driekoningenavond* cheer. The boys, dressed in fantastic garments and wearing gold crowns, carry paper-star lanterns mounted on long poles. As the song indicates, the lads represent the Three Kings of the East following the Star of Bethlehem.

Rosy-cheeked farmers' wives welcome the children in fragrant kitchens and offer candy and cake. Throughout the countryside there are festivities and family parties on this night and itinerant singers never leave homes empty-handed.

Occasionally, as in the nonsense lines that follow, the Kings demand clothing instead of holiday fare:

Three Kings, Three Kings,
Give me a new hat.
My old one is worn out.
Father must not know,
Mother is not home.
Peep, says the mouse in the front hall.

Characteristic of Driekoningenavond celebrations is the special cake which, according to tradition has a bean or an almond in the dough. Whoever finds the bean or nut in his portion is proclaimed King of the Feast and crowned with mock pomp. The King chooses his consort who is also crowned and rules with him.

In some places the King gives a party to everybody else later in the year; in others guests draw lots to indicate the duties of various members of the Royal Household. Thus the Steward serves food;

the Musician improvises entertainment on a paper-covered comb, pots, pans, or other musical instruments he can invent on the spur of the moment; the Jester tries to make everyone laugh; the Wine Taster samples drinks and the Councilor gives sage advice. In other words, each member of the court has a special function to perform. If anyone forgets his allotted role he must pay a forfeit assigned by the Head of the Exchequer.

An amusing variation of the usual custom exists in Denekamp and other eastern communities where three leaves, rather than a bean and almond are baked in the cake. Each of the three guests finding a leaf gives a party to the others some time during the year.

*VASTENAVOND (Fast Eve) (Shrove Tuesday)
The Tuesday before Ash Wednesday

Vastenavond, the day preceding the Lenten fast, is observed with all kinds of feasting and merrymaking. Customs vary widely from place to place. In the southern part of the country the Carnival season lasts for three days, beginning on Sunday. In many places the celebration is confined to one day.

In the provinces of Limburg and Brabant it is customary on Fast Eve to eat pancakes and *oliebollen,* or rich fried cakes. Brabant also specializes in *worstebrood,* a special kind of bread. Outside, the loaf looks like any other; inside, however, it contains a mixture of deliciously spiced sausage meat—the last to be enjoyed until after Lent.

Carnival is very gay in southern Holland. Preparations for the event are made on the eleventh day of the eleventh month, when a council of eleven organizes plans. Eleven, the traditional number of fools, is selected so "anyone can be as foolish as he likes on three days of the year!" In other words, one can get drunk, wear an outlandish costume, dance in the streets. Any sort of foolishness is permissible on the three days preceding Lent. This is a popular season for dances, parades, and masquerade balls.

* Stars indicate movable feasts that depend upon Easter. See Table of Easter Dates and Movable Festivals Dependent upon Easter, p. 246.

Farmers of Schouwen-en-Duiveland, on the island of Zeeland, still observe an interesting old Vastenavond custom. In the afternoon they gather at the village green with their horses. The animals are carefully groomed. Manes and tails are combed out and decorated with gaily-colored paper roses.

The men finally ride their horses down to the beach, making sure the animals get their feet wet.[1] At the head of the colorful procession the leader toots on a horn.

When the men return to the village the burgomaster treats them to a drink and the rest of the evening is spent in dancing and merrymaking.

*Palm Zondag (Palm Sunday)

The Sunday preceding Easter

Palm Sunday (in some places the Saturday before) is a holiday that is impatiently awaited by boys and girls. Dressed in their Sunday best, the children go in procession from farm to farm with the traditional *Palmpaas,* or Easter "palm." As the youngsters march they sing nonsense verses in which they beg eggs for the Easter sports.

The Palmpaas is a curiously-decorated stick which, although differing widely from district to district, usually is decorated with many of the same Easter emblems. The framework of the Palmpaas is a hoop, attached to a stick that is between eighteen and fifty-four inches long. The hoop is covered with boxwood and adorned with colored paper flags, egg shells, sugar rings, oranges, raisins, figs, chocolate eggs and small cakes. Surmounting the structure are little baked dough figures of swans or cocks. In Deventer, in the province of Overijssel, five or more swans decorate the girls' Palmpaas, while the boys' have but a single larger bird. Sometimes competitions are held for the most striking Palmpaas. Originally, this stick, with its fig, egg, and bird decorations, was doubtless a fertility symbol

---

[1] It is possible that this custom originated in some ancient spring purification rite, when horns were blown to drive away evil spirits and the horses' feet made wet as a symbolic cleansing act.

representing the bringing of spring into the village, resurrection after the death of winter.

The children walk through country lanes or village streets, carrying their Palmpaas and little empty baskets. Meanwhile, the youthful voices intone the well known words:

> Palm, Palmpaasen,
> *Ei korei!*
> One more Sunday
> And we'll get an egg,
> And we'll get an egg.

Half speaking, half chanting, the children continue:

> One egg is no egg;
> Two eggs are half an egg;
> Three eggs are an Easter egg

thus indicating that at least three eggs are needed to make one *Paasei* or Easter egg.

Another version of the song, coming from the Overijssel communities of Ootmarsum and Denekamp, reminds householders that Easter eggs are wanted for the popular Dutch sport of *eiertikken,* or egg tapping:

> Palm, Palm Easter
> The hens begin to cackle,
> *Ei korei, ei korei.*
> When next Sunday comes
> We'll get a nice egg for tapping.

In certain Roman Catholic areas the "palms" that decorate the Palmpaas are preserved, after the priest's consecration, as protection against lightning and sore throat during the coming year.

*PASEN, or PASEN ZONDAG (Easter Sunday)

Throughout the country Easter is celebrated as a great spring holiday. In homes there are charmingly laid tables with decorations of colored eggs and early flowers. *Paasbrood,* a delicious sweet bread stuffed with raisins and currants, is one of many traditional feast day specialties which are as much a part of Easter as the joy ously ringing church bells.

Almost every eastern Netherlands hamlet observes the day by lighting Easter bonfires on some hill or high point outside the village. Collection of fuel begins weeks in advance. Everyone con· tributes his share of wood. Even the tiniest child toddles up to the vast pile to lay on a few twigs or sticks.

Generally much friendly rivalry exists between neighboring communities to see which can get the biggest bonfire. As the flames mount villagers join hands and dance about the fires, singing hymns of great antiquity. On Easter afternoon the glow of fires often lights the sky over large areas and fills the air with the tangy scent of wood smoke.

Although each village has its own Easter fire customs and its own songs (often known only in local vernacular), Denekamp, in the province of Overijssel, is unique in featuring two young men who represent the comic characters of Judas *and* Iscariot.

Judas, people tell me, is "the clever man." He is the master of ceremonies while his assistant, Iscariot (Karioter, in Denekamp dialect) is "the stupid man," who acts the part of a brainless clown. There are some who think the character of Judas is simply a Christianized personification of the pagan figure of Winter or Death which was cast from the village in early spring.

The duty of Judas and Iscariot is to prepare the Easter bonfire and to fetch and set up the "Easter pole," a tall fir tree which is annually contributed by owners of the famous Den Beugelskamp estate.

On Palm Sunday Judas and his assistant go with baskets from farm to farm, singing regional Easter songs and begging for money and eggs. Later, the eggs are sold. The proceeds, added to cash already collected, help defray expenses of pine wood for the bonfire.

The following Sunday every detail of dragging the Easter pole to the village is performed according to established custom. In the afternoon a company of men and boys, led by Judas and Iscariot, goes down the long beech-lined avenues skirting the meandering

Dinkel, to Den Beugelskamp, situated a little outside the town. The superintendent indicates the tree assigned to the bonfire. Judas climbs the fir and securely ties a rope to the top. Then the stripping begins. All side branches are removed. Only the feathery top remains. The tree is cut down. The men form in a long line and many pairs of willing hands drag the fir top foremost to the village Church of Saint Nicholas. There the tree is stood up outside the door until after Easter vespers, which all Denekamp attends. Later, the men and boys drag the "Easter pole" (possibly, a substitute for the Maypole of earlier days) to the *Paasbult,* or Easter hill, at the edge of the town. The stripped fir is firmly planted close to the huge unlighted bonfire.

Traditionally, Judas sets a ladder against the tree, climbs up, and starts auctioning it to the highest bidder. Everyone teases and makes fun of Judas, who finally gives over his place to Iscariot. The crowd jeers and hoots at him also. Finally, when the sport becomes tiresome, Judas makes the announcement that the fire will be lighted at eight o'clock that night. Only then do the townsfolk go home to suppers of Easter eggs and other seasonal goodies.

Later, as the great bonfire burns, Denekamp's folk dance far into the night and honor the Risen Christ with a hymn known only to their town. Many of the original words are obsolete or exist solely in native dialect. The verses are given in full since few persons remember them all. Both the archaic expressions and the curious blending of Old and New Testment themes suggest the song's antiquity:

> Today is the great day
> When Christ was raised from the grave
> Early in the morning at this time;
> So let all Christians rejoice.
>
> *Chorus*:
> Therefore, therefore come, all ye mortals.
> Alleluja, alleluja! Let us sing.

THE NETHERLANDS

Samson came at midnight
He, he let the portals fall.
Christ rose by his own strength.
Who will deny it?

Jonas after three days
Was spewed up by the whale.
Christ, to the Jews' regret,
Arises! This will I believe.

False reasons were sought;
O, shame upon the Jews!
The soldiers who were bribed
Lay like the dead beside the grave.

Three Marys with all haste
Came to the grave, afraid
Until they heard the good angel say,
He whom ye seek is risen.

Magdalena stood by the grave
Weeping bitterly;
But when she saw the gardener
Her sadness disappeared.

Christ in darkest night
Has risen in shining glory.
He has broken Satan's power.
Come, let us be glad.

Pharaoh in frantic mood
Pursued Israel's children;
Through the stream of Christ's blood
All sins are washed away.

Pharaoh as if of lead
Is lost in the sea.
The Conqueror of Death
Appears in splendor,

Arising like a god, full of glory.
Then Death was overcome.
Let us rejoice in Jesus' name
That eternal life is won.

Glory to the Father and to the Son,
Glory to the Spirit of both.
May He in His mercy
Lead us to the Heavenly Kingdom.

*VLÖGGELEN ("Winging" Ceremony), in Ootmarsum, province of Overijssel

Easter Sunday and Monday

The old Easter-tide custom of *Vlöggelen,* meaning in local dialect "to wing" or "go as with wings," is practiced only in the eastern Netherlands village of Ootmarsum. The Vlöggelen ceremony is in the nature of a slow, ritualistic dance [2]—probably the survival of some early spring fertility rite. The villagers, who include farmers, housewives, young people and children, form in line in Ootmarsum's narrow cobbled streets. Each person then puts the right hand behind his back and clasps the left hand of the person directly following. A long human chain is thus formed. The line then advances gradually, "like birds on the wing," in rhythm to the constantly repeated words and melody of an ancient Easter hymn. The dancers zig-zag through winding streets and rutted country roads, entering the front doors of shops, inns, farmhouses and barns and emerging by back doors.

The melody of the Easter song is peculiar to Ootmarsum, although the words are familiar to the neighboring village of Denekamp. Each of the nineteen verses ends with an *Alleluja* refrain. Since few people, nowadays, know all the words by heart, it is customary to pin a copy of the entire song to the back of each dancer. In this way nobody falters and the fine old words ring out con-

---

[2] Compare with the Furry Dance of Helston, Cornwall, England. Dorothy Gladys Spicer, *Yearbook of English Festivals* (New York, The H. W. Wilson Company, 1954). "Furry Day," p. 64ff.

tinuously as the dancers wind in and out, up and down, with the traditional message of hope and life eternal:

Christ is risen
From the hands of the Jews;
Therefore let us rejoice
Christ will be our Redeemer.
Alleluja!

*PASEN, or PAAS MAANDAG (Easter Monday)

The Monday after Easter

Paas Maandag, or Easter Monday, is a gay holiday for both children and adults who celebrate the occasion with many kinds of egg games.

Eierrapen, or hunting for colored eggs hidden by their elders in house or garden, is a favorite pastime of the younger children, while *eiertikken,* or hitting together hardboiled Easter eggs, is the day's real sport for boys and girls of all ages.

In country places many children still use coffee grounds, beet juice, onion skins and other vegetable substances to color the eggs collected before Easter. The dyed eggs are then packed in baskets and carried to the meadow or other outdoor gathering place designated for the *eiertikken* contests. The children line up. At a given signal each child matches his green, yellow, or red egg against his neighbor's egg of corresponding color. The trick is to break the shell of the opponent's egg without damaging the shell of his own. The boy or girl who is successful in this feat not only keeps his own egg but collects his adversary's. Of course, the player winning the most eggs is acclaimed local *eiertikken* champion and, as such, holds an enviable position among all the other boys and girls.

FLUITJES MAKEN (Whistle Making), in Ootmarsum, province of Overijssel

About May 1

This is the season when boys and girls in and about Ootmarsum, in Overijssel, welcome spring by making whistles of mountain ash.

The young people soak sections of ash in water until the bark slips off with a few vigorous taps of the jackknife. While the tapping is going on, this traditional nonsense rhyme is chanted:

> Flow, sap, flow.
> When will you blow?
> In May, in May,
> When all birds lay an egg
> Except the quail
> And the godwit.
> They do not lay
> Eggs in the month of May.
> Entirely off, half way off.
> Let's cut off the farmer's head!

The last two lines of the chant refer to the bark which does not come off without a final big rap of the knife.

*VELDGANG (Going to the Fields), in Mekkelhorst, province of
   Overijssel

The Monday preceding Ascension Thursday

On Rogation Monday inhabitants of the little eastern Netherlands village of Mekkelhorst perform the time-honored ceremony of going to the fields to ask God's blessing on all growing things.

At dusk the girls and young men, farmers and gardeners assemble in procession to perambulate the parish and visit an ancient boundary oak. Along the route the group, preceded by the girls and women walking two abreast, pauses to pray for growth of vegetables and grains, the prospering of fruit trees and the granting of rich harvests.

The procession reaches the oak and then goes on to the fields, to kneel before a crucifix and pray for the crops.

The Rogationtide processions of the Christian Church survive from Roman times when, at the end of May, young maidens sang and danced and visited the fields "to drive out the winter." Animals were offered to Mars at these ceremonies and prayers said, to invoke the gods' blessings of increase and prosperity.

*Dauwtrappen (Dew Treading)

Ascension

Dauwtrappen, or "dew treading," is an old folk custom that still is observed in both city and country areas. Townsfolk rise at dawn and take their children to the suburbs where the youngsters tramp through the morning dew and gather early spring flowers. Rural people, on the other hand, visit neighboring fields and meadows and then meet with family and friends at some country inn for a jolly six o'clock breakfast.

> May rain, make me grow, yes grow,
> May rain, make me tall,

is a popular nursery ditty which reflects the old superstition that May rain and May dew possess supernatural power. The delightful dauwtrappen custom doubtless originated in an early belief that Ascension Day dew or rain makes the body both sound and beautiful.

Making immense Ascension Day bread loaves is another folk survival which still is observed at Hengelo, in Overijssel. Centuries ago, people say, farmers of the area had permission to dig all the peat they needed, provided they baked Ascension Day loaves for the parish poor. Custom decreed that any farmer would be fined who baked a loaf weighing *less* than twenty-five pounds. As a special inducement to generosity a bottle of white wine was awarded to the man who produced the heaviest loaf. The winner of the wine was expected to treat all his friends to a party.

Keen competition existed among farmers and their wives to see who could bake the largest loaf. Often the stipulated weight was exceeded by three or four times. Even today immense Ascension loaves, filled with plump raisins and baked to toothsome perfection, are carefully prepared, weighed, and distributed among hospitals and homes for the aged and infirm.

*KALLEMOOI (*Kallemooi*), in Schiermonnikoog, North Coast Islands

The Saturday before Whitsun

The custom called *Kallemooi,* which is celebrated at Schiermonnikoog, in the North Coast Islands, represents the fishermen's welcome to spring. Although both the name of the curious custom and its origin are obscure, there are many speculations regarding the meaning of the word Kallemooi. Some say it can be translated as "calling the May." Others claim it is derived from the word *kalemei,* meaning a "tree without branches," namely a bare tree. This interpretation is preferred by many.

A tall pole with a transverse arm near the top is erected in the center of the hamlet. At the apex of the crosspiece a basket is suspended, with a live cock inside. A group of young men temporarily "borrow" the bird for the occasion from some unsuspecting villager. An empty bottle is hung from either arm of the structure, which is decorated at the top with the Dutch flag, a fresh green May branch and a placard bearing the word Kallemooi.

For three days and nights people give themselves over to the joys of feasting, merrymaking, and playing Whitsun games. Local inns serve a special drink known as "Kallemooi bitters." After the fun is over the rooster is released and returned to his owner's farm.

*LUILAK (Lazy Bones Day)

The Saturday before Whitsun

Luilak, or Lazybones Day, is essentially a festival of youth and is celebrated in Zaandam, Amsterdam, and some other western Netherland towns. The holiday starts at four in the morning on the Saturday before *Pinkster,* or Whit Sunday, when troops of young people begin whistling, beating on pots, kettles and pans, ringing doorbells and raising such terrific racket that sleep is impossible. Indeed nobody can sleep, because any boy or girl refusing to rise and join the fun is branded *Luilak,* or "Lazybones" throughout the coming year. *Luilakken,* moreover, must treat their companions to candy or cakes, besides being the butt of all sorts of taunts, jokes and teasing.

> Lazybones, tucked in his bed,
> Gets up at nine o'clock;
> Nine o'clock, half past nine,
> Then you can see Lazybones!

is one derisive rhyme that greets the late riser.

There is a legend that the name Luilak originated in 1672 with one Piet Lak, a watchman, who was caught napping when French invaders entered the country. Piet Lak, according to the story, became known as Luie-Lak, or Lazy Lak. From this uncomplimentary nickname the term is said to have arisen.

Zaandam and Haarlem children celebrate Luilak by making little wagons which often are shaped like boots and sometimes are decorated with green branches and thistles, known as *luilakken.* The youngsters trundle their wagons over the cobblestones until the wheels become smoking hot and finally catch fire. The children either watch their wagons go up into flames or else dump them into the canals. This rite represents an ancient spring fertility ceremony which long since has been forgotten.

The town of Haarlem, which is situated in the heart of the country's flower growing industry, observes Luilak with a celebrated Whitsun flower market in the Grote Markt, or Great Market.

Following the pealing of the midnight bells in the steeple of Saint Bavo's (the Grote Kerk), floodlights are turned on and the flower market suddenly springs into life. There one sees row upon row of stalls banked with great golden daffodils, pure white tulips with petals like angels' wings, scarlet tulips, blue irises, pink and red geraniums. Cumbersome barrel organs grind out reel after reel of dance music, to the delight of scores of young people who start waltzing about the square.

Herring stalls, ice cream wagons and booths filled with fragrant gingerbreads and delicate pastries, furnish refreshment for the merrymakers and purchasers who surge through the market place.

From midnight until eight in the morning housewives hurry to the Grote Markt to purchase Luilak flowers to be placed in windows or on feast day tables throughout the Whitsun holiday.

In many parts of the country *Luilakbollen,* or Lazy Bones Cakes, are a specialty of the season. Here is a recipe for the delicacy, traditionally baked in the shape of little fat double rolls, and served hot with syrup:

Luilakbollen

2½ cups flour
1 envelope granulated yeast
½ teaspoon salt
¼ cup butter
9 tablespoons tepid milk (about)
1 tablespoon grated lemon peel
1½ cups raisins
1 egg

Sift together flour and salt and add melted shortening. Dissolve yeast in one half of the tepid milk and combine thoroughly with the first mixture. Beat the egg, add the remaining milk, and mix all together. Knead in lemon peel and raisins and let rise for about 45 minutes in warm place. Knead down and shape into 16 rolls. Brush with melted butter and let rise another 45 minutes. Bake about 15 minutes in moderate oven (350°).

*PINKSTER (Whitsunday), in Deventer, province of Overijssel
The fiftieth day after Easter

Making the *Pinksterkroon,* or Whitsun crown, around which neighborhood children dance and sing has long been a community affair in the old town of Deventer. Some time before the festival a committee called *Buurtvereniging,* or "community of neighbors," goes from house to house in the poorer streets to collect funds for making the Whitsun crown's paper decorations. Since people of each street hope to win the annual competition for the most beautiful and original Pinksterkroon, the various neighborhoods take care to keep their preparations secret.

Traditionally, the Pinksterkroon is made over a bell-shaped wire frame that stands at least five feet high and is supported within by five or six wire hoops of graduated size. The top of the structure is adorned by a crown, or by two intersecting hoops. The framework, which is wound with colored paper strips is decorated with brightly-colored paper chains, lanterns, fringes, streamers and small flags. The whole effect has to be airy and transparent, so one can "look through" the crown.

Holland's Pinksterkroon, like England's Maypole, is a gay and charming symbol of early spring. Like the Maypole, the crown is set up on the green, or in the center of a village square where both children and adults can dance about it. The Whitsun crown song, once chanted to accordion accompaniment, now is sung to "recorded" music issuing from a commercial loud speaker. "There is no old charm in it at all," according to a Deventer resident who remembered the original words. "I am afraid this is one of the newer corruptions," she added regretfully, writing down the modern version:

> The Whitsun crown has come again.
> *Hoezee!*
> The flags are waving on all sides.
> *Hoezee!*
>
> We dance about it as of old,
> All together, hand in hand.
> *Hoezee! Hoezee! Hoezee!*

Before the Second World War, Deventer used to have as many as twenty or thirty Whitsun crowns. Nowadays their number is greatly reduced. In former times, after dancing about the crowns in a daytime celebration for children and an evening one for adults, people always set fire to the wreaths and then threw them into the river Yssel.

*Pinkster Bruid or Pinksterbloem (Whitsun Bride or Whitsun Flower), in Volte, Ootmarsum, Markelo, Rijssen, Hellendoorn, Hengelo, and other communities, province of Overijssel

Whit Tuesday

In scattered villages of Overijssel the *Pinkster Bruid,* or Whitsun Bride, accompanied by her maidens, makes an appearance early on Whit Tuesday morning. The diminutive Bride or Queen (also known as *Pinksterbloem,* or Whitsun Flower) wears a white dress and flower wreath. Children walking on either side hold an arch of flowers over the little girl, who marches with the gentle dignity that becomes a queen.

The pretty procession, headed by the Bride, is made up of village girls who wear long white communion dresses. Small boys, also, often participate in the little parade. The children go from house to house in the neighborhood and sing for eggs and money, which later are used for a Pinkster feast. The children's songs vary from place to place, but in Hengelo the words go something like this:

> Here we come with a pretty Whitsun Bride.
> She is dressed so prettily.
> Give something, keep something.
> A rich man lives here
> Who can give much.
> God will reward him
> With a hundred thousand crowns,
> With a hundred thousand bows.
> Here we come with a pretty Whitsun Bride.

Another song, well known at Volte and Ootmarsum, is addressed not to the rich man, but to the lazy child who is reproved by her playmates for not rising in time to join the procession:

> Whitsun Flower,
> You have a bad name
> Because you have slept so long!
> Had you risen earlier,
> You would have been my friend!

THE NETHERLANDS

Many believe that the custom of the Pinkster Bride, or Flower, originated in pagan times and that the little girl who plays the part in the children's modern village drama personifies awakening spring or the returning summer.

LEIDENS ONTZET (Leyden Day)

October 3

This day which marks the lifting of the Siege of Leyden by the Spaniards is celebrated by eating bread and herrings and a special kind of stew, known as *Hutspot met Klapstuk.*

In the year 1574 the people of Leyden were surrounded by the Spaniards. Plague raged in the besieged city and thousands died from disease and hunger. Legend says that a band of desperate citizens finally marched to the Town Hall and demanded that Burgomaster Adrian van der Werff end their misery through surrender.

The Burgomaster, unmoved by the threats and pleas of the townsfolk, replied that he had sworn to keep the city safe; that, with God's help, he would keep his oath. "We shall starve if relief does not come soon, that I know," he continued. "Better it is to die of starvation than shame. Kill me, if you must. Eat my flesh to satisfy your hunger. But while I live, you can expect no surrender."

The heroic obstinacy of their leader so heartened the starving populace that they decided to hold out longer. Relief came shortly, however, for on the second of October a tempest arose, lashing the waters and carrying the Spanish fleet far out to the ocean. Leyden was saved!

Loud were the prayers of thanksgiving and great the rejoicing of Leyden's people, to whom Burgomaster van der Werff became a hero. Today his statue may be seen in Leyden's basilica church of Saint Pancras.

Legend says that the first person to venture from the besieged city on October 3, 1574, was a young orphan boy. Outside the fortresses in the deserted Spanish camp, the boy discovered a huge iron pot (in some versions of the story there were several) containing a savory mixture of meat and vegetables. The kettle's contents, hurriedly left behind by the fleeing enemy, were still hot. The orphan quickly notified the townsfolk of his find and soon everyone gathered round to enjoy the Spaniards' dinner. Hutspot met Klapstuk was the name Leyden's starving people gave to the delicious stew which constituted their first good meal for many months.

When William of Orange's "Sea Beggars," as his sailors were called, finally were able to get to Leyden's rescue, they brought ships loaded with herrings and white bread.

"That is why," explained my informant, "we traditionally eat herrings and white bread for lunch, and Hutspot met Klapstuk for dinner on October third, in memory of the lifting of Leyden's epic siege."

Hutspot met Klapstuk

2 lbs. potatoes
2 lbs. carrots
½ lb. onions
1 lb. boneless beef
Seasonings
3 tablespoons butter

Cook the meat in 3 cups boiling water until the liquid is reduced by one third and the meat is almost tender. Dice potatoes and carrots, slice onions and slowly simmer over low flame until the vegetables are done and the stock almost absorbed.

Remove meat and slice. Season vegetables to taste, mash together until smooth, season and add butter. Serve very hot with the meat.

SINT MAARTEN (Saint Martin)

November 11

On or about November 11 it is customary for boys and girls all over the country to go about serenading householders and begging firewood and goodies "for Saint Martin's feast." Saint Martin's Day, coming as it does at the season when cattle are slaughtered, new wines are tasted, and geese are fat, is looked upon as harvest thanksgiving time in many European countries. In the Netherlands at least forty early churches are dedicated to Saint Martin, the fourth-century patron of Gaul. His feast, with its fire rites and traditional roast goose dinners, is thought to have originated in Roman times when the goose was annually sacrificed as a thank offering for crops.

In many places children build bonfires and march in processions with lighted Chinese lanterns, or with homemade lanterns made from scooped-out turnips, carrots, or beets. During their march the children sing ancient verses about Saint Martin, patron of beggars. The songs, curiously enough, picture the saint as a beggar himself, "with cold arms" and badly needing a fire, rather than as a benefactor of beggars. The songs vary widely from place to place. One of the most amusing comes from North Holland. The first lines, at least, are well known in Hoorn where, for some unexplained reason, boys and girls observe the festival on the fourth Monday in August, rather than in November. After sly reference to "the rich man who can give much," the song speaks of the procession "with a hundred thousand little lights."

> Saint Martin, Saint Martin,
> Calves wear tails,
> Cows wear horns,
> Churches wear steeples,
> Steeples wear bells;
> Girls wear skirts,
> Boys wear breeches;
> Old women wear aprons.
> Here lives a rich man
> Who can give much
> If he gives much
> Long will he live
> And inherit heaven.
> God will remember him
> With a hundred thousand crowns,[3]
> With a hundred thousand little lights.
> Here comes Saint Martin.

[3] The reference is to a piece of money.

141

Venlo, in Limburg, is one of the most important centers for Saint Martin Day celebrations. For days before the festival young people sing through the streets and people toss them "gifts from Saint Martin" from the windows. On the Eve grown-ups as well as children participate in lantern processions. An impersonator of Saint Martin drives through the streets in an open state carriage and the whole affair assumes the character of a civic observance.

In Venlo, where Saint Martin's festival is celebrated much like Saint Nicholas' in other places, children rush home after the procession and dance about a lighted candle, placed on the floor. The rite is accompanied by a traditional song:

> Saint Martin's little bird [4]
> Sat on a little hill
> In his little red skirt.

At the family party that follows Saint Martin often visits the children in person, just as Saint Nicholas calls on December 5. Sometimes the Saint is accompanied by Black Peter the Moor,[5] who also appears with Saint Nicholas. The children dance or sing for Saint Martin, and Peter either throws sweets from behind the door or strews them over the floor.

This custom of scattering goodies is very old. At Utrecht, where the first church in North Netherlands was dedicated to Saint Martin, his day was originally called *Schuddekorfsdag*, the day of "shaking a basket" over the fire. A basket of apples and chestnuts was customarily shaken over a fire until the contents were roasted, and then they were tossed to the children. While scrambling for their share of delicacies the boys and girls sang a verse which is known in both North and South Holland, although in different versions:

> Make a fire, make a fire,
> Saint Martin is coming here
> With bare arms; [6]
> He wants to warm himself.

[4] The spotted woodpecker.

[5] See *Sint Nicolaas Avond,* December 5.

[6] Saint Martin has "bare arms" and is in need of a fire because he traditionally divided his coat with a beggar.

THE NETHERLANDS

MIDWINTERHOORN BLAZEN (Blowing the Midwinter Horn) in the
province of Overijssel

*Beginning of Advent until the
Sunday following Epiphany*

Blowing the Midwinter Horn is a custom peculiar to the province
of Overijssel where, according to one local authority, it probably
originated over two thousand years ago. Farmers of Denekamp,
Ootmarsum, and surrounding communities start making winter horns
at Advent. Blowing them above their frozen wells (which act as
sounding boards) the horns make plaintive music, which carries far
through the still night air.

The winter horn, which generally is fashioned from fitted sections of curving birchwood, has an elderwood mouthpiece and
measures about forty-five inches in length. When soaked in water
the crude instrument gives out a shrill, monotonous tone which carries for great distances across the level countryside. To persons from
other areas the winter horn's notes may sound primitive and barbaric: but to the eastern farmer they symbolically "banish winter and
announce the coming of Christ, Light of the World," to their own
and surrounding communities. In pagan times horns were blown to
expel demons and evil spirits. Today the winter horn brings tidings
of Jesus' birth.

In Oldenzaal, near Denekamp, the champion horn blower of the
district told how he had initiated the modern custom of blowing the
winter horn during Advent from the four corners of the local fourteenth-century church tower. The champion, who has selected by
competition the finest horn blowers from fourteen surrounding
parishes, has arranged a Christmas melody in which each man sounds
a single note on his horn at one time. When the first note stops the
second begins; the third follows the second, and so on, until the
entire tune is played. This composition greets Oldenzaal's inhabitants at five in the morning of Advent Eve and continues until Three
Kings' Day, when Yuletide officially ends. Only on Christmas Day
do the horns follow the church bells' chiming, which begins at half
past four in the morning.

Each community usually has one man who is the district's recognized authority in making winter horns. In Denekamp, there is the local *klompenmaker*, or maker of wooden shoes. A young son nimbly climbed the long ladder to the open attic in his father's small factory and reverently brought the winter horn down from storage. The shoemaker deftly fitted together the various sections of the horn and directed the boy to draw a bucket of water.

"It is dry now," explained the *klompenmaker*, pointing to the horn. "I must soak it a little before it will sound; and then I can give you only an idea of the music as the horn still will be dry."

At last, the instrument was ready to be tried. The master horn maker drew a tremendous breath, puffed out both cheeks and let go with a blast. The three different notes he played possessed a primitive quality that was impressive as well as monotonous. As the creator of the horn proudly explained, "On a winter's night when you hear many horns, sounding from all directions, across ice-sheeted meadows and everything is black and still, then the music is beautiful. The sound carries great distances—sometimes as far as three kilometers."

Like the Pied Piper's flute, the first shrill notes of the winter horn irresistibly attracted great numbers of young boys. Silently they gathered in the small yard and pressed about the shop's open door. They stood transfixed, gazing in fascinated admiration at the curved birch horn like one which in time, they, too, would blow at Advent across Denekamp's frosty fields.

SINT NICOLAAS AVOND or SINTERKLAAS AVOND (Saint Nicholas or
    Santa Klaus Eve)

December 5

Sint Nicolaas, or Saint Nicholas, fourth-century Bishop of Spain, has been the Dutch children's gift bringer for over six hundred years. According to tradition, the long-bearded Bishop, in white robe and red cassock, with tall red miter, white gloves and a golden staff in his hand, comes to Holland each year from Spain. Walking beside the Bishop is *Zwarte Piet,* Black Peter, his Moorish servant who, dressed like a medieval page in plumed hat, doublet and hose, carries a yawning black bag with presents for good children and switches for those who are bad.

Legend says that Saint Nicholas rides over the roofs on a beautiful white horse. In big cities he often arrives officially by boat from Spain; so accustomed has he become to modern ways that sometimes he even arrives by helicopter. The saint jumps on his horse from roof to roof. Zwarte Piet slips down each chimney and fills the children's shoes, which stand in a row awaiting his arrival. The boys and girls leave hay, a cup of water or carrots—sometimes, even, lump sugar and pumpernickel—for the saint's white horse. As we shall see, if the children have been diligent and obedient during the year they find in their shoes, next day, a sweet or a small toy; if naughty, they get a birch switch. After finishing his work, Zwarte Piet climbs up the chimney and the saint and his helper are off to another house.

On Saint Nicholas' Eve the good bishop and Black Peter make an appearance at every village door. The night is popularly called "Strewing Eve," because just before the saint arrives Black Peter supposedly throws *pepernoten,* or pepper nuts, down the chimney. In some homes a door bell rings loudly; then a black-gloved hand, suggesting the presence of Zwarte Piet, opens the door slightly and tosses handfuls of the hard, spicy little round cakes into the room. The children start crawling over the floor, collecting all the pepernoten they can get, singing, meanwhile, little greetings to Saint Nicholas.

The songs vary from place to place, but one of the most popular is:

> Saint Nicholas, good holy man,
> Put your best cassock on.
> Ride in it to Amsterdam,
> To Amsterdam from Spain.

Another well known verse is:

> Saint Nicholas, little [7] scamp,
> Throw something into my shoe;
> Throw something into my boot.
> Thank you, little Saint Nicholas.

Yet another song, which invites the saint's generosity, begins:

> Saint Nicholas, good, good, good Saint Nicholas,
> Throw something into my empty barrel.

While the boys and girls are busy scrambling for sweets, the saint enters the room and questions the little ones on their behavior during the past year. Black Peter, meanwhile puts in an appearance, also, and if the children have been bad he does not hesitate to open his black sack. This gesture terrifies guilty children because it indicates that he will carry them away to Spain and keep them for a year until they become good children and can be returned to their parents! At last the visitors make their farewell and the children are put to bed.

Then their elders have their "surprises"—gifts and bundles mysteriously wrapped and appearing from mysterious quarters. Theoretically, all presents come from Saint Nicholas. Consequently, the actual givers try to keep their identity secret by confusing the recipient with humorous verses and false leads. Often a small gift, for example, has many different wrappings, each addressed to a different person. By the time the article finally reaches the one for whom it is intended, many nonsense rhymes have been read and everyone has had great fun. Sometimes days or months go by before the giver is discovered.

The arrival of Saint Nicholas on December 5 is a civic, as well as a family affair in cities like Amsterdam, The Hague, Rotterdam and elsewhere. Amsterdam, for example, where Saint Nicholas is patron of the city, has a particularly noteworthy celebration. There the

[7] Everything is diminutive in Holland, in accordance with the country's small size. "Little" is a term of familiarity and affection, whether applied to Saint Nicholas, a person, place, or an object.

saint arrives at the Prins Hendrik Kade, or Quay, aboard the steamer *Spanje* (Spain), followed by his retinue on the *Madrid.* Booming guns, pealing bells, the shouts and cheers of millions of spectators all add impressiveness to Saint Nicholas' official welcome. Mounting his faithful horse which awaits him at the pier, the saint, accompanied by the Burgomaster, aldermen and other dignitaries, heads a brilliant procession through the city. The saint is accompanied on his tour by efficient helpers—an entire brigade of Black Peters on foot or mounted on motor scooters or bicycles who distribute gifts to boys and girls in hospitals, schools, and institutions.

SINT NICOLAAS DAG (Saint Nicholas' Day)

December 6

In the homes younger children rise early and rush to the fireplace to see what Saint Nicholas has left in their shoes. Included among the gifts there are sure to be many traditional Dutch sweets, such as *taai-taai* (meaning "tough-tough"), a spiced honey gingerbread, cut into various human and animal figures; *borstplaat,* a creamy bonbon-like candy, made into pink and white hearts and other pretty shapes; and marzipan, simulating small fruits and vegetables, sometimes tiny sausages, or even little pigs.

Occasionally someone gets marzipan that looks like an open sandwich, spread with ham or cheese. All kinds of jokes are attributed to Saint Nicholas for, as we have already seen, he loves "surprises." For this reason marzipan may assume some deceptive guise, such as of a realistic looking piece of toilet soap.

Children prize their initials made in chocolate. *Chocolade letters* is the name of this coveted sweet. Most characteristic of all seasonal goodies, however, is the crisp, spicy *speculaas,* a cooky baked in molds. The making of these gingerbreads is an ancient art that is continued by some old fashioned bakers. Sometimes a child receives a gigantic figure of Saint Nicholas on his horse, or he may have more modest pieces representing girls, boys, toys, or favorite animals.

147

Adults often give and receive *banket letters,* which are almond-stuffed pastries cut into the shapes of the recipients' initials. These initials vary greatly in size, since the warmer the friend, the larger the initial is likely to be. Sometimes young men give huge banket letters to sweethearts, or possibly they present the girl with the entire name spelled out in candy letters.

Eerste Kerstdag (First Christmas Day)

December 25

Christmas is a two-day holiday which is generally celebrated by attending church services and holding family gatherings. In the cities Christmas trees, holly, and other greens are brought up the canals in barges and later sold from stalls in the markets and along the streets.

In some homes the Christmas tree, star-crowned and hung with polished red apples and all kinds of sweets and goodies, is the center of family festivities; but Saint Nicholas' Eve is the old fashioned popular feast in the Netherlands and Christmas is likely to be spent quietly with family and friends.

Among the seasonal foods *Kerstkrans,* the "Christmas Wreath" pastry is a universal favorite. Whenever friends drop in during the holiday—for morning coffee or afternoon or evening tea—a slice of this delicious cake, made with rich almond paste inside and equally rich puff paste outside, is sure to be served. The pastry is baked in a ring and decorated with white icing and all kinds of colorful candied fruits and peels.

Tweede Kerstdag (Second Christmas Day)

December 26

On the Second Christmas Day holiday festivities continue in the homes. In the cities many people celebrate the day by attending theatre parties and concerts or meeting with friends in restaurants and cafés.

THE NETHERLANDS

OUDE JAARS AVOND (New Year's Eve)

December 31

On New Year's Eve it is customary for everyone, including those who are not habitual church-goers, to attend divine service. The minister generally gives a résumé of the year's events and holds a brief memorial for parishioners who have died during the previous twelve months. He never mentions the names of the dead, however, unless they belong to the Royal Family.

After reading the Ninetieth Psalm, "Lord, thou hast been our dwelling place in all generations," the eighteenth-century hymn by the Dutch poet, Rhijnvis Feith, *Uren, Dagen, Maanden, Jaren, Vliegen Als een Schaduw Heen,* is traditionally sung. The hymn begins with the lines:

> Hours, days, months, years flee like a shadow.
> Alas! wherever we look we find nothing lasting here below,

and ends with the thought that, despite the joys and sorrows wrought by the years, "God never changes" and His hand leads us from this life into life everlasting.

Port towns such as Rotterdam welcome the New Year by blowing whistles and the sirens of ships and factories.

Ootmarsum in eastern Netherlands announces the New Year in the old-fashioned way—through the night watchman. He goes through the town at midnight rapping his club on the cobbled streets and calling in loud tones:

> Come, citizens, come at once,
> The New Year has arrived.
> Because of this I wish you
> Happiness, good luck and blessing.

149

8

FESTIVALS OF NORWAY

NYTTÅRSDAG (New Year's Day)

January 1

After attending morning church services many people spend the rest of the day quietly at home, or in afternoon visiting among relatives and friends.

A typical New Year's dinner starts with a table of cold appetizers, known as *koldt bord,* which includes such Norwegian delicacies as *silde salat,* herring salad, smoked salmon, and many other kinds of fish, as well as a great variety of meats, relishes and cheeses. The koldt bord is followed by the main course of roast pork or goose, accompanied by potatoes and other vegetables, and numerous fancy cakes and sweets for dessert. Strong holiday beer and hearty good wishes are passed from host to guest as each bids the other luck and cheer during the coming year.

Once New Year's Day passed without special celebration outside the homes. Gradually, however, the day grew increasingly festive when it became customary, on New Year's Eve, to give a full month's pay to servants who had hired themselves out for a year's service. With pockets full of money, lavish spending and celebration on the first day of the year became widespread among this group.

The second day of the New Year is generally characterized by family parties, dinners and dances. Many organizations hold their annual festivities at this time.

TRETTENDE DAG JUL (Twelfth Day)

January 6

Trettende Dag Jul, sometimes called *Hellig Tre Kongers Dag,* the Three Holy Kings' Day, is the traditional anniversary of the Magi's visit to the Christ Child's manger. In many homes the three-pronged Yule candle still is lighted at night in honor of the Three

Kings. Some years ago young students commemorated the festival by carrying a paper star lantern about the streets and singing ancient carols concerning the Wise Men.

One of the oldest songs of the season comes from the province of Telemark. The twelfth-century heroic ballad known as the *Draumkvedet* (Vision of Heaven and Hell), describes the dream of Olav Aasteson, who fell asleep on Christmas Eve and did not waken until Epiphany, when people were going to church. During the twelve days of his sleep Olav had dramatic visions of souls in purgatory.

TYVENDEDAGEN (Twentieth Day, after Christmas)

January 13

"Saint Knut drives Christmas away," is an old folk saying which explains why, in many country areas it was customary on this day to hold the traditional "Christmas race." People piled into their sleighs and sledges and drove madly across ice-bound lakes and frosty roads to the accompaniment of joyous shouts and merrily jingling bells; for, according to ancient superstition trolls, led by the troll woman herself, Kari-Tretten, or Kari the Thirteenth, raced over the frozen countryside on the night of January 13.

On *Tyvendedagen,* which marks the official end of Yuletide and is the last day the greeting *"Glaedelig Jul,"* "Merry Christmas," is used, Christmas trees are dismantled and decorations carefully packed away until the following year. Generally the tree is chopped up and burned in the fireplace. The last Christmas parties are held, the final festivities attended on this day.

*FASTELAVN (Shrovetide)

The Sunday preceding Ash Wednesday

The Sunday [1] before Lent is a holiday which boys and girls await with great impatience. Following old tradition the children rise at

---

* Stars indicate movable feasts that depend upon Easter. See Table of Easter Dates and Movable Festivals Dependent upon Easter, p. 246.

[1] Formerly the Monday preceding Ash Wednesday.

daybreak, arm themselves with *fastelavnsris,* or decorated birch branches, and go about the house trying to switch all the "lazy" people they can catch lying abed. This curious custom of switching with branches doubtless originated in an ancient pagan rite of bringing into the village the fruitfulness of spring.

The *fastelavnsris* are made with great artistry. Sometimes the children tie the switches together and decorate them with sparkling tinsel and paper streamers of red, orange, yellow, or green. Sometimes they tie a small doll with stiff, outstanding skirts to the topmost branch, and sometimes they ornament the twigs with bright colored paper roses or other flowers.

The youngsters enter into the switching game with great zest, since custom decrees they shall receive a delicious hot cross bun for every victim they spank. Grown-ups, of course, feign sleep as the children slip into their rooms and start beating the bedclothes. Sometimes parents and grandparents seem to waken slowly, but even so, the coveted bun is always produced, and the boys and girls troop off happily, counting their spoils and seeking further conquests.

*LANGFREDAG (Long Friday)

The Friday preceding Easter

Langfredag, a "long day to the suffering Christ," is celebrated in all churches with religious services in memory of the Passion of Jesus.

*PÅSKE (Easter)

Although Easter is a church holiday which many celebrate with religious observances, excursions to mountain resorts are increasingly popular among large groups of people. From Holy Thursday through Easter Monday towns and cities are deserted and every small mountain hotel and inn is packed to overflowing with those who come for skiing, tobogganing, skating and other winter sports. Ice carnivals, sports competitions, dances and concerts are popular features of the holiday festivities while many mountain centers hold special out-of-door Easter services.

In the homes Easter is always a festive event for the children. Weeks in advance the boys and girls start hoarding eggshells. They either bore holes in the shell ends and blow out the contents, or else carefully cut the shells in half. Often the empty shells are filled with small candies and then pasted together with strips of paper. The children ornament the fragile containers with gay paper cutouts or colorful painted designs.

Easter morning is egg hunting time. Dyed and decorated eggs are hidden in flower pots, doll beds and all sorts of odd places. The boys and girls, bursting with excitement, hide the offerings they themselves have prepared for other members of the family and shout with delight as they find the eggs concealed for them.

*PINSE (Pentecost or Whitsun)

The fiftieth day after Easter

Services are held in all churches. *Pinse* is the great spring holiday when everybody tries to get to the country. Everyone, that is, except members of the country glee clubs who like to hold conventions in the cities. Members of city glee clubs, on the other hand, customarily make trips to the country. Singing contests are held from village to village and town to town.

JONSOK (Saint John's Eve)

June 23

Jonsok, Saint John's Eve, is celebrated in Norway, as in all Scandinavian countries, with bonfires, dancing, singing and other festivities. "As high as you jump over the *Sankthansbål,* or Saint John's bonfires, so high will the grain grow in the coming year," is an old folk saying which refers to the time-honored custom of dancing all night about the midsummer fires and then vaulting over the dying embers.

153

Built on every height and along beaches and on the shores of small islands, the fires, made from logs and tar-soaked barrels, burn long and fiercely and are seen for many miles. Young people dressed in colorful regional costume dance about the blazing piles to the merry tunes of valley fiddlers. As one fiddler "plays himself out" another takes over, so no break in music occurs the long night through.

Often the dancers, singing old folk songs of their valleys, go out on the water in flower-decked boats and watch the bonfires; often, also, young lovers wander hand and hand through the birch groves:

> They sit among the birches
> In the beautiful Midsummer;
> And before the sun goes down
> They swear faithfulness to each other,

according to a Setesdal folk song.

Jonsok is as important to children as to their older brothers and sisters. In many regions a little village girl is chosen midsummer queen. Crowned either with flowers or with a traditional bridal crown, she is led through the community by a gay procession of boys and girls. The village fiddler, playing a native wedding march, precedes the children who wear flowers and are dressed in native costume.

The traditional aspect of the midsummer festival is preserved in all its beauty in the open air museum in Maihaugen, in the city of Lillehammer, and at the Norwegian Folk Museum at Bygdøy, near Oslo.

OLSOK (Saint Olaf's Day)

July 29

The anniversary of the death of Olaf Haraldson, who fell at the Battle of Stiklestad, near Trondheim, in 1030, is celebrated throughout Norway. Olaf, a pagan prince, set forth from his native shores a Viking and returned a Christian. He ruled Norway as king from 1015 to 1028, converted his people to the Christian faith, consolidated the kingdom, and finally became his country's patron saint.

Annual vesper services in honor of Saint Olaf are held at Trondheim Cathedral, while special observances take place in Maihaugen in the city of Lillehammer, and at the Trondheim Folk Museum. During recent years, an open air pageant representing the Battle of Stiklestad and King Olaf's death, has been given at Stiklestad on this anniversary.

MIKKELSMESSE (Michaelmas)

September 29

About this time of year herd girls drive the cows and goats back from the *sæters,* or mountain farms, to the valley homesteads. The return of both girls and animals is the occasion for great rejoicing —for dancing, singing and feasting.

Almost all farms of any importance have sæters. These summer camps, operated by the women, are important in rural economy. Cattle and other animals are put out to lush mountain pasturage, and the girls—generally the eldest daughters of the family—milk, tend the beasts and make the butter, goat's cheese and other dairy products for sale or for use on the farms throughout the winter.

When the girls return home in the autumn with fat, flower-decked animals and full butter tubs, the joy of the valley folk knows no bounds.

FLYTTEDAG or FAREDAG (Moving Day)

October 14

In Bergen and other large towns servants in search of employment go about from place to place on this day, looking for new positions. Peasant girls and men from all parts of Norway come to town. Dressed in the colorful costumes of their respective valleys, they often ride in little carts or wagons, which are piled high with gaily-painted hope chests or bundles bulging with clothing and other worldly possessions.

Market places and streets are thronged with city folk and peasants who meet to buy and sell animals, chickens, eggs, goat's milk and cheeses, as well as hand weavings, carvings, and other types of handiwork.

City-dwellers hold interviews and select help for the year from among the scores of rosy-cheeked country servants who crowd into the towns, hoping to find city employment.

April 14, as well as October 14, is a popular *Flyttedag.*

JULAFTEN (Christmas Eve)

December 24

Christmas preparations start weeks in advance. The family pig and calf are slaughtered in November and the meat made into all sorts of delicacies, such as the pork and veal sausages which, when sliced, reveal various decorative patterns of stars, spirals or geometric designs. Then there is the pickled tongue which holds place of honor in the center of the table and has the legend *God Jul,* Merry Christmas, written on it in red. There are also the hams, the cutlets and the pickled pigs' feet—all important to two weeks of Yuletide hospitality.

The *lutefisk,* or Christmas cod, is slowly dried to give it strong flavor. Then the fish is soaked in a lye solution until it swells to a trembling jellylike mass. Among the seasonal baked delicacies are fancy gingerbreads and animal cookies for the Christmas tree, as well as many kinds of delicious coffee breads and small cakes to accompany steaming coffee or holiday punch. In many places it is traditional to have fourteen different kinds of small cakes—one kind for each of the fourteen days of Christmas entertaining. In addition to the cooking, the semi-annual family washing is done, brasses and coppers are polished, curtains hung, and enough wood chopped to last for two weeks of holiday fires.

To Norwegian country people *Jul* is the season of peace on earth and good will to all of God's creatures. Nobody thinks of hunting or harming wild animals or birds during the Christmas season. A sheaf of wheat, attached to a pole and placed in the yard or on top of houses or outbuildings, furnishes plentiful cheer for birds. Generally the poles are made from spruce trees, with little tufts of branches left at the top, so that while eating the birds can have both firm foothold and protection against snow and winter winds.

Horses and cows have extra feedings of the best oats and barley on *Julaften*. In olden days the animals received their holiday rations with the traditional greeting, "It is Christmas Eve, good friend. Eat well."

There is a story from the valley of the river Driva about the careless farm girl who neglected to feed one of the cows on Christmas Eve and so brought dire misfortune upon herself. The girl, thinking she had given extra food to all the cattle, sat down on the gate. Suddenly she heard a voice from the barn:

> I wish, I wish that she were blind
> Who sits upon the gate.

The story states that the voice came from the cow the girl had forgotten to feed; and that, from then on, she was blind.

Christmas eve starts officially at four in the afternoon with the ringing of the village church bells. By then everything is in readiness for the holiday. Stores and shops are closed and the "Christmas peace" descends over every Norwegian town and hamlet. In homes the entire family, including the father, mother, children, guests and servants, gathers round to partake of the traditional *mølje,* or rich broth in which the Christmas meats are cooked. Mølje is served hot with *fladbrød,* the paper-thin Norwegian bread, which each one dips into the soup. In rural areas where country.people still wear their regional costumes for this ancient Christmas Eve ceremony, the scene about the soup kettle is especially picturesque. In cities, of course, formal clothes are customarily worn on this occasion.

For supper the usual hot and cold appetizers are served in staggering array. Then the lutefisk appears which, after its lye bath, has been boiled and is served with drawn butter and boiled potatoes. Then there are *ribbensstek,* pork ribs, accompanied by boiled potatoes and sauerkraut. Cakes and sweets and *risengrynsgrøt,* or rice porridge, end the meal. The porridge is made with a single almond in it, and whoever finds it will either "have luck" throughout the coming year, or will be first to wed!

After supper the closed doors, which have been hiding the Christmas tree from the children, are thrown open and the glittering tree is revealed in all its breathless beauty. The tree is lighted with white tapers and decorated with all kinds of tempting cooky animals, gilded nuts, eggshell toys, red apples and gingerbread figures. The father of the family usually reads the Christmas story from the Bible. Old and young join hands and walk about the tree, singing well-loved Christmas carols.

Often the *Julenisse,* the gnome who wears a red pointed cap and has a long flowing beard, brings the children's Christmas presents. Traditionally, the little man dwells in attic or barn and is guardian of the family's welfare. It is wise to please the Julenisse because he is apt to mix up the milk tins, tangle the horse's manes, and even make the cows sick, if he doesn't like your household. Consequently, every family tries to keep things orderly and pleasant, without harsh words or needless bickering. The children are careful to do their share, too, and every Christmas Eve they remember the little man with a bowl of risengrynsgrøt—which surely is appreciated, because by morning it always is gone.

JULEDAG (Christmas Day)

December 25

Everybody attends Christmas morning church services. Generally the rest of the day is spent quietly at home. In the afternoon boys and girls try out new skis, skates, or sleds, but few parties are held until Second Christmas Day.

Throughout the Yuletide season breakfast is a gay and tremendous meal. Long tables, decorated in the holiday spirit, groan under sometimes as many as thirty or forty different kinds of delicious hot and cold dishes. *Aquavit* and other strong drinks accompany the food and make the holiday breakfasts really festive occasions.

Annen Juledag (Second Christmas Day)

December 26

The Second Christmas Day is a time for parties and visiting. Factories, places of business, and civic organizations have parties for their employees on this day. Many children's parties are given in mid-afternoon while adult gatherings often start in the evening and continue throughout the night. In rural districts Christmas hospitality is at its height. In some places people adhere strictly to the old tradition that passers-by, regardless of age or social status, must stop in at every farm along the way and partake of food and drink.

In olden times the day after Christmas, known as Saint Stephen's Day, was devoted to the mad sport of horse racing over the icy roads. There is an old rhyme which says that:

> Saint Stephen was a stable boy,
> He watered his five foals.

Nyttårsaften (New Year's Eve)

December 31

In some places young people often dress in masks and fancy costumes on New Year's Eve and go visiting in groups of ten, fifteen or more. The visitors stop at every house for dancing and refreshments and finally wind up with breakfast at the house of some friend or neighbor.

FESTIVALS OF PORTUGAL

Ano Novo (New Year's Day)

January 1

The New Year starts with special services in the churches. Friends and relatives visit from house to house, greeting one another with *"Boas Festas"* and exchanging good wishes and congratulations. In northern Portugal children go about the neighborhood singing old songs called *janeiras* which are thought to bring luck in the coming year. In return for their greetings the boys and girls receive gifts of food and coins. In some places the village band goes through the streets playing stirring airs. Whenever the musicians happen to pass the house of one of their members they stop and play a special selection.

Peasants of the Minho have the saying that a person will act during the twelve months as he behaves on the first day of the year. For this reason youngsters look well to their manners and older people conduct their affairs with care. If anyone pays a debt on *Ano Novo,* for example, he is likely to be paying throughout the year. On this day it is well to have a coin in the pocket, something new on one's back, and extra food in the larder.

Dia de Reis (Day of the Kings)

January 6

All over the country peasants perform Epiphany plays in honor of the Magi. Bands of carolers go about, singing greetings and begging gifts, for they, like the Three Holy Kings, are weary and come from afar.

In some places family groups visit one another from house to house. The guests stand at the door and beg admittance, so they can sing to the Christ Child. After receiving a hearty welcome and singing special carols in honor of the Infant Jesus, the guests are entertained with wines and sweets.

Gifts are exchanged on *Dia de Reis* and special entertainment is provided for children. Mothers give them a party and a ring-shaped cake called *bolo-rei*. Baked inside the cake are all sorts of little amulets and fortune-telling trinkets, as well as a single dried broad bean. The child finding the bean in his portion is crowned king of the party and promises to "make the cake" for his playmates the following year.

When adults hold Dia de Reis parties, in some regions, the person finding the bean is expected to pay for next year's cake.

São Vicente (Saint Vicente)

January 22

Saint Vicente, murdered by Saracens of Algarve in 1173, is Lisbon's patron saint. Tradition says two ravens miraculously guided a boat, carrying the saint's coffin, up the river Tagus to the harbor of Lisbon. The inhabitants were so grateful to both winged pilots and magic bark for returning their saint that they depicted the event in Lisbon's coat of arms.

Saint Vicente's Day is celebrated in weather omens and folk traditions, no less than in processions and prayers. Farmers feel that a good way to predict harvests in the coming season is to light a resin torch, carry it to a high hill and then note what happens: if the flame is extinguished in the wind, crops will be abundant and an extra helper needed; if, on the contrary, the torch burns in spite of the wind, the season will be bad and a farm hand must go.

Nossa Senhora de Fátima (Our Lady of Fátima), in Fátima, province of Estremadura

May 13 and October 13

The Sanctuary of Fátima, at Cova da Iria, in a brief time has become one of the world's greatest pilgrimage centers. Thousands of pilgrims—often more than a hundred thousand at one time—throng this Portuguese Lourdes on the thirteenth of May and October, to pray, seek spiritual grace, or miraculous cure at Our Lady of Fátima's shrine.

Until May 13, 1917, Fátima consisted of a handful of peasant huts, and the Cova da Iria, now dominated by the modern basilica and the vast open space before it, was nothing but a grassy slope. Here three young shepherds, Lúcia de Jesus and Jacinta and Francisco Mato tended their sheep. On that fateful thirteenth of May, the sky suddenly darkened above the children at noon. Thinking a storm threatened, the three shepherds prepared to drive the animals back to their village of Almoster.

As the children started to leave, a beautiful lady clothed in white appeared to them from the branches of a holm-oak. She told the frightened children to return to the same spot on the thirteenth of each month, until October, and to "say the Rosary every day to obtain peace for the world and the end of the war."

Word about the monthly appearances of Our Lady of the Rosary spread. She visited the children for the last time on October 13, in the presence of an estimated seventy thousand persons who gathered on the grassy slope to witness the miraculous apparition. The message of the Virgin was always the same: a warning of need for sacrifice, prayer, and consecration, and a promise of the conversion of Russia and peace to the world, when "a sufficient number of people" do what Our Lady asks.

Today Lúcia, the only one of the three children to survive, is Sister Maria Dolores of the Carmelite Convent of Coimbra. The image of Our Lady of the Rosary has circled the globe and visited seventeen or more countries in a mission to bring the message of peace to all peoples. The Chapel of Apparition stands on the reputed site of the little shepherds' vision. A new place of pilgrimage has arisen in central Portugal's remote and barren moors.

Pilgrims travel long distances—on foot, by donkey, in automobiles—to bring their sick to Fátima. May 13 and October 13 are the great pilgrimage days, since they mark the first and last apparitions of Our Lady, but many minor pilgrimages are made on the thirteenth of the intervening months and also at other times. Families crouch about small fires built on the bare earth and cook simple meals. Then, huddling in the vast arena before the church, the pilgrims await the moment when the small image of Our Lady is carried out of the basilica in procession. In the warm glow of thousands of lighted candles the Virgin makes her rounds. Mass is performed and the sick and crippled receive the Sacrament.

When Nossa Senhora de Fátima is returned next day to her place in the basilica, the pilgrims wave their handkerchiefs in sad farewell.

*CARNAVAL (Carnival)
The Sunday, Monday and Tuesday preceding Ash Wednesday

The last three days before Ash Wednesday culminate the pre-Lenten festivities, which begin several weeks earlier. Throughout the country masked balls, parties, confetti battles and dances are held at this season.

Even as recently as a little over a century ago the Lisbon carnival was characterized as a time of license, with obscene jokes, coarse horseplay, and battles with eggs, oranges, flour and water predominating. Today public festivities in Lisbon are restricted for the most part, to processions of gay flower-decked cars, music, and parades of revelers in fancy costume.

In rural areas Carnival continues to be celebrated with much of its old time gaiety and abandon. Battles of flowers, mummers and musicians, the burial in effigy of King Carnival, old folk plays and dramas are features of the festivities.

*DOMINGO DE RAMOS (Palm Sunday)
The Sunday preceding Easter

In northern Portugal people take to church *ramos*, or branches bent into half loops and decorated with spring flowers. The priest

---

* Stars indicate movable feasts that depend upon Easter. See Table of Easter Dates and Movable Festivals Dependent upon Easter, p. 246.

blesses the ramos, which later are carried in procession. These hoops are carefully preserved in homes and burned during storms, as a protection against thunder and lightning.

*Semana Santa (Holy Week)

The week preceding Easter

During Holy Week, sometimes throughout Lent, there are exhibits in the churches and processions through the streets of scenes from the Passion of Jesus.

The church of *Senhor dos Passos,* Our Lord of the Way of the Cross, in the city of Guimarães, shows a different Passion tableau each day of Holy Week "to remind people of the sufferings of Our Lord."

Two of the most famous Passion processions are in the city of Covilhã on the slope of the Serra de Estrêla, and in the town of Vila do Conde. In many places these processions are attended by bands of *anjinhos,* children dressed as little angels, with crowns on their heads and fluffy eiderdown wings attached to their shoulders. The figures of Jesus, which have lashes, real hair, and crystal tears, are sumptuously clad in robes of purple velvet. The clergy's vestments and all processional properties are violet in color, and frequently the worshipers lined up to watch the procession, toss violets to their suffering Lord.

*Páscoa (Easter)

Many churches are decorated with white flowers. Old and young, rich and poor attend the Easter Masses which are characterized by magnificent Resurrection music. After the services families eat a holiday meal and visit among friends and neighbors.

Folar is a popular Easter cake in many places. This is made of sweet dough baked in a round flat shape and decorated on top with hard-boiled eggs. People exchange presents of little colored paper cornucopias filled with sugar covered almonds.

*QUINTA-FEIRA DA ESPIGA (Ear of Wheat Thursday or Ascension Day)

The fortieth day after Easter

On this day peasants make bouquets of olive branches and wheat sheaves, poppies and daisies. The olive and wheat symbolize wishes for abundant harvest; the poppy stands for peace, the daisy for money. A bit of wheat is kept in the house as a sign of prosperity throughout the coming year. People often gather medicinal plants and herbs on this day, preparing them later for home remedies or magic spells.

*PENTECOSTES (Pentecost, Whitsun)

The fiftieth day after Easter

The anniversary of the descent of the Holy Ghost on the Disciples is celebrated with special church services. In some towns of the Azores, local Holy Ghost societies issue free food tickets to the poor. Long elaborately decorated tables, laden with all kinds of bread, meat, and other tempting foods, are set up in the main streets. Food and drink are distributed to the community poor while bands play and villagers who have contributed to the feast act as hosts and hostesses to their less fortunate neighbors.

The distribution of food usually continues until Corpus Christi, eleven days after Pentecost.

*DIA DE CORPO DE DEUS (Corpus Christi), in Ponta Delgada, on the island of San Miguel, the Azores

The Thursday following Trinity Sunday

Since medieval days Corpus Christi, the feast that honors the Eucharist, has been one of the most sumptuous of all religious observances both on the Portuguese mainland and in the Azores.

In the city of Ponta Delgada, on San Miguel, on Corpus Christi Sunday [1] the inhabitants make a magnificent flower petal carpet—

---

[1] The Sunday following Corpus Christi Day.

almost three quarters of a mile in length—over which the procession passes. High-ranking clergy wearing gorgeous vestments and walking under an embroidered canopy, are accompanied by acolytes who swing censers and hold tall white candles. Hundreds of red-robed priests follow, then a charming group of first communicants—little boys in dark suits and scarlet capes and little girls in white frocks and filmy veils.

The climax of the ceremony comes when the bishop, in vestments woven with gold and silver thread, slowly raises the silver monstrance and exposes the Blessed Sacrament, symbol of the Body of Christ. Worshipers sink to their knees. As if to enhance the solemnity of the moment, the setting sun often drenches the bowed heads of the vast throng with warm glowing light. A spectacular backdrop of purple, rose, and gold suddenly unfurls in the sky as the chanting of priests and the devout responses of the people fill the evening with somber melody.

SANTO ANTÓNIO (Saint Anthony)

June 13

One of the country's most popular saints is Saint Anthony of Padua, who was born in 1195 in the Alfama, Lisbon's oldest and most crowded quarter, where the small church of Santo António da Sé now stands. When the church was destroyed by the earthquake of 1755, even the boys and girls of the Alfama began collecting pennies for its reconstruction. The children set up little street altars which they decorated with white paper lace cut-outs, flowers, tapers, and gaudy pictures of their saint. The youngsters begged "a little penny for Santo António" from all who passed. The "little pennies" and the children's example must have prompted many substantial gifts, because the present building, completed in 1812, was paid for by these alms.

The custom of begging for Santo António still continues in the twentieth century. Throughout the month of June in Lisbon, children prepare altars in the saint's honor. Boxes and tables are covered with white paper "altar cloths" and decorated with candles, images and pictures depicting the life and works of the saint. "Little pennies" are still demanded, but nowadays for a children's feast.

António is the matchmaker saint. On the Eve of his day young girls try various methods of finding out whom they will wed. One favorite way is for a girl to fill her mouth with water and hold it until she hears a boy's name mentioned. The name she hears is sure to be that of her future husband!

Young people write letters asking António to furnish sweethearts. These epistles are dropped into a box in Santo António da Sé. When love affairs prosper and suitable mates are found, the box receives thank offerings from the grateful lovers.

A charming custom of the day is for young men to present a pot of basil to the girls they hope to wed. A frilled and fluted tinsel-trimmed paper carnation of various colors "blooms" in each pot. Within the petals is a verse or message which indicates the young man's passion. Often the flower is accompanied by a painted toy, a pretty fan, or some other trifle calculated to appeal to a maiden's fancy.

VÉSPERA DE SÃO JOÃO (Saint John's Eve)

June 23

On the night dedicated to São João Baptista many traditional rites connected with fire, water, and love are observed. In some places boys and girls strip a pine tree, decorate it with flowers and greens, and ceremoniously carry it into the village. There the *facho*, as the tree is called, is set up in the center of a great bonfire of brush and pine logs. When the fire is lighted young people dance about it, singing ancient songs dedicated to São João. Hand in hand the couples leap over the flames.

Mothers often hold children over the embers, as the saint's fires are thought to possess curative virtue. Cattle and flocks are driven through the ashes so the animals will prosper throughout the coming year. Even the dead embers are gathered and carefully preserved, for they are thought to be efficacious against storm and evil influences.

People say that Saint John's Eve water possesses great healing power. Before dawn both cattle and children are bàthed in rivers or dew, to ensure health and strength. Young girls and women like to wash their faces in spring water or early dew, so they will be lovely throughout the year. Often peasants deck the springs with garlands, and water from seven different springs either is drunk, or carried home in flower-wreathed jugs.

On Saint John's Eve, night of love, young people exercise powers of divination. Three beans slipped under the pillow at night, cakes in which a grain of maize is hidden, fig leaves passed through the São João fires and touched with midnight dew—all these are good devices for learning whom one will wed. In Oporto, lovers exchange gifts in the marketplace at dawn. Boys give their sweethearts little pots of marjoram, girls present the boys with a large leek, which must be kept "for luck." In other places a boy sometimes bestows a purple thistle, which the girl promptly burns in the bonfire. She then plants the blackened stem in the ground. If a flower appears by morning, the true love has been found.

Portuguese peasants, who like to feel their saints can enjoy their own *festas,* have many charming folk songs in which the saints are tenderly addressed. São João, being a favorite saint, is showered with loving attention on his day.

These verses, known at Braga, Amares, and Póvoa do Lanhoso, are typical of many delightful Saint John's Day songs:

If Saint John knew
When his day occurred
He would come down from heaven to earth
With pleasure and joy.

O, my Saint John the Baptist,
Of what do you wish your chapels made?
Of carnations and of more roses,
With little yellow carnations.

DANÇA DO REI DAVID (Dance of King David), in Braga, province
of Minho

June 24

Portugal celebrates Saint John's Day widely with parades,
pageants, bull-fights, fireworks and other popular amusements.
Vila do Conde, Viseu, Évora, Vila Nova de Famalicão and many
other places have special observances, while the day is popular
among gypsies of the Alentejo for weddings and colorful festivities.
One of the most interesting folk ceremonies is at Braga, where the
Dança do Rei David, Dance of King David, is performed in the
streets.

The role of King David is hereditary in a certain family living
near Braga, and the dance itself possibly originated in medieval
times or earlier. The King, wearing a tall crown and voluminous
cape and strumming a guitar, is accompanied by ten shepherds (or
courtiers, according to some) in brilliant velvet coats and turban-
wound fezzes. The shepherds play ancient tunes on a variety of
musical instruments, including fiddles, flutes, and triangles. During
the course of their parade through town the group frequently halts
to perform a curious ritualistic dance, first King David alone, then
the King accompanied by his followers.

SÃO PEDRO (Saint Peter)

June 29

São Pedro, patron of fishermen, like Santo António and São
João, is a favorite June saint whose day is celebrated widely in both
towns and villages. Sintra (Estremadura), Montijo (Estremadura)
and Alcanena (Ribatejo) all have traditional festivities which
include fairs, fireworks, singing and dancing. In Lisbon there are
torchlight parades in the saint's honor and, as in most popular
festas, young people dance in the streets at night and refresh
themselves from sidewalk stalls with huge platefuls of rice and
succulent sardines, grilled with tomatoes and green peppers.

Since São Pedro, like António and João, looks upon lovers with an indulgent eye, his night is considered favorable for all sorts of divination games. One favorite way for young girls to find out whom they will marry is to knock at nine different doors without uttering a word. If absolute silence is maintained throughout the ceremony, the first man seen from the window in the morning will be the girl's lover.

In some places children erect little shrines to São Pedro on the doorsteps. The altars are charmingly decorated with flowers, holy pictures, and lighted tapers. Whenever the children see someone coming they run out and beg coppers "for the poor saint."

FESTA DA RAINHA SANTA ISABEL (Festival of the Holy Queen
    Isabel), in Coimbra, province of Beira Litoral
First fortnight in July, in even years

Rainha Santa Isabel, Holy Queen Isabel, is patroness of Coimbra, Portugal's first capital and ancient university center. Every two years Coimbra observes the festival of her pious Queen with a week of elaborate religious processions, fireworks, speeches, concerts and popular amusements. So devoted is Coimbra to the Rainha Santa that her image is incorporated in the city's coat of arms. Isabel, whom people claim "saved the city from pestilence and calamity," was beatified by Pope Leo X in 1516 and canonized by Urban VIII in 1625.

Isabel of Portugal, who was born in 1271, was daughter of Pedro III of Aragon and wife of Dom Diniz, Portugal's poet king. Of all her good works the Rainha Santa is probably best loved for the legendary "miracle of roses." Dom Diniz, who was unsympathetic to his wife's frequent errands of mercy for the poor and afflicted, once demanded to know what she carried in the upheld folds of her robe. "Roses," said Isabel, who was hiding bread for the hungry. She opened her robe and lo! her alms had been transformed into roses.

Historically, Queen Isabel exercised a strong influence for peace in the tumultuous times in which she lived and prevented Portugal from becoming embroiled in civil war. When her husband died in 1325, she retired to the convent of Santa Clara which she had founded, and joined the Third Order of Saint Francis. Throughout the country the Rainha Santa was famed for her miracles, many of the blind and paralyzed claiming she had cured their ills.

The ruined convent of Santa Clara stands on the banks of the Mondego, where it is partly buried in the sands. People still point to the door where the miracle of roses occurred. The saint's reputedly incorrupted body once rested in the old church, but was removed in the seventeenth century to the Convento de Santa Clara a Nova, the "new" Convent of Santa Clara, built high on the Monte da Esperança, the Hill of Hope.

The Rainha Santa procession starts at nine in the evening from this convent. The image of the Holy Queen is solemnly carried beneath the gaily-painted wooden arches that span the streets between tall poles. The poles are alternately decorated with gilded crowns and baskets of red and white roses, illumined from within. Garlands of flowers and plaster replicas of Queen Isabel with her robe full of roses, add further color to the line of march. The spectacular procession accompanied by music and fireworks advances slowly down the steep winding hill, goes across the Ponte de Santa Clara and to the Igreja da Graça. There religious ceremonies are held and the image remains until the last night of the festa, when it is returned to its place on the altar of the convent church.

FESTA DOS TABULEIROS (Festival of the *Tabuleiros* [2]), in Tomar, province of Ribatejo

> *About the second week in July, every third year in odd years (1959, 1961, 1963, and so on)*

For over six hundred years the city of Tomar has celebrated the *Festa dos Tabuleiros* in token of thanksgiving for harvest foods and of the city's charity for the poor and afflicted. Every third year the

---

[2] *Tabuleiro*, literally "tray," refers to the headdress worn by the girls in the procession.

171

festa is celebrated for four days, toward mid-July, both in the homes and on the streets. For four days there are bands, dances, concerts, processions, fireworks, bullfights and feasting. For four days Tomar's population is doubled or tripled, for rich and poor alike pour into the town from far and near.

The outstanding feature of the celebration is a magnificent procession of six hundred girls selected from Tomar and surrounding communities. The girls wear huge headdresses constructed with small loaves of bread and adorned with flowers. "Once the flowers were real," people told me. Now they are made of colored paper —a wise provision, surely, for a four-day festa.

The *tabuleiro,* as the traditional headdress is called, weighs about thirty-three pounds and "must be as tall as the girl who carries it." The foundation is a round basket, such as the Portuguese use for serving bread. From the basket (which is covered with an embroidered linen cloth) rises a framework of bamboo sticks and wires. The bamboo pierces thirty small bread loaves, arranged in five rows, six to a row. The intervening wires are covered with rainbow-colored flowers. A Maltese cross or a white dove makes a finial to the massive structure. The dove (of cotton batting with red tinsel eyes and an olive branch in its tinsel beak) "symbolizes peace and the Holy Ghost," while the cross stands for the ancient Order of Christ, which once flourished in Tomar.

The city has lived for centuries with the cross as her symbol. The twelfth-century Templars' monastery castle is silhouetted against the sky on the hill west of the town. It was in Tomar that the "new" Order of Christ took firm root in 1356, following the suppression of the Templars whose Grand Master, in 1160, built the forbidding castle above the Nabão. The square Maltese Cross of the Order of Christ is therefore repeated endlessly both in the town's sculptured monuments and in all festa decorations.

The Festa dos Tabuleiros though intermingled with secular entertainment, is primarily religious in character. The event is so old that nobody in Tomar can tell when or how it started. Everyone agrees, however, that the procession which honors the Holy

Ghost, represents an annual thank offering; that the bread, wine, and flesh—three symbolic elements featured in the procession—which are blessed by the priest and distributed to the poor, are gifts of plenty from the rich to their needy neighbors. The Portuguese word *peça*, "a word impossible to translate," according to one informant, "but meaning the giving of these three foods to the poor, has come down through the centuries and is known only to Tomar."

As with all ceremonials that have been observed for hundreds of years, there are many conflicting theories concerning the origin of the Festa dos Tabuleiros. One favorite supposition is that it has come down from early Roman times and the processions honoring Ceres, goddess of the harvest. Another explanation links the giving of bread to the poor with the legend of Queen Isabel I, who was known as the Rainha Santa.[3] Yet a third legend associates the custom with the name of Donna Maria Fogaça, a rich and pious woman, who lived long ago when Tomar and the surrounding countryside were ravaged by locusts. All the grain was destroyed. The poor, deprived of daily bread, died by hundreds. Donna Maria ordered that a great loaf be made from her own stock of grain. Distributing the food to the starving people, she urged them to make an annual procession and to beseech God always to provide them with sufficient bread.

Since I arrived in Tomar in advance of the festa, I had ample opportunity to observe the elaborate preparations going on in every quarter of town. For weeks beforehand housewives had indulged in orgies of cleaning and polishing. Confectioners turned out tons of the regional *estrelas, fatias, queijinhos,* and other *doces,* or sweets, for which Tomar is justly famous, while local hostelries frenziedly set up extra beds and stocked extra foods for the expected influx of guests.

One of the most delightful folk aspects of the whole affair was the original and often very artistic way in which various little communities worked out decorative plans for their own neighborhoods.

[3] See *Festa da Rainha Santa Isabel,* p. 170.

There was Rua do Camarão, the Street of Shrimp, for example, one of Tomar's more humble quarters, which won both first and second prizes as the most beautiful street in town.

Rua do Camarão is long and slightly twisting. The modest whitewashed cottages with gaily painted half doors, crowd close to the cobbled lane. On the eve of the festa every man, woman, cat, dog, and chicken was busily running hither and yon. I was invited to look into a dark cellar which overflowed with beautiful paper flower decorations. People were stringing electric lights against house walls. Fresh greens were being woven into long garlands adorned with pink, blue, yellow, and red artificial flowers. Festoons were hung from house to house across the narrow alley. One old man was busy making what I took for a shrine in a jog of the wall. He beckoned me to come closer. Unwarily, I leaned over, to be suddenly drenched by a tiny hidden fountain!

The Rua do Camarão was gay with paper flower festoons over doors and windows. At either end of the street inverted paper umbrellas, with panels of red, yellow, blue and white swung merrily, with tissue covered "pails," lighted from within, dangling from each point. Smaller umbrellas, also illumined, lined the street close to the houses.

But while Rua do Camarão artists were busy with decorations, her poets were busy writing little hand-printed rhymes which they tacked up against the walls and framed with flowers. One verse read:

> This street so humble
> Where we are very happy
> Is the most beautiful of all streets,
> This street of Camarão.

Another verse, not only flower framed but decorated with green leaves and two pink-eyed doves, emphasized the peace theme, so often evident in Portuguese thinking:

> O, thou who passeth by singing,
> Indifferent and unheeding,
> Pause here a moment
> And pray God for peace.

174

Yet another verse expressed much the same idea:

> To see a white dove flying
> Fills my breast with rapture
> And reminds me of the Holy Spirit.

Decorations in the Rua do Camarão grew increasingly elaborate as the festa progressed, so it was fun to visit the quarter each night and see what new ideas had developed during the day. One night hundreds of fairy lamps made from lighted wicks floating in tiny terra cotta saucers, shone like glow worms along the cobbled street, close to the houses. For centuries primitive lamps such as these have been used by humble folk in this ancient land. By the end of the festa, flower pots adorned the tops of walls, flowers bloomed from trees and many other colorful touches appeared in the narrow street.

Tomar's ancient ghetto, like the Street of the Shrimp, also was bursting with festa spirit. I paused to chat with an old man who was attaching sprays of green, adorned with bright red artifical cherries, to a morning-glory vine which sprawled voluptuously across the front of his tiny cottage. The vine, I noted, not only bore its own great purple flowers, but a profusion of red, green, and silver tinsel blossoms. Everywhere people took childlike joy in producing colorful effects. Throughout the town a great deal of artistry and skill went into the decorations, which cost little but displayed community planning and effort.

Serpa Pinto, Tomar's business street, was as gay as the town's more humble quarters. There were paper lanterns and roses, fluttering banners and balcony decorations. The motifs of the Cross of Christ and the Holy Dove were repeated many times. Shops vied with each other in displaying original verses, figures of girls carrying the tabuleiros, and all kinds of Tomar sweets, together with regular merchandise. Some shopkeepers showed a real flair for modern advertising. One accessory store, for example, exhibited women's

175

scarves, handbags, gloves, and dress materials, along with comforting hints such as these:

> Don't walk along sadly
> Because nobody loves you
> You can be so pretty
> You won't have to stay single!

And again:

> Miracles are not necessary
> If you want to get married;
> With so many pretty things
> You will soon become a bride!

Against this background of gaiety and color the Festa dos Tabuleiros officially opened with processions of bands and soldiers. By day, firecrackers, set off at intervals, announced the approach of bagpipers and drummers. All night loudspeakers blared forth song hits and jazz—Portuguese, French and American—while the amusement park was the scene of a products' fair, family picnics, and unbelievably noisy merry-go-rounds. By midnight the noise reached a deafening crescendo when fireworks were shot off from the Templars' castle on the hill. One night there was a great naval battle in the air. Another time the mighty eight-hundred-year-old fortress seemed smoldering in flames. Of course, nobody slept until he fell down from sheer fatigue.

Sunday, the high day of the festa, dawned bright and hot. Everybody seemed too exhausted by the fireworks, bullfights, and parades of the first two days to get the celebration under way on time. The bagpipers, who kept circulating in streets and taverns, began to look decidedly worse for wear. Housewives were out early, nevertheless, to seek festa bargains. I saw many hurrying home before noon with huge bouquets for the table and chickens or rabbits for the pot. Solemn High Mass at São João Baptista's was late, and the old Gothic church, hung with feast day scarlet, overflowed with peasants, kneeling in Sunday best. Dinners were late all over town, but once eaten, everybody hastened to the church square to witness the great Tabuleiros procession. The grandstand was erected before the beautiful eighteenth-century palace, now the Town Hall, directly opposite São João Baptista's door. Spectators lined the streets all about the square, which was cleared except for cameramen.

After a long wait the repeated firing of rockets announced the approaching procession. Two firecracker men slowly advanced, passing before the grandstand. They wore white shirts and trousers, broad red sashes and green and red knitted caps. One man held a bundle of rockets. His partner preceded him, lighting one rocket at a time and sending it aloft with a terrific din that immediately dislodged all the gray doves in the church belfry. Out they flew, a silver phalanx against the deep blue sky; then they settled back in their hidden ledges, only to fly out again with the next explosion.

Following the firecracker men came the bagpipers, resplendent in red satin shirts, their waists twined with red and black paper garlands. Tomar's briskly stepping band came next, then the city standard bearer with a red satin banner embroidered with a gold dove. Close behind were three men, each bearing a silver crown displayed on a scarlet cushion.

At last the tabuleiros approached—the procession of six hundred girls carrying on their heads beautiful crowns with the bread to be blessed. From a distance they looked like moving columns of brilliant flowers—green, blue, cerise, purple, orange, pink. Each girl wore the traditional simple white cotton dress, high-necked, long-sleeved, of ankle length. The close fitting blouses had little lace-edged peplums, and the full ruffled skirts were also trimmed with lace. Ribbons about four inches wide, of pink, blue, red, or other colors were passed over one shoulder, about the waist and tied in a bow with long streamers at the opposite side.

Straight and strong the double line of girls approached, each with a ribboned *sogra,* or padded ring on her head, to support the tabuleiro of bread and flowers. Modern caryatids, these stately girls bore their heavy burdens with the grace of young goddesses. Each girl had an escort—a young man in dark trousers, red sash, and white shirt who strode beside her on the outside of the line.

177

The girls with the tabuleiros marched past the grandstand, on into the square. Their escorts lifted the headdresses to the ground. Line after line filed by, each group of girls preceded by the parish standard-bearer, each with the special flower or fruit selected by the parish. Tiger lilies, poppies, roses, tulips, lemons, and cherries all were represented in the headdresses. Many girls made the flowers themselves, I was told. Sometimes a well-to-do citizen donated a headdress to be carried by a girl in the community. Each village or hamlet developed its own decorative theme in an individual way. One parish wrapped the small loaves in cellophane tying the ends with scarlet bows.

One of the prettiest tabuleiros was made with geraniums, shaded from salmon pink to deep maroon. The flowers were charmingly emphasized by green leaves. As in all headdresses, rows of bread alternated with flowers. The pretty girl bearing the geraniums was small, with long gold earrings and maroon sash.

At last, all six hundred girls and their escorts had filed into the square where they stood motionless, their symbolic crowns beside them. A solemn hush fell over the crowd. The time of benediction had come. Even the doves seemed to settle back into the shadows of the old belfry, the circling swallows to cease their screaming. The priest appeared, robed in gold and white, and accompanied by two altar boys in scarlet and white. Slowly the priest passed down one long line of the motionless girls and up another, blessing the loaves as he went.

This gift of bread for the poor is symbolic, rather than actual, I was told. Each family receiving a Festa dos Tabuleiros loaf cherishes it throughout the year against sickness and disaster. A bit of the blessed loaf, when swallowed by man or beast in time of crisis, is thought to possess healing power. Many peasants keep in the holy place not only current *festa* loaves, but those acquired in previous years.

The benediction service completed, the church bells rang joyously. Almost simultaneously the escorts lifted the tabuleiros, replacing them on the heads of the erect young girls who began marching out of the square and into the street. Then came one of the most picturesque features of the procession: Three two-wheeled ox carts, each drawn by a yoke of golden brown animals with flower decked horns, passed by the stand and followed the marching girls. The first two carts, decorated with wheat and poppies, (in symbol of the gift of bread), each carried a little girl with long corkscrew curls and swansdown angel wings. The third cart, representing the gift of wine, contained a decorated wine cask under a bower of grapes and leaves. Then came three pair of oxen with decorated horns. These beasts—the gift of prosperous citizens—were destined for slaughter. Tomorrow their flesh would be distributed to the needy. The blessed bread, the wine, the flesh—these three elements comprised Tomar's *peça*—her traditional festa offering to old people in the workhouse on the hill, to the poor for miles about.

The distribution of peça started next day from the Misericordia Church, where the loaves had been locked up throughout the night. By ten o'clock the procession was slowly forming close to the church, before the interested eyes of small boys, a few old peddlars, and a handful of spectators. The continuous celebration of the previous three days and nights seemed to rob this last ritual of much enthusiasm on the part of Tomar's citizens.

The peça procession, like that of the tabuleiros, was preceded by firecracker men, bagpipers, and drummers. One of yesterday's wheat-and-poppy-decorated ox carts was piled high with the blessed bread, the other with newspaper wrapped packets of meat. As on the previous day, the little angels presided over the carts. Stocky men in white suits and red sashes strode beside them, guiding the animals and assisting in the distribution of peças. Following the bread and meat carts came the one with the wine cask.

All day the little procession passed up and down through Tomar's twisted streets. All day food was given to ragged and poor, old and infirm, and all day the traditional rite was accompanied by the playing of bands, shooting of rockets and the fanfare of bagpipes and drums.

179

But the festa was not over. Once more magnificent fireworks exploded most of the night, loudspeakers roared, merry-go-rounds blared. Streets and roads were filled with peasants returning home with baskets and bedding, for the morrow would find them toiling at their nets and in the fields.

The next day Tomar gradually huddled back into her accustomed quiet beneath the shadow of the Templars' castle on the hill. Secular though the great celebration is in many respects, the Dove of Peace hovers over the standard of the ancient town and the Cross of Christ is hewn in her twelfth-century ramparts. Peace for Portugal and bread for the poor—this is the real significance of the Festa dos Tabuleiros.

FESTA DO COLETE ENCARNADO (Red Waistcoat Festival), in Vila Franca de Xira, province of Ribatejo

Some time in July

The *Festa do Colete Encarnado* derives its name from the red waistcoats of the *campinos,* or bull herders of the Ribatejo. These men still wear their traditional eighteenth-century costumes, consisting of bright red sleeveless waistcoats, blue breeches, stocking caps, white woolen hose and red sashes. The campinos carry slender eight- to ten-foot staves with sharp arrow-pointed metal tips. These staves are used in the province of Ribatejo to herd and control the bulls.

The campinos parade on horseback through the streets of Vila Franca de Xira amid the wild acclaim of onlookers; for these hardy men breed and care for the black bulls for which the district is famous.

The high point of the festa comes when the bulls are let loose in the streets and start on their way to the ring. Chased by the campinos and goaded on by the yells, taunts, and teasing of the foolhardy, the enraged animals often charge at their tormentors who seek to exhibit their prowess as amateur matadors. Hundreds of spectators cheer and shout as they view the dangerous sport from the safety of balconies, windows, and barriers.

Bullfights, fireworks, folk dancing and great regional suppers, featuring whole roast oxen and native red wine, characterize this, picturesque event in honor of the red waistcoat wearers.

FESTAS GUALTERIANAS (Festivals of Saint Walter), in Guimarães, province of Minho

First Sunday in August, for four days

Guimarães, Portugal's twelfth-century capital and birthplace of Dom Afonso Henriques, the country's first king, is indeed "the cradle of the nation." Each year this ancient town, proud in palaces and tradition, rich in treasure of silver, wood and stone, but poor in livelihood to many of its humble citizens, is the setting of the *Festas Gualterianas,* the festival honoring São Gualter (Walter), patron of the town. For four days and nights people from all over the Minho pour into Guimarães. There are magnificent processions, dazzling fireworks, animal fairs, picturesque displays of food and merchandise —all to the deafening accompaniment of brass bands, and of loud-speakers playing the jazz hits of the nations.

"The noise starts a month before the *festa* and continues for a month after it is over," a nun complained.

"Who was São Gualter?" I inquired, curious to know about the saint who inspired the noise, the fireworks, the showy adornment of the square with huge yellow, pink and blue parasols, surmounted by stars and electric lights; the white-pillared streets, festooned with green and white garlands that were caught up with great shimmering, green-and-white dragonflies. "Oh, he was a Franciscan saint, contemporaneous with Santo António and São Francisco," said my informant, who added, "His story is 'made up', not real."

Before the festa commenced I made São Gualter's acquaintance at Senhor dos Passos, Our Lord of the Way of the Cross, the blue-and white-tiled church which overlooks the public garden from a high terrace. In the nave stood a platform with the image of a slender young Franciscan monk, a book in his hand, a halo on his head. Blue hydrangeas and tall white tapers surrounded the image, which soon would be carried in triumphal procession through the town, in celebration of the medieval saint's fiftieth anniversary as patron of Guimarães. Barefoot peasant women in gaily striped skirts, toil worn men in festa black and little girls in fluttering white Communion veils quietly slipped into the church, prostrated themselves before the image, and left a few coppers for the saint.

The balconies and windows of Senhor dos Passos, now more a museum than a church, were hung in festa scarlet. Other draperies, of blue and white, were for Portugal's first flag—a white cross on blue background. Many processional properties were on exhibition— the scarlet and gold embroidered canopy beneath which the archbishop would walk; sumptuous gold and red vestments for high-ranking clergy; the silver mace; the handsome white satin standard of Saint Gualter, with the name worked in gold threads. One of the most interesting exhibits was a handwoven natural colored linen standard, embroidered in blue with the city's coat of arms and in gold with a representation of *Nossa Senhora da Oliveira,* Our Lady of the Olive Tree, patroness of a tenth-century Guimarães abbey. This beautiful symbolic banner was made as an anniversary gift from the city of Guimarães to Portuguese countrymen in Goa.

The *Procissão Gualteriana* of Sunday night was a magnificent spectacle. The image of the saint, accompanied by the Archbishop of Braga and distinguished churchmen of both Portugal and Spain, priests, divinity students, bands and standard bearers, was carried from the church of Senhor dos Passos through the picturesquely decorated streets. Thousands of spectators watched the solemn procession, then spent the rest of the night enjoying fireworks, folk dances in regional costume and, most of all perhaps, the shooting galleries, side shows and merry-go-rounds in the public garden that is dominated by the church of Senhor dos Passos. The sanctuary's doors, windows, and rococo façade were now outlined by strings of red, green, yellow, and blue electric bulbs. Even the figures of the four huge granite saints near the portal were wreathed in blazing lights.

Pandemonium seemed let loose as the night wore on. A singer dressed half in scarlet, half in white, with bulbous red nose and raucous voice, kept popping in and out of one side show. Another exhibited an 'animated *crèche*. Joseph and Mary lifted their arms, while donkeys, cows, and sheep moved heads up and down as the Infant Jesus jerkily raised tiny hands and feet.

Vendors of green and purple grapes, ices, household wares, and foods thronged the streets. Even at two in the morning many peddlars sat by their stalls hopefully awaiting customers. Others wrapped their children in blankets and bunked them up against the sides of buildings. Occasionally a weary woman dropped her head on her arms for a snatch of sleep. Barefoot peasant women, gracefully balancing classic looking terra cotta jugs on their heads, strode through the streets selling draughts of water. Some vendors sold bottles of soft drinks cooled by an oblong block of ice in a pail, while specialists in hot foods squatted over little charcoal braziers close to the curb.

The most fascinating of all merchandise, however, were the tiny pink and black flower-painted cocks, the miniature jugs, the whistles, and pretty hand-woven baskets, spread out in endless array. Each small item was a perfect example of peasant handicraft, the flowering of centuries of poetic imagination, of dwelling close to the soil in the beauty of field and flower.

Then there were the festa breads and fancy cakes. There were great round fragrant loaves designed for family picnicking and little dough dogs and birds to please the children. There were oval sugar-coated cakes and round ones with holes in the middle, strung on pink, blue, or red cords. *Vareirinhas,* large sugar-coated buns, were sold in pairs for three-and-a-half escudos (about ten cents), while cellophane bagfuls of *alfacinhas,* cakes that looked like fat peppermints, were even dearer.

As the days passed the festa increased progressively in noise and tempo. The *Marcha Gualteriana,* a midnight procession of twelve allegorical floats, exhibited to the stirring music of the saint's march, culminated official festivities in a triumph of color. music, and fantasy.

Possibly the most interesting peasant event of the festa came on the final day when the prize-winning animals from various outlying districts were selected and led through the streets by pretty girls in regional dress. Young men and women in costume followed, singing their village songs with great gaiety and flair.

The prize-winning oxen were magnificent golden brown beasts, with enormous lyre-shaped horns adorned with bright paper streamers. The animals' wide, brass-studded collars were hung with flowers. Led through the streets by a comely girl in black pleated skirt and apron, the stately oxen symbolized the Minho, where the rhythm of life changes little through the centuries and festa and song lighten the task of tilling the earth and gathering the harvest.

DIA DE NOSSA SENHORA DA ASSUMPÇÃO (Assumption Day)
August 15

In the churches special services are held to crown Our Lady, Queen of the Angels, in commemoration of her ascent to heaven.

Religious processions accompanied by bands, bagpipes, and drums, go through the streets of many towns and villages. At the small coastal village of Póvoa de Varzim in the Minho, the benediction of the fishing boats is one of the festival's main events.

NOSSA SENHORA DA NAZARÉ (Our Lady of Nazaré), in Nazaré, province of Estremadura
September 8-18

High on the steep cliff overlooking the sea, Nazaré has a little chapel dedicated to Our Lady, the object of ten days of pilgrimage and of both religious and secular ceremonies for fisherfolk from miles about.

Local legend says that one Dom Fuas Roupinho built a chapel on this promontory in gratitude to Our Lady of Nazaré for miraculously saving his life. According to the story Dom Fuas went doe hunting on September 8, 1182. Through the heavy fog which enveloped the scene like a curtain, the huntsman saw the deer he was following vanish into nothingness. His horse, in hot pursuit, suddenly stopped and pawed the air, for he was on the edge of a cliff that dropped three hundred feet to the sea. Both man and horse would have quickly followed the animal, except for the huntsman's vision of Our Lady of Nazaré, whose image had been found by shepherds in a nearby grotto. Dom Fuas prayed for the Virgin's help. As he did so, the horse, poised on the brink of death, drew back into safety. The grateful petitioner had a chapel built for the image. Soon the shrine became the object of veneration to fishermen from throughout the district.

Today it would be hard to find along the coast a cottage without a holy picture of the miraculous rescue of Dom Fuas. The chapel of Our Lady, reconstructed in the seventeenth century, is said to occupy the spot where the vision occurred.

Beginning with September 8, anniversary of the miracle, religious processions, bullfights, dancing, feasting and a fair commemorate *Nossa Senhora da Nazaré,* whose help is sought against all perils of the sea.

DIA DE FINADOS (Day of the Dead)

November 2

Masses are said for the repose of the souls of all the deceased. Processions of the faithful go to the cemeteries and visit the graves of the dead. In olden times food offerings for the departed probably were eaten at the graves. Today, however, *magusto,* or open air feasts of wine and chestnuts, are prepared for the living.

On November 1 bands of children go about singing for "bread for God," and are rewarded with food and drink. Sometimes the singers receive *bolas de festa,* special Day of the Dead sugar cakes, flavored with cinnamon and herbs.

SÃO MARTINHO (Saint Martin)

November 11

The Feast of São Martinho, which is popularly associated with frequent draughts of red Portuguese wine, chestnuts roasted over glowing embers, and the annual slaughter of the family pig, is widely celebrated. At Golegã, in Ribatejo, the traditional Saint Martin's Fair features a famous horse show, with exhibitions of some of the country's finest thoroughbreds. Penafiel, in Trás-os-Montes, also has a Martin's Fair, while towns and villages throughout the country hold parades and revels to honor this saint whose festival has a strongly pagan flavor.

> "Children born on Saint Martin's Day
> Will be born both happy and gay,"

is a current saying which would seem to justify special celebration on the part of all Portugal's many Martinhõs.

DIA DO NATAL or DIA DA FAMILIA (Christmas, or Day of the Family)

December 25

Christmas to the Portuguese is primarily a family festival, characterized by reunions of as many relatives as can be gathered together. In many parts of the country, the *cepo do Natal,* or Christmas log (traditionally of oak), is burned on the hearth while the family feasts and drinks late into the day. The charred remains of the log are gathered up and carefully preserved. They are burned, later on, to keep the house from harm, when endangered by thunder or sudden storm.

In some primitive districts people share the *consoada,* or Christmas repast, with the spirits of the dead, who are thought to return to their former homes at this season. Sometimes crumbs from the feast are sprinkled over the hearth, or food is left on the table so the hungry ghosts may have a part in the family's cheer.

The night before Christmas groups of carolers go through the streets singing hymns about Jesus and his birth in Bethlehem's humble manger.

PORTUGAL

Véspera de Ano Novo (New Year's Eve)

December 31

Throughout the country the devout attend religious services in the churches. At midnight the bells ring and people hasten to the village squares to speed the Old Year and welcome the New with fireworks, blaring trumpets, and beating drums. In certain localities everyone goes to the rooftops at midnight, to recite appropriate improvised verses and "blow away" the dying year through megaphones. An almost universally observed custom is to pick and eat twelve grapes from a bunch of grapes, just as the bells strike twelve. This act is said to ensure twelve happy months in the coming year.

In some places little groups of masked children go about from house to house singing *janeiras,* or ancient New Year songs. The *janeireiros,* or singers, address their words to the owners of the house, praising them when generous, and insulting them when stingy with their traditional presents of wine, apples, sausages or nuts.

10

FESTIVALS OF SPAIN

Año Nuevo (New Year)

January 1

Tradition says that the luck of the entire year depends upon the first day. If you have a gold coin in your pocket, there will be plenty of gold during the next twelve months, while empty pockets mean a lean year ahead. If you eat good food and drink good wine, you are certain to have an abundance of food and drink the whole year round. Meeting a rich man is a propitious sign, but coming face to face with a beggar is bad luck.

Family reunions, visiting, feasting, and the exchange of cards and presents are generally characteristic of the day.

Día de los Reyes Magos (Day of the Kings, or Epiphany)

January 6

Children eagerly await Epiphany Eve when the Magi Kings—Gaspar, Melchor and Baltasar—who take the place of Santa Claus to Spanish boys and girls—travel through the land on their way to Bethlehem and leave gifts of sweets and toys.

On the Eve of Epiphany children fill their shoes with straw or grain and place them on the balconies or by the front door. By morning the horses of the Kings have eaten the food. In its place the monarchs leave cookies, sweets, and all kinds of pretty baubles. Parents often blacken the cheeks of the sleeping children with charcoal. The next day the boys and girls rush to the mirror to see if Baltasar, the Black King, has kissed them in the night.

At Palma, Mallorca and Las Palmas, Canary Islands, as well as in many cities throughout Spain, people turn out on Epiphany Eve

188

to witness the splendid spectacle of *Los Reyes* making official entrance into town, to the accompaniment of military bands and drumming by musicians in medieval attire.

The procession at Palma is a gay torchlight affair. First come the city officials on horseback, then the kingly visitors in Eastern costume. The Kings, who ride horses led by faithful attendants, are followed by retainers in colorful Oriental garb. In the Canary Islands the procession is even more exotic, since there the Kings customarily ride on camels.

In Madrid groups of men and boys used to go out on Epiphany Eve "to meet the Kings." The men carried a tall ladder and made terrific din on horns, trumpets, and drums, as they went about searching for some credulous person they could induce to join in the search for the Magi. Once a victim was found, he received a bell-decked mule collar and was ordered to take the ladder.

From time to time his tormentors told him to climb the ladder and look about for the Kings. Often the rude jesters let the ladder fall at the risk of the poor simpleton's neck. Such practical jokes finally went so far that city authorities banned the custom of "meeting the kings."

DÍA DE SAN ANTÓN (Day of Saint Anthony)

January 17

Saint Anthony is patron of horses, asses, mules, and other four-footed beasts. On his day farmers in towns and villages throughout Spain decorate their animals with flowers, ribbons, and bells and drive them to a church dedicated to Saint Anthony. There the priest administers a barley wafer to the odd communicants, sprinkles them with holy water and invokes Saint Anthony's blessing against accident and disease during the coming year.

All day processions of animals pass through the streets, much to the entertainment of bystanders who watch the antics of balky mules, horses, and oxen as they are led toward the sanctuary.

FESTIVALS OF WESTERN EUROPE

FALLAS DE SAN JOSÉ (Bonfires of Saint Joseph), in Valencia
March 12-19

Valencia's custom of burning *fallas,* or bonfires, on March 19, Saint Joseph's Night is said to have originated in medieval times when members of the Carpenter's Guild annually swept out shops and made bonfires of accumulated chips and trash. The burnings were in honor of Saint Joseph, father of Jesus and patron of carpenters.

Modern Valencia, one of Spain's most famous furniture-making centers, continues the Saint Joseph's Day tradition with at least a week of festivities which feature not only bonfires, but bullfights, parades, and religious processions. The climax of the whole affair is the spectacular midnight burning of over a hundred giant effigies, of canvas, plaster, and papier maché, made over wooden foundations.

These fallas, ingenious, larger-than life-sized creations, sometimes three or four stories tall, are made by highly skilled craftsmen. The effigies usually have a sharply humorous or ironic twist. They poke fun at some world, national, or local problem, or possibly caricature a well known personality or illustrate a current fad, scandal, or trend. The gigantic figures which are filled with explosives are set up throughout the city—at intersections, in plazas, on top of tall platforms.

The fallas are executed secretly, months in advance of the festival, under direction of district committees. These committees commission artists to follow plans already approved by the various community groups. Expenses are defrayed by local contributions. Each group, of course, hopes to win the competition for the most clever and original falla. Each year all fallas are burned. A small-scale model of the falla that is popularly accaimed the best is made and placed on permanent exhibition in the local museum.

Saint Joseph's fiesta commences about a week before March 19, when the City Beadle reads an official proclamation of the event from the City Hall balcony, then from the various public squares. This ceremony, accompanied by shooting of rockets and a great deal of band playing, marks the beginning of a ceaseless round of merrymaking. The city is adorned with flowers; balconies are draped with banners and rich tapestries; countless illuminations make night brighter than day, and thousands of people surge through the streets in carnival mood.

There is a spectacular parade of fallas before they are judged and finally mounted throughout the city on their platforms. A fallas Queen, selected from among Valencia's most beautiful girls, presides over official ceremonies, which include concerts, dancing, banquets, and bullfights.

On Saint Joseph's Eve, Valencia's young girls from sixteen to twenty years old, carry through the streets the image of the *Virgen de los Desamparados,* Virgin of the Forsaken, patroness of the city. The girls, dressed in colorful native costume, place flowers at the feet of the statue. This is a striking event, not only because of the beauty of the girls in provincial dress, but because of the vast quantity of flowers—often more than three tons—which is offered before the image.

The climax of the fiesta comes the following night as the city chimes strike midnight. At this moment bands begin to play, fallas are set afire and fireworks explode. Saint Joseph, patron of carpenters is honored on an immense scale as the effigies of animals, gods, and human beings are silhouetted in changing, flashing color against the midnight sky. For hours the dramatic fires continue amid deafening explosions, bursting rockets, and dancing in the streets.

*CARNAVAL (Carnival)

The three days preceding Ash Wednesday

The last three days of Carnival, which culminate the pre-Lenten period of merrymaking and amusement, are devoted to eating and all kinds of entertainment. Every town and village celebrates with bull fights, parades, feasting, masquerades and dancing. Valencia, like many other cities, is the scene of picturesque revelry at this season when orange trees are in bloom and the air is filled with

* Stars indicate movable feasts that depend upon Easter. See Table of Easter Dates and Movable Festivals Dependent upon Easter, p. 246.

delicious fragrance. Battles of flowers, showers of confetti, and throngs of vendors selling trinkets and sweets crowd the town, which suddenly is transformed into a gigantic fair.

*Domingo de Ramos (Palm Sunday)

The Sunday preceding Easter

Early in the morning people go to church to have palms blessed by the archbishop. The consecrated branches, which come from Elche's famous palm trees,[1] are reverently carried home and fastened to balconies as a protection against storm, lightning, and other evils during the next twelve months.

Palm Sunday is the occasion of many confirmations. Processions of little white-veiled girls and shy young boys in fresh new suits fill all the streets, as children go to or come from their first communion.

*Semana Santa (Holy Week)

From Palm Sunday to Easter

Throughout Spain *Semana Santa,* or Holy Week, is characterized by deep religious fervor and magnificent processions which are estimated at over three thousand in number. Although some of the most outstanding observances occur in Seville, Granada, Málaga, Cartagena, Murcia and Valladolid, every town and village gives realistic portrayals of the final seven days of Jesus' life. Every Spaniard regardless of age, sex, or social position, participates in the ceremonies.

Seville's Holy Week processions, which surpass all others in splendor and realism, typify Spain's *Semana Santa* celebrations. *Pasos,* or large platforms with life-sized sculptured images portraying different episodes in the Passion story, are brought out of churches and paraded through the streets. The pasos, of Byzantine origin, are of marked originality in Andalusia, those of Seville being

---

[1] Elche, in the province of Alicante, has the only palm groves in Europe, and supplies the entire country with the six-foot palm fronds which are universally used in the Palm Sunday processions.

the most elaborate and ornamental of any in the country. Each parish has at least one *paso,* or group of figures, and one figure of either Christ or the Virgin. Forty eight *cofradías,* religious lay brotherhoods, or trade guilds, direct Seville's processions. These organizations are very old, many having existed since the Middle Ages. The members dress alike except for the color of their costumes. These are long full silk robes and tall pointed hoods which completely cover the head and face. Two slits are cut for the eyes. Originally the hoods were intended to hide the identity of repentant sinners. Rope or silk girdles are tied about the waist. Each brother carries an immense lighted beeswax candle throughout the procession.

Many pasos are masterpieces of fifteenth or sixteenth century wood carving. The Last Supper, the agony in Gethsemane, the trial before Pilate, the Crucifixion—all are represented with remarkable workmanship and attention to realistic detail.

The pasos, which are very heavy, are borne on the shoulders of sometimes as many as sixty porters, who crouch beneath the platform. The bearers, hidden from view by velvet curtains, shuffle along, unable to see, stopping to rest only when their leader, who walks outside, gives the order.

The life-sized statues of the Virgin, magnificently arrayed in velvet robes, embroidered with gold and precious gems, are carried beneath rich canopies. Flowers and hundreds of lighted wax tapers adorn the platforms and give the Madonnas added splendor and impressiveness.

"*Viva la Macarena,*" shouts the crowd tumultuously as *La Macarena,* the Virgin of Good Hope, Seville's most sumptuously decorated image, appears on Good Friday night. The crowd goes mad. Women weep emotionally. Now and again a *saeta*—an impromptu wailing song of sorrow and repentance, delivered in minor key—pierces the darkness. The procession stops. The heavy paso shudders to the ground. The saeta ends and the procession moves once more. This kind of interruption occurs many times during the slow march through the city.

At last the Macarena is returned to the church which houses her throughout the year. Then the hidden bearers begin tipping the paso up and down and rocking it from side to side, "to make their Virgin dance." The spectators shout and clap their hands in delight. Finally the Macarena is replaced on her altar.

Easter in Seville, as elsewhere in Spain, begins on Holy Saturday. The church bells, silent since Holy Thursday, peal forth the Resurrection tidings. The black veil shrouding the front of the sanctuary, is torn aside, revealing the altar in a blaze of light. Vehicles, immobilized since Holy Thursday, now resume their usual breakneck course through the streets. People discard mourning attire for brightly colored gala clothes. Cabarets open, gypsies dance. The Lenten fast is broken with rich foods and sparkling wines. The joy of the Resurrection is celebrated by colorful bullfights where famous matadors exhibit their skill before thousands of frantically cheering, wildly waving spectators.

*FERIAS (Fairs)

Some time after Easter

After Easter many Spanish cities hold colorful *ferias,* or fairs, which attract thousands of people from surrounding communities and are celebrated with parades, processions, bullfights, music, folk dancing and, in some places, with livestock markets and exhibits of fine horses and cattle. Trading, however, is incidental to having a good time, meeting old friends, drinking, and enjoying various amusements.

Each town celebrates its fair with its own customs and in its own individual way. Seville, Jerez, Murcia and Ronda all have famous fairs, as well as many smaller towns all over Spain.

Seville's Spring Fair is probably the most picturesque of all these events. Many beautiful costumes are seen, for the Sevillian, wearing short jacket and broad brimmed hat, parades through the streets on his most spirited horse. Many times a lovely, dark-eyed sweetheart in high comb, lace mantilla, flower-embroidered shawl and frilly, flounced skirt, rides pillion behind the horseman.

Jerez, home of the sherry vineyards, and noted for its splendid horses, also celebrates its fair with picturesque cavalcades. As at Seville, the men wear regional costume. Many of the women, in vivid Andalusian dress, ride in flower-decorated open carriages.

Murcia's feria starts on Easter Monday and continues for four to five days. Battles of flowers, parades, and the traditional *Entierro de la Sardina,* or Burial of the Sardine, are features of this spring festival. Toward the end of the fair, the Sardine is buried at midnight with great pomp, following a torchlight parade. The meaning of this ancient rite is unknown, but there are some who think the ceremony may have originated in an old fertility custom of burying Winter in early spring.

SAN ISIDRO LABRADOR (Saint Isidore the Ploughman), in Madrid
May 10-17

Madrid honors San Isidro, patron of the capital and of farmers, with eight days of bullfights at the Plaza de Toros, colorful parades and street dancing.

Isidro was reputedly born in the twelfth century, on the site of modern Madrid. Peasants from surrounding towns and villages look upon San Isidro as their friend and patron, for he was a simple peasant like themselves. Legend says he labored for Don Juan de Vargas on a farm outside Madrid. Isidro was a devout, hard working man. Jealous tongues began to wag, however, claiming he was lazy and that he preferred praying to guiding the plough.

One day the master spied upon his servant. To his amazement, Vargas beheld an angel and a yoke of white oxen ploughing at Isidro's side. The vision finally convinced the master of his servant's faithfulness—for Vargas knew Isidro was beloved of God.

May 15, Saint Isidro's feast day, is a memorable occasion. In some neighborhoods near Madrid street vendors sell fruits and sweets, pictures of the saint, and little glass or pottery pig bells which when rung are thought to dispel harm from thunder and lightning. Then there are tiny whistle-stemmed glass roses which everyone toots, thus adding a cheery accompaniment to the music, feasting, dancing and general fiesta merriment.

Although San Isidro is especially loved by the peasants, since 1595 his memory has also been greatly revered by people of high rank. In that year Philip the Third was dying. The remains of the saint were carried in solemn procession to the village where the king lay. The monarch rallied and recovered. From then on, the pious Isidro was honored by the rich and powerful no less than the poor and humble.

*LA PROCESION DE LA PENITENCIA (Procession of Penitents), in Roncesvalles, region of Navarre

> *The week preceding Pentecost* (Whitsun)

At Roncesvalles, in the Pyrenees near the French border, the week before Pentecost is annually observed by black-clad penitents, with crosses tied to their backs, who toil up the steep pass to attend mass at the Monastery of Roncesvalles. The penitents come from five surrounding villages. On each of five separate days one of the five parishes performs its penitential march.

Tradition says this procession originated long ago as an act of penance among twenty-three families seeking atonement for sins committed during the year. The penitents wear black robes and hoods having only slits for the eyes. The men stretch out their arms to support the heavy crosses. As the penitents make their weary two-mile ascent from the village to the monastery they chant a *Miserere* which echoes solemnly through the hills.

*ROMERÍA DEL ROCÍO (Pilgrimage of the Dew), in Almonte, region of Andalusia

> *Friday before Pentecost to the Tuesday following*

The *Romería del Rocío,* or Pilgrimage of the Dew, is one of Spain's gayest and most picturesque processions. It is in honor of the Virgin known as *La Blanca Paloma,* the White Dove, at the Santuary of El Rocío, in Almonte in the province of Huelva. For days preceding Whitsunday roads all over Andalusia are crowded with caravans of two-wheeled, white-hooded farm carts, flower-decked and oxen-drawn. Entire families occupy the high swaying wagons, for this romería is half-pilgrimage and half-picnic. Often pretty girls, in embroidered shawls and ruffled, coin-dotted crinolines, sit in the open backed, bower-like wagons and flirt with their mounted escorts who ride beside them. Many times, however, sweethearts ride pillion behind the men, who sit, proud and erect in close-fitting white jackets and stiff, broad-brimmed hats.

Every town or village represented by a lodge of the Brotherhood of the Dew has a separate cavalcade which joins the passing procession. Each group is preceded by a cart with its own image of the Virgin. These lovely moving shrines, covered with white silk and decorated with flowers and wax tapers, are also drawn by oxen. The beasts with their tinkling bells, their flowers and ribbon streamers, are as picturesque as the rest of the procession. Many pilgrims, carrying colorful standards, walk beside the wagons.

The rapidly growing procession of rocking covered carts and people in regional costumes moves slowly through the countryside. At night the pilgrims camp beside their wagons, in fields or ancient olive groves. The older women busy themselves with preparing suppers of spicy sausages, fresh crusty bread and native wine, while youths and girls walk hand in hand beneath the gnarled and twisted trees. As night falls and the stars come out, guitar strings are plucked and the still air is filled with sounds of laughter, dancing feet and songs that originated in Moorish times.

On Whitsunday pilgrims with lighted tapers and embroidered standards file past the church of El Rocío and pay homage to the small statue of La Blanca Paloma. At midnight there are fireworks, then dancing and singing until dawn.

Monday brings the climax of the festival, when the image of the Virgin is carried in solemn procession through Almonte's streets. Pilgrims reverently bear the statue on their shoulders—a highly-coveted privilege, sought by those wishing special indulgence during the coming year. The progress of the image through the streets is accompanied by the chanting of priests and hoarse shouts of *"Viva la Blanca Paloma"* from hundreds of devout pilgrims. At last the Virgin, her annual tour of the town completed, is returned to her place of honor on El Rocío's altar.

Throughout the night and the day following, cavalcades again crowd the country roads. Again one hears music and laughter. But the romería is over for another twelve months. Now a tinge of sadness creeps into the songs that rise hauntingly at night from the dim shadows of the ancient olive trees.

*CORPUS CHRISTI (Corpus Christi), in Sitges, region of Catalonia
The Thursday after Trinity Sunday

Days before Corpus Christi inhabitants of Sitges, the little fishing town some twenty-five miles south of Barcelona, start harvesting the vast fields of flowers for which the locality is famous. Carnations, roses, bougainvilleas, sunflowers, and violets—all are needed to make the fragrant flower carpet which marks the processional path of the Sacred Host.

Early in the morning of the festival day all Sitges starts making the flower carpet. People of each block execute their own design, which has been made in secret, in the hope of winning a coveted money prize. The patterns, which are varied and elaborate, first are chalked on the streets, then filled in with thousands of fresh flower petals. The resulting flower tapestry is sprinkled with water from time to time to keep it fresh. There are colorful geometrical arrangements which glow with the beauty of Oriental rugs; sacred pictures of David and Goliath, or Saul playing his harp; flags and intricate heraldic motifs, or full-rigged ships ploughing across azure seas.

No foot touches the completed carpet until evening when the procession of the Holy Eucharist emerges from the church. People kneel in adoration beside the street as the Host, accompanied by chanting priests and richly robed church dignitaries, is carried beneath a sumptuously embroidered canopy. The spring night is heavy with the fragrance of crushed flower petals, dripping beeswax, and pungent incense—all intermingled with the soft smell of the sea.

The Eucharist passes. Bells ring, rockets flare and musicians, beating out an old melody on little drums, lead forth the *gigantes.* These are fifteen- to twenty-foot-tall effigies of King Ferdinand and Queen Isabella, dressed in robes of crimson velvet, with gold crowns upon their heads. The figures (which are popular at most Spanish fiestas) jig, dance, and whirl upon the shoulders of stalwart men hidden inside.

At last the King and Queen lead off the dance of the evening and return to the Town Hall. Then the people of Sitges take over with the *sardana,* the ancient Catalonian circle dance which has many beautiful figures and variations.

The inhabitants of Orotava, in the Grand Canary Islands, like those of Sitges, also celebrate Corpus Christi by covering their streets with flower petal carpets. Throughout Spain the festival is observed with splendor, especially in such places as Barcelona, Gerona, Cádiz, Toledo, Granada, Seville and Valencia. Nowhere, however, is the scene more beautiful than when the Sitges procession of the Eucharist passes at dusk over the carpet fashioned from millions of sweet scented petals.

La Víspera de San Juan (Saint John's Eve)

June 23

"Saint John's is the feast for youth" declared a stout, middle-aged Mallorcan. "I remember how as a young man I used to think the sun danced with joy on his day; for, after all, was it not Saint John who baptized our Lord?"

Throughout Spain, *la Víspera de San Juan* is dedicated to youth, and also, to fire and water. Fireworks are widely displayed and *hogueras,* or bonfires, lighted in honor of San Juan, saint of the summer solstice. Everywhere, also, old folk sayings and delightful old practices surround the anniversary of the kindly Juan, whose name is borne by many Spanish men. Pastry shops do a brisk business in making name's day cakes, many of which are baked in J-shape and decorated with pink sugar roses and elaborate scrolls. All day on June 23 and 24 people scurry through the streets with large cardboard boxes containing cake offerings for Juans. The Juans, meanwhile, take the day off from work and settle down to enjoyment of their festival with feasting and gatherings of relatives and friends.

According to tradition, if people walk through the dew or bathe in the sea on this day, the skin will be lovely and the body healthy and strong. Young girls resort to charms and omens, for San Juan is said to help one look into the future. One favorite device is to place a bowl of water outside the window and break an egg into the water just at midnight. A clever girl can readily read her destiny in the shape the egg assumes. Another method is to pour melted lead into a bowl at noonday. If the lead looks like a scythe the future mate will be a farmer; a hammer shows he will follow the carpenter's trade, while a fish indicates his living will come from the sea.

San Juan's is considered a good time for sowing, and when the sun shines on his day, nuts will be abundant during the coming year.

On *El Día de San Juan,* Saint John's Day, it is customary at San Pedro Manrique, in the province of Soria, for youths to jump barefoot across the bonfires, carrying others on their backs.

XIQUETS DE VALLS (Human Towers of Valls), in Valls, region of Catalonia

June 24

One of the most spectacular Saint John's Day celebrations takes place in the city of Valls, where a Catalan *comparsa,*[2] or traveling acrobatic company, presents the *Xiquets de Valls,* the "human towers of Valls."

The towers are formed by dancers who stand on each others shoulders, often making figures that rise to eight times a man's height. Four or five men may form the base of one of these astonishing human edifices, while one or more children stand at the top.

---

[2] *Comparsas,* or itinerant companies of acrobats, musicians, clowns and other performers, originated in sixteenth-century Spain. The entertainers, often wearing grotesque make-up and striking costumes, specialize in mysteries and farces, as well as astonishing gymnastic feats. The province of Catalonia is famous for these comparsas.

The *pila de sis,* always a popular figure, stands to the height of six men, upon a base of six. The actors make all their figures in rhythm to the musical accompaniment of the *gralla,* the sharp-noted native oboe.

The climax of the act comes when the children on top of the structure salute the audience. Suddenly the music ceases. For a few seconds the human tower stands immobile. Then, with incredible ease and swiftness, the great pyramid falls apart.

FIESTA DE SAN FERMÍN (Feast of Saint Fermin), in Pamplona, region of Navarre

July 6-20

For centuries Pamplona, city of San Fermín, in the province of Navarre, has celebrated its patron's feast with bullfights. Legend says that the modern dangerous custom of running bulls through the town on July 6 originated in olden times, when the city's standard bearer led bulls through the streets to the arena. He was assisted by men who prodded the animals from behind to keep them on their course. Later, we are told, scatter-brained boys, eager to display their daring, began rushing out before the bulls and plaguing them into charging.

Quite aside from the custom's origin, animals destined for killing in San Fermín bullfights are not taken to the Plaza de Toros in closed stalls, according to usual procedure. Instead, the snorting, angry beasts are turned loose from the corral in early morning and coursed through the town to the ring by a wild, teasing, tantalizing crowd of daredevil youths. Now and then the young men strike the bulls or pull their tails, thus infuriating the animals to the point of attack.

Immense crowds regard the helter skelter, heaving mass of bulls and the reckless, yelling youths from the safety of barricades, balconies, and windows. Later in the day everyone attends the afternoon *corrida* and witnesses the killing of the bulls by some of the world's champion matadors.

Between the afternoon fight and the next day's bull running everyone in Pamplona attends contests by men dancing to the accompaniment of native flute and drum. Many of the participants, dressed in the typical northern Spanish costume, consisting of white shirts and trousers, with red kerchiefs and sashes, carry handsome fraternity banners inscribed with words, *Viva San Fermín.*

Parades of the *gigantes* are another great holiday attraction for the crowd, while firework displays enliven all plazas and squares at midnight. Merrymaking, feasting, and dancing continue until dawn, when the bulls again run through Pamplona's streets.

FIESTA DE SANTIAGO APOSTOL (Feast of Saint James the Apostle), in Santiago de Compostela, region of Galicia

July 25

On July 25 and the days following, the anniversary of Saint James the Apostle—patron of Spain and of the city of Santiago de Compostela—is celebrated widely, but with greatest splendor in the city itself. Religious pilgrimages, secular processions, bullfights and the famous *La Fachada* fireworks display, all combine to make this one of the country's most spectacular events.

Since the eleventh century pilgrims from all parts of the world have traveled the Pilgrim's Way, or the "Way of Santiago," to kneel before the saint's tomb in the crypt of Santiago de Compostela's twelfth-century cathedral.

The twelfth-century Calixtine *Codex* describes the steady flow of pilgrims to the sanctuary in terms that might almost apply to modern times; for today, also, people bring their own musical instruments and speak many different dialects:

Some sing to the sound of the zither, others to that of the lyres, others to that of the kettledrums, others to trumpets, others to fiddles, others to British reels, others, to psalms, others to divers types of musical instruments.

There is no language or dialect which is not heard there. The doors of the basilica do not close, neither in the daytime, nor at night, when the darkness never shrouds the holy place, which glows as in the daytime, with the light of lamps and wax tapers.

202

The fame of Santiago de Compostela rests on the ancient tradition that Santiago (Saint James the Apostle), Son of Zebedee, visited Spain in the first century. For seven years he walked the length and breadth of the land, preaching Christianity to the heathen inhabitants. He then returned to the Holy Land, where he suffered martyrdom. Later, followers returned the Apostle's body to Spain, where they buried it in the Holy Mountain, close to modern Compostela.

For a time the grave was venerated. Then the Roman persecution of Christians began and the holy spot, neglected at first, was finally lost. Many futile attempts were made through the years to find the grave. Finally, the legend goes, in the ninth century, its position was miraculously revealed by a star. A shrine was erected on the spot. About it a town grew up—*Sant-Yago,* or Saint James, of *Compostela,* the "field of the star."

Saint James the Apostle not only became patron of the country but of the Order of the Knights of Santiago. On July 25 a sumptuous procession of the Order follows the Archbishop, dressed in silver vestments, as he enters the Cathedral nave. The chief feature of the impressive religious ceremony is the swinging of the *Botafumeiro,* the six-and-a-half-foot tall censer which is supported by cords from a metal base in the dome. The immense censer (which is kept in the Cathedral Library, except for special occasions) is swung above the transept in a hundred-and-thirty-foot arc, to the almost barbaric accompaniment of wooden *chirimias,* or Arab oboes.

During the Middle Ages it was customary to use a *botafumeiro* during pilgrimages to purify the air in the Cathedral when hundreds of people were gathered for worship.

Fireworks, singing, and Galician bag-piping are all part of the secular observance of Santiago's Feast.

EL MISTERIO DE ELCHE (Mystery Play of Elche), in Elche, region
 of Valencia

August 14 and 15

Each year on the Feast of the Virgin's Assumption, Elche's Church of Santa Maria is the scene of a medieval drama, *El Misterio de*

Elche, the Mystery Play of Elche, which is performed from a raised platform in the sanctuary transept.

The first part of the play is given on August 14; the second on August 15. The theme, of Apocryphal origin, centers about the Death and Assumption of the Virgin. Some think that the *Misterio* (which many consider one of Spain's greatest religious dramatic survivals) dates from 1226; others claim it originated in 1370. The score has been variously attributed to Ginés Peréz de Orihuela, an organist at the Cathedral of Valencia, in 1581, and to the anonymous author of a manuscript dating after 1639.

All parts in the remarkable liturgical drama are taken by male singers, female roles being sung in the high soprano of young boys. The language used is the traditional Limousin dialect.

The first part of the play opens with the appearance of Mary and the Holy Women, to the accompaniment of trumpets, bells, and organ. The conclusion of the first day's mystery comes when the Virgin dies and the *araceli,* or throne carried by five angels, descends from above to secretly bear *Nuestra Señora's* soul to heaven. This act is interpreted by an angel chorus, followed by the thundering of organ, flageolets, bells, and crackers.

In the second part of the *Misterio* the dead Virgin is buried after some moments of struggle between Apostles and Jews. Then the Gate of Heaven opens. The araceli with the five angels descends for a second time and takes away the Virgin. Our Lady is crowned at the heavenly portal as trumpets resound, the organ bursts out triumphantly, bells ring, and crackers explode.

On September 15, 1951 *El Misterio de Elche,* also called *La Festa,* was proclaimed a national festival.

Fiesta de la Vendimia (Vintage Feast), in Jerez de la Frontera, region of Andalusia

Some time in mid-September

The *Fiesta de la Vendimia,* or annual thanksgiving for the grape harvest, is held in Jerez Cathedral, in honor of Saint Gines de la Jara, patron of vineyards.

The fiesta opens with brilliant cavalcades, featuring the magnificent Andalusian-bred horses. The horsemen, wearing wide-brimmed Cordovan hats, close fitting black jackets with neck and wrist ruffles of white, and handsome leather boots, ride through the town beside the open flower-decked carriages of the women. The girls are strikingly beautiful in their deeply flounced polka-dotted frocks and sheer lace mantillas draped over high carved combs.

The morning is devoted to church services and parades of the horsemen and girls. In the afternoon there are bullfights, horse racing, and other sports events; but in the evening people sit and sip the famous golden sherry of Jerez and listen to the haunting improvisations of *flamenco* singers. As darkness deepens and the stars come out, guitars begin to strum and couples dance until dawn of the soft September night.

Virgen del Pilar (Virgin of the Pillar), in Saragossa, region of Aragon

October 11-21

The annual Feast of the Virgin of the Pillar commemorates an ancient legend that the Virgin appeared in Saragossa to Santiago, or Saint James the Apostle, when he was laboring to evangelize Spain. According to tradition, the Virgin revealed herself from the top of a pillar. The Apostle interpreted the vision as meaning he should build a chapel at the place where the column stood.

Nuestra Señora del Pilar, one of Saragossa's two cathedrals, is thought to occupy the site of Santiago's original sanctuary. This great pilgrimage center for people from far and near, has a chapel dedicated to a fourteenth-century statue of the *Virgen del Pilar.*

The Feast is observed by special masses and processions in honor of El Pilar. Fireworks, dancing and parades of the *Gigantes* and *Cabezudos,* Giants and Dwarfs, are important in the secular part of the celebration. The giant and dwarf figures, which are housed at the Lonja, or Exchange, during the year, are brought out for special occasions. The *gigantes*—some of them twenty to thirty feet tall—are walking cardboard and canvas figures, concealing men who dance and perform to the traditional music of the *gralla,* or flute, and *tamboril,* or small drum. The giants often represent Spanish kings and queens, or famous literary and historical figures. The *cabezudos,* on the other hand, are grotesque dwarfs with immense heads. These puppets caricature different professions or personalities.

Contests of the *jota,* Aragon's regional folk dance are a feature of this feast of the Virgen del Pilar. There are several exciting variations of this supposedly Moorish dance, which is performed to the passionate musical accompaniment of guitars, mandolins, and lutes.

NOCHEBUENA (Christmas Eve)

December 24

Almost every Spanish town and village celebrates *Nochebuena,* the Good Night, as Christmas Eve is called, with elaborate markets. Streets and plazas are crowded with stalls where livestock is sold. Country people exhibit squawking turkeys and quacking ducks. Thoroughfares are lined with stalls heaped high with oranges, lemons, melons and bananas, flowers of every color, children's toys, piles of *turrón, mazapán,* chocolate and other favorite Christmas sweets.

Streets are flooded with music and laughter, with the jostling crowd, good-natured men and gaily dressed peasant women; everywhere eager dark-eyed children run from booth to booth admiring, touching, exclaiming over the little *nacimientos,* or nativity scenes, which hold place of honor in every Spanish home. Some of these scenes are made of cardboard, some of plaster or wood. Many figures of Jesus, the Holy Family and the manger animals are so modestly priced as to be well within the means of even the humblest purse. Others are elaborate in workmanship and sell for large amounts.

Toward evening crowds on the streets thin out and housewives, with baskets overflowing with foodstuffs and toys, turn homeward to prepare the evening meal. Crude oil lamps are lighted before household altars as families gather about the table for the *Nochebuena* feast.

As twelve o'clock strikes, church bells peal forth and everybody hurries to Midnight Mass. Clergy in gorgeous vestments perform the *Misa del Gallo,* or "Cock Crow Mass," to the accompaniment of hymns and chants by choir boys and priests.

In some places Nativity plays are a feature of Christmas Eve ceremonies. In most cities, however, the hours between Mass and dawn are devoted to street dancing and singing, for:

> *Esta noche es Nochebuena,*
> *Y no es noche de dormir,*

which means this is Christmas Eve (literally, the Holy Night) and therefore it is not meant for sleep.

NOCHEBUENA EN MONTSERRAT (Christmas Eve Midnight Mass),
at the Monastery of Montserrat, region of Catalonia
December 24

On Christmas Eve pilgrims from many parts of the world come to the Benedictine Monastery of Montserrat for Midnight Mass, which is followed by a spectacular procession in honor of the image of the Black Virgin. Tradition says that the wooden image was carved by Saint Luke and brought to Barcelona A.D. 30 by Saint Peter on a missionary expedition to western Europe.

When the Moors invaded Spain in the eighth century the image was said to have been hidden in a cave among Montserrat's jagged peaks. There the sacred relic remained until the year 880, when the Bishop of Vich tried to have it more suitably placed. Several attempts were made to remove the small statue from the grotto, but all met with failure. Finally it was realized that the Virgin wished to have her chapel built where the image had remained undisturbed for over a hundred and fifty years.

Today the reputedly miraculous image is enshrined on a marble throne above the high altar of the abbey church, built near the site of the original chapel. The face and hands of Virgin and Child are so blackened by the burning of countless votive tapers throughout the centuries that the image has earned the name of *La Moreneta,* "The Little Black Virgin."

At the annual Christmas Eve service *La Moreneta* is carried in a glittering ecclesiastical procession. It is lifted high on a platform surrounded by flowers and candles. The Virgin's image is accompanied by magnificently robed clergy and boys of Montserrat's world-famous *Escolanía,* who sing old Gregorian chants and *villancicos,* or medieval carols. Since the thirteenth century the monastery has maintained a boys' choir with an average strength of forty voices to sing to the honor of the Virgin before the high altar.

The setting of the midnight ceremony is both dramatic and symbolic. Montserrat, "toothed and serrated mountain," rises four thousand feet above the Llobregat river valley. Both abbey church and monastery buildings are dwarfed and insignificant in comparison to the awe-inspiring backdrop of gigantic, barren monoliths. These fantastic peaks gave rise to the medieval legend that identified Montserrat with Monsalvat, the sacred mount to which angels carried the chalice from the Last Supper, entrusting it to the care of the "Knights of the Grail."

PASCUA DE NAVIDAD (Feast of the Birth)

December 25

Everybody attends Christmas Day church services after which the holiday is devoted to feasting and merrymaking. For dinner the traditional turkey is eaten in many homes. In rural areas the priest and the doctor receive gifts of turkeys, cakes, and farm produce at this season, while well-to-do people always make a practice of sending food and luxuries to their less fortunate neighbors.

On Christmas morning it is customary for patrons to receive calls and cards, or little holiday verses, from washerwoman, elevator boy, bootblack, baker's boy, radio service man, garbage collector and many others who have rendered services during the year. It is also usual to receive similar greetings of a "Merry Christmas and Happy New Year" from many who have rendered no services but hope to be patronized in the year to come. All who present holiday greetings, as well as family domestics, expect to be remembered with *aguinaldos,* or gifts of money. It is even customary to give presents (although not of money) to the local policeman. In Madrid and other large cities, it is not uncommon to see a policeman on duty surrounded by parcels of all sizes and shapes, as he directs street traffic on Christmas Day.

Crowds fill streets and plazas, greeting friends and enjoying the holiday processions of the *gigantes,* or giant figures, which dance to the accompaniment of fife and drum. Often the immense figures appear with a pair of Spanish gypsies, who collect coins and gifts from spectators.

NOCHE VIEJA, New Year's Eve

December 31

New Year's Eve in Spain as elsewhere is devoted largely to merrymaking and parties, to sending the old year out with laughter and song, and to welcoming the new with toasts and gaiety.

In the vicinity of Jerez, heart of the country's vineyards and of the sherry industry, people hang bunches of grapes from ceiling beams so the fruit will be ready for eating on New Year's Eve. According to old folk tradition, when the clock strikes twelve at midnight on *Noche Vieja,* everyone swallows twelve grapes, one with each stroke of the hour—as a precaution against witches and evil spirits. This custom of swallowing grapes is widely practiced throughout Spain, and is by no means confined to the Jerez area.

11

FESTIVALS OF SWEDEN

Nyårsdagen (New Year's Day)

January 1

After morning services which everyone attends, the day is spent quietly at home. The New Year's Day dinner almost duplicates the Christmas feast and always includes *smörgåsbord,* a magnificent array of appetizers, which serves to introduce the main meal; *lutfisk,* a specially prepared stockfish, usually served with light cream sauce and boiled potatoes; holiday ham, and *risgrynsgröt,* or rice pudding dessert, with a "lucky" almond inside.

Trettondag Jul (Twelfth Day, Epiphany or Holy Kings' Day)

January 6

Trettondag Jul, a church holiday which commemorates the Magi's finding of Jesus in the manger, was celebrated during the Middle Ages with ecclesiastical folk plays. In towns and cities it is still customary for *Stjärngossar,* or Star Boys, to present pageants which dramatize the march of the Holy Kings from the East. The lads wear white garments and white cone-shaped caps, adorned with pompons and astronomical emblems. The boys always carry large transparent paper star lanterns, mounted on long poles and illumined from within by lighted candles.

In many country villages the youngsters, dressed in all kinds of fantastic costumes to represent various biblical characters, go about from house to house singing old folk songs and hymns that have been handed down from generation to generation for hundreds of years. Judas is one traditional character who often accompanies

210

the Stjärngossar. He wears a huge false nose and carries a money bag jingling with the thirty pieces of silver.

The day following Trettondag Jul is a legal holiday.

TJUGONDAG KNUT (Saint Knut's Day)

January 13

Saint Knut's Day, the twentieth day after Christmas, brings the Swedish Yuletide to an official close. The occasion is celebrated with dances and, finally, by dismantling the Christmas trees lighted for the last time on this night.

In some places young people dance about the Yule table while their elders sing,

> Twentieth day Knut
> Driveth Yule out.

According to some authorities Saint Knut's Day originated in the laws of Canute the Great, written between 1017 and 1036, which decreed that fasting between Christmas and the Epiphany Octave should be eliminated.

*FASTLAGSAFTON (Shrove Tuesday)

The Tuesday preceding Ash Wednesday

The traditional luncheon treat for the last day before Lent are *Fettisdagsbullar,* or hot cross buns. These buns, which are filled with almond paste or a mixture of chopped almonds, confectioners' sugar, and cream, are served in soup plates with hot milk.

*FASTLAGEN (Lenten Period)

The forty day fast (excluding Sundays) that precedes Easter

During Lent, when trees are still bare and the ground often covered with ice and snow it is customary to cut birch branches and decorate them with chicken or rooster feathers that have been dyed

---

* Stars indicate movable feasts that depend upon Easter. See Table of Easter Dates and Movable Festivals Dependent upon Easter, p. 246.

red, yellow, purple, orange, or green. As the weeks advance the twigs gradually produce feathery green shoots. The unique decoration of the green branches with their fluffy colored feathers adds gaiety and charm to many an indoor window ledge.

In early times people switched one another with birch branches as part of spring purification rites. Today the branches serve only as picturesque symbols of awakening spring.

*Skärtorsdag (Holy Thursday)

The Thursday preceding Easter

There are many folk beliefs associated with Holy Thursday, the time when people once thought witches rode broomsticks to a Blåkulla mountain rendezvous, where they stirred steaming cauldrons and uttered evil spells. Farmers tried to protect house and barn from the Easter Witch by marking crosses in tar above the doors and placing pieces of steel across thresholds. Of course, ploughs had to be placed under lock and key, and no brooms could be left about, lest witches ride them away. Bonfires were built on hilltops and rifles shot into the air to further discourage the prowling powers of darkness.

Today old witch superstitions are the joy of Swedish boys and girls who impersonate the old crones by donning horrible masks and dressing up in gaudy colors. The children often decorate their playrooms with clever paper silhouettes of hags on broom handles, black cats, and coffee pots presumably containing witches' brew.

*Långfredagen (Good Friday)

The Friday preceding Easter

The day is observed with special church services and musical programs in commemoration of Christ's Passion and crucifixion. In Stockholm and other metropolitan centers, theatres and many restaurants are closed and newspapers suspend publication.

SWEDEN

In olden times families observed the Good Friday custom of "birching," or switching each other with birch branches, in remembrance, people said, of the lashings Jesus suffered before the Crucifixion.

*PÅSKDAGEN (Easter Sunday)

Throughout the country the egg, symbol of life and resurrection, is featured in all Easter foods and Easter games. Every household has egg dyeing parties. Often eggs are decorated with delightful flower designs, accompanied by amusing rhymes; others are colored plain red, blue, green, or orange. In some places children tuck the brightly dyed eggs among rose bush branches or garden shrubbery. Egg rolling contests are the favorite Easter activity of younger boys and girls.

Since winter sports are at their height in Dalarna, Jämtland, and many of the northern provinces at this season, thousands of people from Stockholm and other southern cities board special excursion trains and spend the Easter holidays in the country.

*ANNANDAG PÅSK (Easter Monday)

The Monday after Easter

This church holiday commemorates Jesus' walk to Emmaus with the two disciples whose "eyes were opened" as He sat with them at meat, blessed bread, and broke it.

Friends and relatives spend the day visiting and sipping tall glasses full of *äggtoddy,* or egg toddy. This beverage—a delicious mixture of egg yolk, sugar, sherry and boiling water—is as traditional to Easter as *glögg* is to the Yuletide festivities. Wherever groups of friends gather at this season äggtoddy is served.

MARIE BEBÅDELSEDAG (Annunciation, Lady Day)

March 25

Ever since the seventh century Annunciation Day has been a church holiday. This is the only day dedicated to the Virgin Mary

213

which the Church accepted when, in 1593, the Lutheran faith became Sweden's state religion.

In olden times people regarded March 25 as important in predicting weather for the coming months. In the province of Värmland, particularly, many quaint customs were observed on Annunciation Eve. People "honored the sun," for example, by eating supper before sunset and retiring without lighting candles. Since cranes arrive in Sweden about this time, parents always told children that the birds would come into the house with lights, to make sure everyone had gone to bed.

Annunciation, or Lady Day, is popularly called Waffle Day, since waffles customarily are served at breakfast, lunch, or dinner. Some think that the word *Våffla* meaning waffle, originated from *Vår Fru,* Our Lady, and that in time the two words became slurred and corrupted, first into *Våffer,* then to *Våffla.*

VALBORGSMASSOAFTON (Walpurgis Night)

April 30

This festival has survived from Viking days, when warriors of old celebrated an annual feast in honor of returning spring. Bonfires lighted on mountain tops were thought to frighten away demons of darkness and gloom. Today people observe the festival throughout the land by lighting fires on hills and mountain peaks in symbol of welcome to the lengthening days.

This is the night when university students at Upsala, Lund, Stockholm, and elsewhere, wear their white velvet caps for the first time, pin sprays of spring flowers in their lapels and march from their fraternity and clubhouses, singing traditional Swedish spring songs. The bonfires that blaze from every height flare dramatically against the dark sky.

In Stockholm thousands of people celebrate the festival at Skansen, the city's outdoor museum and animal park, where the tremendous bonfire of logs and tar barrels which blazes from the top of the Reindeer Mountain, is visible for many miles.

SWEDEN

If spring comes early many townspeople go to the country to search for the first spring flowers and spend the day out-of-doors.

*KRISTI HIMMELSFÄRDSDAG (Ascension Day)
The fortieth day after Easter

Many old peasant superstitions exist in regard to Ascension Day, which is celebrated by special church services. One saying is that the person who fishes from dawn until night on this day will learn the hour when fish bite best and will be a lucky angler during the next twelve months.

Another folk superstition is that "the dragon who guards hidden treasures throughout the night, exposes them to view on Ascension, when he sets them out to air."

*PINGST (Pentecost or Whitsun)
The fiftieth day after Easter

Whitsun, "time of ecstasy," according to the Swedish poet, Esaias Tegnér, is a two-day religious festival which is widely observed with excursions to the country, picnics, and visits to rural estates.

City as well as country people decorate their houses with branches of green in welcome to the returning spring. Even the old brewer horses of Stockholm share in the holiday since their masters decorate their collars and wagon shafts with sprays of green.

Annandag Pingst, Whit Monday, is a general holiday.

MIDSOMMAR (Midsummer)
June 23

Midsommar, the festival of the summer solstice, is celebrated throughout Sweden. Every town and village erects a *majstång,* or maypole, on the village green. The pole, usually made from the peeled trunk of a tall spruce, is characterized by a transverse bar placed near the top. Wreaths of greens and field flowers are suspended from either arm of the bar. The pole itself, wound round with evergreen garlands, interspersed with sprays of tender young birch, is crowned by the Swedish flag.

Raising the majstång is a traditional rite in which every man, woman, and child likes to have a hand. Once the pole is in position the village fiddlers strike up merry dance tunes which have been handed down for generations in different localities. Old and young dance about the maypole the whole night through as the witching music floats through the sweet summer air. Since pagan times Midsommar has been the night of rejoicing and merrymaking over the return of spring. Nobody ever thinks of going to bed. In some places dancing is held in village barns rather than out of doors.

In Rättvik, on Lake Siljan, in Dalarna, the dancers hold their festivities on the pier of the bridge. Often somebody tumbles into the water when merrymaking and excitement reach a boisterous climax. Leksand, another village in the same province, is especially famed for its Midsummer celebration which is one of the most traditional in the country. Throughout Dalarna, indeed, the festival is particularly colorful not only because of strict adherence to the old customs, but because of the richness and variety of the regional costumes.

Since Midsummer Night is kind to young lovers, village girls used to practice all sorts of romantic charms which were thought to evoke visions of their future mates. One favorite rite was to pick nine different kinds of flowers which, when hidden under the pillow would surely cause a clear image of the beloved one's face.

MÅRTEN GÅS (Martin's Goose Day)

November 11

From Skåne, the province famous for geese, comes the old-time custom of feasting on goose in the fall of the year. The typical foods which are eaten at the great family *Mårten Gås* parties are roast goose, luscious with stuffings of apples and prunes, sauerkraut and green cabbage. Blood soup is also highly esteemed. This concoction is made from the wings and neck, as well as the blood, heart, and liver of the goose. Additional ingredients are dried apples and prunes, with flavorings of ginger, pepper, vinegar, sugar, and wine.

In some northern provinces *surströmming*, a fermented delicacy made from the small Baltic herring, is a special gastronomic delight of the season.

LUCIADAGEN (Saint Lucy's Day)

December 13

The Swedish Yule begins on December 13 with *Luciadagen,* Saint Lucy's Day. Although essentially a home festival, the day is widely observed in factories, offices, hospitals and other organizations throughout the land. Saint Lucy, represented by a young girl wearing white dress, crimson sash and lingon-leaf crown with white lighted candles, visits each household at dawn with a tray of coffee and cakes. This charming custom originated in the legend of Santa Lucia, a fourth-century maiden who was condemned to death during the reign of Diocletian.

Lucia as already seen, was born in Syracuse, Sicily.[1] Tradition says she had her eyes plucked out because their beauty attracted a heathen nobleman. She was denounced as a Christian and martyred for her faith. The story of Lucia's death was carried to Sweden. Since the saint's day comes at the season of deepest winter darkness, the legend of the young martyr whose name means "light" took deep root in popular imagination in the north. Observance of Lucia's festival in Sweden, as elsewhere, has come down through hundreds of years.

In some parts of the country old people used to say that the Lucia Bride, clothed in white and crowned with light, might be seen at dawn moving across the ice-bound lakes, with food and drink for the parish poor. Perhaps this tradition has given rise to the

[1] See Santa Lucia, p. 101.

modern custom of the Lucia Bride. In the homes Lucia usually is represented by the oldest daughter in the family. In towns and villages some young girl is elected to re-enact the role by taking a tray of coffee and cakes to each household. In Stockholm, Lucia is chosen by popular vote, in much the same way that beauty queens are selected in the United States. Of course, in large communities there are many Lucia Brides. In urban centers morning trams and buses are crowded with members of the Lucia group, still in costume, who have been making rounds since dawn and are going to their offices to repeat the ceremony.

In smaller places Lucia sometimes makes her rounds alone. Often, however, she is accompanied by girls and boys of the parish. The girls wear long white gowns and carry white candles. The boys, known as *Stjärngossar,* or Star Boys, also wear white, and have tall peaked silver caps, decorated with star and moon cutouts. One boy holds an illumined paper star lantern which is fastened to a pole and revolves like a pinwheel. Sometimes Lucia is attended by baker boys who carry *Lussekatter,*[2] or "Lucia cats," delicious cardamon-flavored buns made in X-shapes, with curled up ends and raisin eyes. These buns, together with crisp *Pepparkakor,* or ginger cookies, and steaming hot coffee are the usual refreshments.

This is Mrs. Hannah Johnson's family recipe for:

Lussekatter (Lucia Buns)

1 cup milk, scalded
1/3 cup butter
2/3 cup sugar
Dash of salt
1 yeast cake, crumbled
1 egg, beaten
4 cups sifted flour
1 cardamon seed, crushed
Raisins

Add milk to butter, sugar, and salt and stir until dissolved. Cool to lukewarm and add the yeast. Stir well, then add egg. Gradually stir in

[2] From the author's article, "Start Your Christmas Entertaining with a Lucia Fest." *American Home,* 39:92+. December 1947. Reprinted by permission.

flour and the crushed cardamon and beat thoroughly. Place dough in a greased bowl, cover and let rise in a warm place until double in bulk. Knead on a floured board for a few minutes. Roll a small portion at a time and cut into strips about 5 inches long and 1/2 inch wide. Place two strips together to form the letter X on a greased baking sheet. Brush with beaten egg. Cover and let rise for 1 hour.

Bake in moderately hot oven (400°F) for about 12 minutes.

Yield: Twenty-four to thirty buns.

Lucia and her little band, like Christmas carolers of other countries, sing old Yuletide songs as they visit the various homes. Contrary to usual custom, however, the Swedish boys and girls offer, rather than expect hospitality.

As they enter the house the young people sing these words [3] to the tune of *"Santa Lucia:"*

> Night goes with silent steps
> Round house and cottage.
> O'er earth that sun forgot
> Dark shadows linger.
> Then on our threshold stands
> White clad, in candlelight
> Santa Lucia, Santa Lucia.

Many interesting folk practices exist in connection with Luciadagen. The year's threshing, spinning, and weaving must be put in order for the Christmas holidays. Before this day young people finish making their Christmas presents; the housewife completes her weeks of holiday baking and finishes making the tallow dips for table and Christmas tree decorations. Floors are scrubbed, pewter, brass and copper scoured and polished; and most important of all, *lutfisken,* the traditional holiday fish, is buried in beech ashes so it will be sweet and tender for the Christmas feast.

JULAFTON (Christmas Eve)

December 24

The period between *Luciadagen* and *Julafton* is devoted largely to baking Christmas cakes, cookies, and breads and making the

---

[3] English words by Holger Lundbergh.

unique decorations which beautify every Swedish home at the holiday season. There are, for example, intricate paper cut-outs to put
on the walls; festoons, stars, wooden toys, and straw animals—the
Julbockar, or Yule goats, and the *Julgrisar,* or Yule pigs—to hang
on the Christmas tree. The straw animals, which are found throughout Sweden, are intimately related to ancient Norse mythology; for
the modern figures originated in legends of the sacred animals of
the gods—the goat of Thor, the thunder god, and the pig of Frey,
god of the sun.

Before Christmas Eve, all the presents are wrapped and sealed
with red sealing wax. Each offering is accompanied by an appropriate jingle which generally tells something about the article or
its use. These verses are read aloud when the gifts are distributed,
adding much merriment to the occasion.

A few days before Christmas the men of the family go to the
woods with a sledge on which to bring back a fine straight hemlock
or spruce tree and branches of juniper and pine. Soon the house
assumes a festive air. The tree, set up behind closed doors, is
decorated with homemade candles, with shining red apples, nuts,
gingerbread figures, the straw goats and pigs and all the other
delightful trifles various members of the family have made. The
national flag often holds place of honor on top of the tree, while
smaller flags decorate the branches.

On Christmas Eve the family gathers at six o'clock around the
kitchen stove for the time-honored ceremonial of *Dopp i grytan,* or
"Dipping in the Kettle." The room is festive with paper garlands
and candles in three branched candlesticks. The freshly-scrubbed
pine floor is strewn either with straw—in memory of the manger
birth—or with fragrant juniper twigs. On the stove there is a big
kettle of appetizing broth containing sausages, ham, pork, and other
hearty meats.

Each person, including members of the family, guests, and
household servants, sticks a slice of *vörtbröd,* that is wort bread,
on a fork, dips it into the pot and eats it with a slice of pork or a bit

of sausage. Traditionally this bread is eaten "for luck" before the Christmas feast begins.

Then toasts are drunk—sometimes in *glögg,* the concoction of wine, rum and spices, which is lighted and poured over lumps of sugar, sometimes in another type of beverage. After laughter and jests and the exchange of wishes for a *God Jul,* the company sits down in the dining room to the meal which begins with an elaborate array of *smörgåsbord,* or appetizers, followed by *lutfisk,* served with boiled potatoes or with green peas and drawn butter. The preparation of this delicacy, which requires fully three weeks of soaking, cleaning, and scrubbing, is the most important item on the holiday menu. Lingon berries stewed in sugar, the Christmas ham, roast goose with prune stuffing and all kinds of preserves are among the many rich foods that may be served on this occasion.

Dessert consists of *risgrynsgröt,* or the rich rice pudding which also is eaten on New Year's Day. The *gröt* is cooked with milk and sugar and is decorated on top with intricate designs in cinnamon. Inside a single almond is hidden. Whoever gets the almond will be first to wed during the coming year. According to custom each guest should make an original jingle before taking his portion of *gröt.*

At last the long feast ends. The moment comes when doors are thrown open and the tree is revealed in all its glory. The father of the family sits beside the twinkling branches and reads the story of the Manger Birth. Then follow old carols in which everyone joins.

Suddenly there is a knock at the door. The children jump up excitedly to admit *Jultomten,* the Swedish Santa Claus, who arrives by sleigh, drawn not by reindeer but by Julbockar, the goats of the ancient thunder god. Jultomten (usually impersonated by an uncle, brother or other male member of the family) wears a long white beard, red tunic and trousers and carries over his shoulder a sack bulging with sweets and presents for "good" boys and girls.

Originally Jultomten, the little white-bearded, red-capped gnome who is so old nobody remembers when he first appeared, belonged to rural Sweden; but of late years he has found his way to the cities where he now seems equally at home. Traditionally Jultomten was guardian of the farm, where he dwelt in the hayloft and kept a sharp eye to all that went on. If cows were to give milk, horses to foal and crops to prosper, Jultomten had to be treated with respect—especially at Christmas time, when he always received a big bowl of risgrynsgröt as his holiday treat.

After the gifts Jultomten brings have been distributed and enjoyed, the Christmas Eve ceremonies end with the gay dance song about the tree:

> Now 'tis Yuletide again, and Yuletide will last, methinks,
> 'Till Easter; no, this cannot be, as 'twixt the two comes Lent!

JULDAGEN (Christmas)

December 25

Regardless of how late the family lingers about the tree on Christmas Eve, everyone—in cities as well as rural districts—is up in time to attend *Julotta,* the six-o'clock church service.

In country places candles twinkle in the windows of almost every farmhouse. The winter stars hang low and bright in the sky. Chimes peel joyously through the crisp air. Sleighs drawn by prancing horses carry loads of worshipers across the frosted earth. Each sleigh is lighted by a pine torch which casts eerie shadows against the blackness of the sky. When people arrive at the church they throw their torches into a great pile, which flares up dramatically in the blackness.

The church is lighted with hundreds of candles. Hundreds of voices sing well-loved Lutheran Nativity hymns to stirring organ accompaniment.

"God Jul," says one Swede to another on Christmas Day. *"God Jul,"* is the hearty response. "May God bless your Christmas and may it last until Easter."

Christmas, which is a church holiday, is spent rather quietly with family and friends.

SWEDEN

ANNANDAGEN (The Day after Christmas)

December 26

The day after Christmas is also a church holiday. From *Annandagen* until *Tjugondag Knut,* on January 13, parties, dances, and all kinds of festivities are held from house to house in the neighborhood. Old and young consume quantities of rich holiday foods and indulge in general merrymaking.

12

FESTIVALS OF SWITZERLAND

Switzerland is a country of fête days and festivals. Yet, with the exception of August 1, Anniversary of the Founding of the Swiss Confederation, the country's one nationally celebrated day, other holidays are almost entirely local in character. Just as each canton has its own beautiful traditional costumes which have been passed down from father to son and from mother to daughter for many generations, so each canton possesses its own unique festivals.

The Confederation of Switzerland consists of twenty-two cantons, three of which—Appenzell, Basel and Unterwalden—are subdivided into half-cantons. Since each canton is like a small sovereign state, it is not surprising that two cantons seldom celebrate the same holiday in the same way, or even on the same date.

Religion plays an added part in creating festival differences. An estimated fifty-seven per cent of the population is Protestant, forty-one per cent Catholic and two per cent of other faiths. Festival observances naturally vary considerably according to religious beliefs. The geographical location of the cantons is also important, since festivals have a distinct German, Austrian, Italian, or French flavor, according to the nationality of the closest neighboring country.

Switzerland has four national languages—German, French, Italian and Romansch [1]—not to mention countless dialects. Dialects, like festival customs, vary widely from valley to valley and canton to canton. Because of these language differences the names of the festivals that are described are given in the language or dialect of the area in which they are celebrated.

---

[1] Romansch, which was recognized as a national language in 1937, has two dialects—Surselva and Ladin—and sounds like a mixture of French, Italian, and Latin. Romansch is a *national*, but not an *official* language.

SWITZERLAND

NEUJAHRSTAG (New Year's Day)

January 1

Amateur dramatic performances, visiting among friends, and general merrymaking characterize the first day of the New Year, which generally is observed as a quiet holiday.

In some places roast goose with chestnut stuffing is traditional to the day. Goose necks, filled with ground giblets, seasonings and other ingredients, are a favorite delicacy when thinly sliced and served with between-meal snacks. Housewives vie with one another in making special New Year's bread rich with milk, butter, eggs, and raisins, while *birewegge,* or pear pie (which looks like a shiny loaf of bread and has a rich filling of pears and raisins) is a popular seasonal treat.

On New Year's morning children love to hide and pounce out at startled elders with the first "Happy New Year" greeting. The boys and girls then start village rounds to homes of relatives and friends. After singing "Good day and good cheer" and inviting largess, the children are asked inside and treated.

In peasant lore January first is associated with all sorts of omens and predictions. A red sky, for example, signifies storms, fire, and war in the coming year. In some places meeting a woman the first thing on New Year's Day is thought to bring bad luck, while encountering a man or a child is looked upon as a good sign.

BERCHTOLD'S TAG (Berchtold's Day)

January 2

In many areas the second day of January is devoted to gay neighborhood parties in which nuts play an important part. In early autumn children begin hoarding supplies of nuts for Berchtold's Day, when they have "nut feasts." Nut eating and nut games, followed by singing and folk dancing are features of these Berchtold Day gatherings. One favorite stunt of the boys and girls is to make "hocks." Five nuts make a hock—surprisingly difficult to construct—four nuts placed close together, with a fifth placed on top.

225

FESTIVALS OF WESTERN EUROPE

Festa di Sant' Antonio (Feast of Saint Anthony), canton of Ticino

January 17

In Bellinzona, Locarno, and other towns and villages throughout the canton of Ticino, the ceremony of Blessing the Animals is an important rite. Owners curry their horses, mules, and donkeys until their coats shine, then adorn the beasts with bells and ribbons and take them in procession to church. Often the family dogs attend the parade, barking and jumping joyously as the larger animals are driven in state toward the sanctuary doors.

The strange communicants wait at the doors until after Mass. Then the priest comes outside and blesses the creatures in the name of Saint Anthony, patron of four-footed beasts.

Chalanda Marz (First of March), in Engadine, canton of Grisons

March 1

On the first of March boys of the Engadine "ring out the winter" and announce spring's arrival with a picturesque old custom. The youths put on herdsmen's costumes with wide leather belts from which they suspend as many large cow bells as they can collect. Smaller bells hang from their necks or are strapped across their chests. Other lads, who represent the cows, put bells around their necks and follow the "herdsmen." The children go about from house to house, clanging their bells with enough uproar to make winter speedily retreat, and serenade housewives with an old spring song:

> The first of March, the first of April,
> Let the cows out of the stable.
> Grow grass, grow!
> Go away, snow, go!

Housewives give the boys such gifts as freshly baked cakes, apples, small rolls and eggs—sometimes a few coppers. The food is pooled for a jolly evening feast, followed by games and dancing. The money goes to the village schoolmaster who uses it, later, for a class picnic or excursion.

SWITZERLAND

Sᴇᴄʜsᴇʟäᴜᴛᴇɴ (Six Ringing Festival), in Zurich, canton of Zurich
Some time in April

For over six hundred years the city of Zurich has symbolically driven out Winter and welcomed Spring with the traditional *Sechseläuten,* Six Ringing Festival, which is observed on a Sunday and Monday early in April.

The festival originated in the Middle Ages when the trade guilds governed the city. On the Monday following the spring equinox (March 21) it was customary for the cathedral bells to start ringing at six, instead of seven o'clock—the usual time—to announce the end of the guild member's working day. This first day of change from winter to summer schedule was celebrated as a guild holiday. For centuries the bells rang as a signal to cease work. Gradually the general public sought to join in festivities. Finally the Six Ringing, which started as a purely guild holiday, became an affair in which all of Zurich's citizens shared.

The festival opens on Sunday with a school children's parade and pageant, followed on Monday by a splendid procession of the various guilds, some twenty-four of which still exist. The city presents a gala appearance with bunting, cantonal flags and pennants fluttering from houses and public buildings. Immense crowds from surrounding areas gather to see the procession. School children in regional costume precede a float on which is enthroned a pretty girl personifying Spring, surrounded by flowers, garlands, and numerous attendants.

Then comes *Böögg,* traditional embodiment of Old Man Winter, whom the crowd boos and derides as he goes past on a moving platform. Böögg is a huge snow man, fashioned over a wooden frame and stuffed with firecrackers and explosives of all kinds. Böögg's attendants, in contrast to Spring's fair young companions, are a crowd of jeering, dancing clowns who stick out their tongues and add their own quips and insults to those of the spectators. Böögg is carried to the Bellevue Platz overlooking the Lake of Zurich. Lifted high on a pole above an immense unlighted bonfire, the personification of Winter awaits his fate at six o'clock on the following day.

227

On Monday tradespeople and craftsmen from country districts come into Zurich to participate in the guild procession. Members of the barbers', bakers', hat makers', butchers', weavers', and other guilds are dressed in historic costume and carry the traditional symbols and standards of their various trades and professions. The barbers, for example, may carry a pair of scissors as tall as a house, the bakers toss rolls to the crowd, or the hat makers sport about a gigantic hat. All the capering and marching is accompanied by numerous bands, including the fifers and drummers for which the area is famous.

The colorful procession proceeds before cheering crowds, marches along the banks of the Limmat and comes to Bellevue Platz, where Böögg is impaled above his pyre. Promptly at six o'clock the bells start ringing. Fife and drum bands play loudly the stirring *Zürcher Sechseläuten Marsch*. The people shout with joy. The bonfire under Böögg is lighted. Suddenly the flames spring upward and the explosive-filled figure of the snow man ignites. White-robed horsemen gallop about the fire as firecrackers explode and parts of Böögg fly in all directions, amid a deafening roar of noise and confusion. Round and round the horsemen ride, forming a magic circle about Winter, to prevent his escape from the flames.

The symbolic rite which has come down through the centuries from pagan times is one of Switzerland's many ceremonies to dramatize Winter's expulsion and universal joy in returning Spring.

KUHKÄMPFE (Cow Fights), canton of Valais

Some time in April

Organized cow battles are unique to the canton of Valais. Each spring during April the Queen Cow of the village herds is determined by pitting the cows against each other in battle. The cow that holds her own against all opponents and comes through the encounter victorious, is proclaimed Queen Cow of the year.

Crowned with a flower garland between her horns and with the largest bell hanging from her artistically designed collar, the Queen

Cow, acknowledged leader of the herd, walks at the head of the procession of animals that migrates annually to summer pasture in the mountains.

ALP AUFZUG (Procession to the Alps)

Some time in April or May

Alp Aufzug, the procession of animals driven to upland pastures in early spring, is a picturesque sight and a festive occasion in every valley hamlet. Every year the village men and older boys set out in early spring for crude mountain huts, situated at an altitude of six to eight thousand feet, to look after the cows and goats and make butter and cheese for autumn marketing. The women and children remain at home, tending crops and gardens and bringing in the hay.

On the morning of the Alp Aufzug the whole village tingles with suppressed excitement. The air is filled with the barking of dogs and the melodious ringing of cowbells. Herdsmen dressed in vivid peasant costume, with flowers in their hats and, sometimes, a brass ring in one ear,[2] assemble the long procession of animals for the slow march to the mountains. The sleek herds, each preceded by their flower-crowned Queen, wear garlands and gay streamers. Enormous bells swing from the collars of the choicest cows, while smaller, but no less musical bells, adorn the necks of the more humble creatures.

Behind the cows, dogs and youths round up goats and sheep. Once in the mountains, these rugged smaller animals seek higher more stony pastures than the cows. At milking time the boys drive the goats down to the dairy hut and later join the older men in a simple supper of black bread, cheese, milk, and mountain fruits.

The rear of the procession is brought up by flower-decked wagons, or sometimes by mules, laden with cheese molds, cauldrons, pans, and other necessary dairy equipment, as well as enough blankets and household articles to last through the summer.

[2] The brass earring worn in some areas symbolizes the milk bowl.

FESTIVALS OF WESTERN EUROPE

As the colorful procession of herdsmen and animals slowly starts from the village, good-byes are called, hands waved, a few tears shed; for girls will miss their sweethearts, women their men, and life in the mountain pastures is lonely and monotonous.

*FASTNACHT (Carnival)
Some time before Lent—usually the Sunday, Monday and Tuesday preceding Ash Wednesday

One of Switzerland's most magnificent spectacles is the Basel Carnival which opens in the market square at four o'clock in the morning with fife and drum performances by the bands of various companies. Just as Basel's clocks strike four lights go out all over the city. From every direction fifers, drummers and masked marchers in fantastic costume, pour into the square. In the procession that follows, four men in each group carry immense transparencies which, like many of Valencia's *fallas*,[3] mercilessly satirize local politics and politicians. Other marchers carry colorful lanterns attached to the ends of long poles. The transparencies, like the fallas, are created in secret by professional artists. Later awards are given for the most unique or original contributions.

At five o'clock the city lights are turned on, the fifing and drumming ceases and spectators hurry to inns and taverns to warm themselves with bowlfuls of the thick brown flour soup which is Basel's Carnival specialty.

Carnival is celebrated extensively throughout the country, with each town and village following its own local traditions. At Flums, near the Wallensee, for example, celebrants in wooden masks (many of which are handed down from father to son for generations) parade through the streets. It is thought that these horrible and terrifying masks, some of which symbolize abstract ideas such as war, death or disease, originally were made to dissipate the very forces they so hideously represent.

---

* Stars indicate movable feasts that depend upon Easter. See Table of Easter Dates and Movable Festivals Dependent upon Easter, p. 246.
[3] See *Fallas de San Jose,* p. 190.

SWITZERLAND

At Einsiedeln, in Schwyz, "Carnival Runners," wearing grotesque false faces and with enormous bells attached to their backs, run through the streets continuously from Sunday to Ash Wednesday morning. The bells, which are so heavy the men have to bend their backs to support the weight, clang incessantly as the Runners course through the town. This ceremony, like the masks of Flums, also survives from ancient times when primitive people "drove out Winter" with deafening noise and fearsome faces and "rang in" their welcome to the Spring.

*OSTERN (Easter)

After attending morning church service, which features magnificent music, Easter Sunday generally is spent in merrymaking and festivity.

Games and gaily-decorated Easter eggs are important to the young people, especially those living in towns and smaller villages. Parents often hide colored eggs under the trees and in the garden, and then call the children to "see what the Easter Hare has left for them." The boys and girls receive additional presents of little chocolate and marzipan rabbits, sugar eggs, and chocolate eggs with colored sugar flutings.

Boys love to match eggs with friends since the one who smashes the most eggs reaps the largest reward. In some places there is a lively egg competition in which one group throws a given number of eggs into a flat basket while another covers a certain distance on foot or horseback.

SANKT GEORG'S TAG (Saint George's Day), in Turtmann, canton of Valais

April 23

The blessing of Saint George, fourth-century patron saint of domestic animals, is solemnly invoked at Turtmann's parish church on the anniversary of the saint's martyrdom.

Farmers interrupt their work in the fields to bring their donkeys, mules, and horses to the sanctuary. There the village priest sprinkles them with holy water and gives the beasts his benediction as protection against accident and disease throughout the coming year.

MAITAG VORABEND (May Day Eve)

April 30

The custom of planting the *Maitannli,* the May pine tree, on May Day Eve, is celebrated widely in villages of the cantons of Vaud, Solothurn, Zurich and Ticino. In the little town of Kaiserstuhl, in Aargau, a fairly typical ceremony takes place. The village's bachelors go out at night and cut down small pine trees, which they decorate with flowers and ribbons and plant before the homes of girls they admire. Usually the pine tree is set before the sweetheart's bedchamber window. Sometimes it is placed before the gate, occasionally on the roof. Frequently a girl is so popular that she wakens on May Day morning to find she is the recipient of not one, but several trees.

The following Sunday evening the girls entertain the boys who have left the May trees, and not infrequently, this is the time when many young people get engaged. The little *Maitannli* remain where they have been planted until the end of the month when they are gathered up and burned outside Kaiserstuhl's ancient town walls.

Only girls of good character are recipients of the *Maitannli.* Girls who do not command respect from the village boys are likely to find a grotesque straw puppet, rather than pretty pine tree, on May Day morning.

At Sargans and surrounding communities in Eastern Switzerland, church bells ring in the month of May. In local tradition the bells may be rung only by young men of blameless reputation, who are native to the region. As the bells ring prayers should be offered for crops; for, according to superstition, good spirits spin from the music of the bells a web over vineyards, meadows, and pastures, thus ensuring blessings and bountiful harvests.

SWITZERLAND

*PFINGSTEN (Feast of Pentecost), in Lucerne, canton of Lucerne
The fiftieth day after Easter

The deeply moving Pentecostal candlelight procession which starts from Lucerne's Hofkirche, or Cathedral, and winds up a narrow road to the Wesemlin, an old Capucin monastery in the hills, is typical of many religious ceremonies of the season.

It was nearly eight o'clock as I mounted the steep flight of stairs leading to the Cathedral court. It had rained all day but suddenly snow-capped Pilatus emerged from its curtain of mist. Bright sunshine flooded the court and bathed the Cathedral's slender twin spires in golden radiance. There were hundreds of worshipers waiting in the court, and everyone held lighted candles, inserted into small paper plates to catch the dripping wax.

By half past eight it was growing dark. The crowd stirred expectantly as the Cathedral doors opened and priests and choir came down the steps with a golden image of the Virgin. A scarlet-robed prelate followed, then acolytes with tall white tapers in golden candlesticks.

The lay procession formed quickly behind the clergy. First were the Boy Scouts with a huge rectangular lantern painted with sacred scenes. Then other youth groups followed, all wearing fresh uniforms and carrying their organization standards.

Finally the men formed in line. The lighted candles illumined the bronzed, careworn faces and toil-stained hands of country men from surrounding villages. Last of all, came the women. I walked beside a mother with two young sons. Behind me was a tall, gaunt woman in close-fitting cap and shabby peasant clothes. The procession began to move, accompanied by the deep melodious chanting of the priests and the devout responses of the worshipers.

Night deepened as the procession walked up the narrow stony Kapuziner Weg, past numerous Stations of the Cross, toward the monastery on the hill. Wayside altars, lighted with candles and decorated with fragrant flowers, were set up at intervals all along the line of march. Doorways were outlined with lights and festooned with flowers. The wind blew slightly now and then causing the candles to flicker.

After what seemed like a long climb in the darkness, the procession reached the Wesemlin. The arched door of the church was outlined by stubby lighted candles; the interior was crowded with worshipers and heavy with the scent of fading flowers.

Later, when the crowd had gone, I stood looking down at the lighted city below.

*FRONLEICHNAMSFEST (Corpus Christi Feast)
The Thursday following Trinity Sunday

In many parts of Switzerland *Fronleichnamsfest,* or Corpus Christi, is celebrated with distinctive ceremonies that have come down from the Middle Ages. Customs vary widely from town to town and canton to canton, but this festival which commemorates the institution of the Sacrament is almost universally observed with sumptuous processions of clergy in gorgeous vestments, people in picturesque regional costume and soldiers in uniforms of former days.

In Blatten and Kippel, in the Lötschen Valley, for example, the "Lord's Grenadiers," an honor guard in .traditional uniform, stands watch over the Monstrance on *Segensonntag,* or Benediction Sunday.[4] In Fribourg, where the festival assumes magnificent proportions, people decorate the façades of their houses with precious Gobelins as the Bishop of Fribourg, walking beneath a richly embroidered canopy, carries the Holy Sacrament through the streets. In Fribourg, also, as in Blatten and Kippel, the honor escort wears traditional uniform.

In the canton of Appenzell processions featuring the old Swiss uniforms are seen, together with women in native costume, somberly garbed Capuchin monks and fresh young girls with white dresses and flower-wreathed heads.

[4] The Sunday following Corpus Christi.

SWITZERLAND

In many places church doors are thrown open on Corpus Christi and both altar and aisles are decorated with garlands and branches of green. Often outdoor village altars, beautiful with flowers and candles are erected in secluded spots. The priest, stepping on carpets of fragrant flowers, bears the Sacrament to the kneeling worshipers on whom he bestows his benediction.

HOCHSOMMER FEST (Midsummer Festival)

June 24

On this day valley people make excursions to the Alpine pastures to visit their friends and relations who have been with the goats and cows since the opening of the season. Families load their mules with baskets containing such satisfying picnic foods as hams, eggs, and home baked bread and ascend the steep mountain paths to the herdsmens' huts. The special bread of the season has a sweet anise flavored dough base, made with butter, and baked in fancy shapes.

After a hearty outdoor meal at which the good valley foods are supplemented with pastoral fare such as cheese, butter, milk, cream and wild berries, the young people dance, play games, and gather mountain flowers.

At dusk everyone brings out flutes, accordions, and alphorns. Soon the mountains echo and reecho with the old folk melodies indigenous to the Alpine regions.

"Praise ye the Lord," sings the herdsman, offering a prayer something like this for the animals entrusted to his keeping:

> Watch over our herds, O God.
> Make our mountain pastures green;
> Keep our cows from harm
> Of storm, or snow, or sliding rock.
>
> Praise ye the Lord!
> Praise ye the Lord!

SANKT PLACIDUSFEST (Saint Placidus Festival), in Disentis, canton of Grisons

July 11

An impressive religious procession is held on July 11 at Disentis in honor of Saint Placidus, who reputedly was murdered near the great Benedictine Abbey he helped to found. Tradition says that Saint Sigisbert and Saint Placidus, patrons of Disentis, established the Abbey in 614. Placidus, a wealthy landowner, gave the ground, joined the religious order as a monk, and later was beheaded for defending the Abbey's ecclesiastical rights.

Each year the relics of the two saints are carried in solemn procession from the Abbey to the parish church and back through the village to the Abbey. During the ceremonies parishioners in colorful folk costume chant the old, and very long, Song of Saint Placidus.

LES PRÉMICES DES ALPES ("First Fruits of the Alps" Sunday), in Vissoie (Val d'Anniviers) canton of Valais

Fourth Sunday in August

On the fourth Sunday in August dairymen of Vissoie, in the beautiful Val d'Anniviers, hold an impressive service at which they present the parish priest with cheeses known as *les prémices des Alpes,* the "first fruits of the Alps." These gifts are made in appreciation of faithful spiritual service the priest has rendered to the members of his flock who annually migrate with their herds to high alpine pastures.

In early spring the men leave the valley with their animals and dairy equipment and slowly ascend the steep passes to summer huts perched in the mountains where the grass is green and lush. Throughout the season the priest regularly visits the men to read Mass and administer Holy Sacraments. Traditionally, the dairymen dedicate to the priest all the milk their herds yield on the third day after their arrival in the mountains. This milk they make into cheeses, which are large or small according to the number of cattle in the herd.

At the end of summer, the Justice of the Peace of Val d'Anniviers, his assistant and recorder, count, inspect, and weigh the cheeses brought back to Vissoie with the returning herds. The cheeses then are displayed so all can admire them. After High Mass, the fifteen dairymen of the district march in procession to the altar, each man carrying his own cheese. The dairy master of the Alp Zatelet Praz comes first, since his cheese, which weighs eighty pounds, is the largest. The other masters of the Alpine pastures follow in order, according to rank. The procession ends with the Alp Ponchette pasture's offering, which weighs approximately eight pounds.

The dairymen stand in a line before the altar, with Vissoie's red-and-black-robed magistrates on either side. After the ceremony of giving the "first fruits of the Alps" to the priest, the dairymen once more form in procession and march to the parsonage. There the village celebration ends with feasting, toasts, and speeches beneath the chestnut tree in the priest's pleasant courtyard.

SCHÄFER SONNTAG (Shepherd Sunday), in Belalp, canton of Valais
The second Sunday in September

The return of the sheep from summer pasture in the mountains is a time of great rejoicing in Belalp, as in all other sheep raising areas.

As the sun rises on the Alpine plateau of Belalp sheep owners and peasants gather at open air Mass to pray for the safe return of flocks. The shepherds, meanwhile, assemble their animals on the mountain and start them down on their perilous journey toward the plateau. The villagers anxiously watch for the appearance of the beasts. As they descend the mountain everyone lends a hand in penning the sheep in a great overnight enclosure. A hearty "Sheep Dinner" brings the day to a fitting close as shepherds are reunited with families and young girls with their sweethearts.

The day following, owners sort their sheep, wash them in the lake and prepare for the task of shearing.

Zybelemärit (Onion Market), in Berne, canton of Berne

Some time in November

Each year the historic *Zybelemärit,* or Onion Market, is held in Berne where all housewives of the area stock their larders with winter supplies of onions. The picturesque market is filled with countless stalls which are hung with strings of onions, both large and small. Bins of onions and baskets of onions of all varieties, sizes and shapes furnish lively interest to prospective purchasers.

The Onion Market is a festive as well as a commercial event. Crowds of young people surge through the arcades laughing and pelting each other with bright-colored confetti. Later many groups meet to sing and dance far into the night.

Samichlaus Abend (Santa Claus Night)

December 6

Swiss Christmas festivities officially begin on December 6, *Samichlaus Abend,* Santa Claus Night. *Samichlaus,* a sack of nuts, apples and cookies slung over his shoulder, often parades through the streets and rewards good children with his coveted gifts, bad ones with a switch. Samichlaus is both loved and feared. His costume varies from place to place, as does the date of his visit. Each village or canton has its own traditions concerning the ancient bishop saint, patron of all children, but especially of school boys. Each community observes his festival in its own peculiar way.

One of the most spectacular Samichlaus celebrations is in Zurich where the saint, wearing a red coat and carrying a bulging bag over his shoulder, leads a procession of teen-aged boys and girls. The young people who are known as the *Wollishofer Kläuse,* or "Klauses" from Wollishofer, a Zurich suburb, wear long white robes. On their masked heads are magnificent headdresses fashioned from cardboard and ornamented with intricate cut-out designs, covered with colored silks. The headdresses, illumined from within by lighted candles, are reminiscent of the traditional jewel-incrusted miter of Saint Nicholas, Archbishop of Myra, and precursor of the modern Samichlaus. The Klauses, whose illumined hats glow like rich stained glass, ring bells, blow trumpets and toot horns to frighten away the evil spirits that once were thought to roam abroad at Yuletide.

Similar processions occur in many parts of Switzerland. In the Aegeri valley, for example, school boys wear illumined hats and carry mountain lanterns. They drag about large sacks for goodies. Parading through village streets, they clang huge cowbells and stop at every door for contributions.

At Kaltbrunn, in the canton of Saint Gall, the paraders also wear magnificent headdresses. The youths dress in white, as at Zurich, but enliven their costumes with gaily embroidered suspenders and broad herdsmen's belts.

The burning of many lights and making a terrific racket—these two customs in Swiss Samichlaus processions come from pre-Christian times; for light and noise were the means primitive peoples used to frighten away midwinter's demons and devils.

HEILIGER ABEND (Christmas Eve)

December 24

Christmas Eve, possibly more than any other holiday, is cele-brated differently in different parts of Switzerland. In some places children think that *Christkindli,* the Christ Child, makes village rounds in a sleigh drawn by six fine reindeer. *Christkindli* carries a load of toys and gifts, as well as glittering Christmas trees which are well laden with oranges, apples, nuts, and cookies baked in many delightful shapes.

In the vicinity of Hallwil, in the canton of Lucerne, *Christkindli* is impersonated by a young girl in white, who wears a sparkling crown on her veiled head and is accompanied by white-robed children, with lighted lanterns and baskets of gifts. Youngsters eagerly await the sound of the tinkling bell which announces *Christkindli's* arrival at the door. As soon as she enters a house the Christmas tree candles are lighted. *Christkindli* and her attendants sing carols and distribute presents. Then *Christkindli* shakes hands with everyone and slips away to visit other neighborhood children.

In many homes the Christmas tree is kept behind closed doors—a carefully guarded secret—until after Christmas Eve supper. Then the doors are flung open and the tree is displayed, beautiful with its lighted red tapers and simple ornaments. The branches are hung with polished red apples, silver bells, white cotton snowballs, candies, and cookies cut out in animal shapes. Children and adults gather about to listen to the Nativity story and sing "Stille Nacht" before looking for the presents which are hidden in all sorts of odd places. Children's gifts often consist of practical items, such as knitted mittens, socks, a bright new cap, warm jacket or pretty frock, or perhaps a knife, some hand carved toys, or even a home-made doll.

For weeks before the holiday housewives are busy preparing the many fancy breads, cookies and cakes, both baked and fried, which are served in enormous quantity together with coffee, throughout the Christmas holidays. In the Valais *Ringli,* or huge doughnut-like cakes and hot chocolate are eaten after Midnight Mass. Perhaps the most traditional of all Yuletide cakes, however, are Zurich's golden brown *Tirggel* which people say originated as pagan offertory cakes. Made of flour and honey, as in olden times, these cakes which once were cut in cow, sheep, pig and other sacrificial animal shapes, now include, also, an endless variety of modern motifs. The Tirggel dough is pressed into elaborate molds representing story book cartoons, fairy tale episodes, portraits and many other subjects. Triggel, which are thin, hard, and shiny, are sometimes as large as window panes. Often the cakes, which keep for months, even years, are so unusual or artistic that people use them as decorations.

Bell ringing and carol singing characterize the Swiss Christmas Eve ceremonies, while Midnight Mass is widely attended throughout the country. In 1540, the Brotherhood of Saint Sebastian instituted one of the most unusual carol services when the town of Rheinfelden, in the canton of Aargau, was swept by plague and the Brotherhood (which was started by twelve men and still maintains the same membership) invoked its patron's aid.

On Christmas Eve before Midnight Mass, twelve Brothers, dressed in sombre garments and tall black hats, assemble in Rheinfelden to commemorate the tragic event of over four centuries ago. The Brothers, who are led by a lantern bearer, go through the town stopping to sing a traditional carol at each of seven different fountains. Three times during the singing of the carol mention is made of the Son of God. Three times the Brothers remove their hats in His honor. After the ceremony at the seventh fountain the Brothers join Rheinfelden's other citizens in attending Midnight Mass.

Many naïve folk superstitions exist regarding the miracles of Christmas Eve. One is the widespread belief that dumb animals are blessed with power of speech at midnight because they were present at Jesus' birth. For this reason peasants give their horses, cows, goats and other creatures extra portions of grain, salt, and hay on the Holy Night, but farm hands take care not to linger near the stables lest they overhear what the animals are saying and so invite misfortune. Some housewives clip their chickens' wings between eleven and twelve o'clock, so their fowls will be saved from beasts of prey; and old folk predict weather for the next twelve months by peeling off twelve layers of onion skin and filling them with salt.

Christmas Eve is auspicious to young lovers. It is said that those wishing to foretell future events should drink from nine different fountains while the midnight church bells are ringing. Then the girl or boy must hasten to church, where the future mate will be seen standing on the steps.

WEIHNACHTEN (Christmas)

December 25

Christmas marks the beginning of winter sports, such as skating, skiing, sledding, and tobogganing. Between Christmas and New

Year's Day, especially in mountain villages, people continuously visit neighbors, relations and friends. *Jass,* the national Swiss card game is a perennial favorite at these gatherings, which end with a *Kaffeeklatsch,* or coffee served with many varieties of homemade holiday cakes.

SILVESTERABEND [5] (New Year's Eve)

December 31

In Appenzell and other cantons of eastern Switzerland there is an old folk tradition that spirits of darkness walk abroad on *Silvesterabend,* the last night of the year. The demons must be frightened away with lashing whips and ringing bells, lest they linger and work evil on men and beasts. For centuries men and boys have masqueraded at this season as *Silvesterkläuse,* or Silvester Klauses, in costumes characterized by enormous bells and grotesque headdresses. Sometimes the headdresses represent bridges or houses, sometimes jesters or other characters. The men playing the feminine roles wear round painted masks and brightly decorated round hats. Strings of round bells, graduated from large to small, hang from either shoulder, over gaudy peasant costumes.

The Silvesterkläuse who are especially associated with the towns of Herisau and Urnäsch, perform dances and antics that are sufficiently noisy and fantastic to route the most persistent demon hordes.

In Geneva Silvesterabend is celebrated in quite different fashion. Great crowds gather at the square before the Gothic Cathedral of Saint Pierre to listen to the midnight chiming of the bells. The ringing of *la Clémence,* the bell Swiss people claim is the oldest and most beautiful in all Europe, is one of the impressive attractions of the occasion. As the New Year is ushered into the world, people dance in the streets, embrace, and wish each other health and prosperity in the coming months.

[5] See note, p. 21.

Children rise early on this day because of the saying that whoever gets up last in the morning will be *Silvester* in the home, and whoever reaches school last will be Silvester at school. Both at home and school these sluggards are greeted with deafening shouts of "Silvester!"

In many rural areas bonfires built on the mountains and village church bells rung in joyous harmonies announce the passing of the Old Year and the arrival of the New.

PART II
FOR FURTHER REFERENCE

TABLE OF EASTER DATES

And Movable Festivals Dependent Upon Easter to 1988

Year	Shrove Monday	Shrove Tuesday	Ash Wednesday	Palm Sunday	Holy or Maundy Thursday
1958	Feb. 17	Feb. 18	Feb. 19	March 30	April 3
1959	Feb. 9	Feb. 10	Feb. 11	March 22	March 26
1960 *	April 30	March 1	March 2	April 10	April 14
1961	Feb. 13	Feb. 14	Feb. 15	March 26	March 30
1962	March 5	March 6	March 7	April 15	April 19
1963	Feb. 25	Feb. 26	Feb. 27	April 7	April 11
1964 *	Feb. 10	Feb. 11	Feb. 12	March 22	March 26
1965	March 1	March 2	March 3	April 11	April 15
1966	Feb. 21	Feb. 22	Feb. 23	April 3	April 7
1967	Feb. 6	Feb. 7	Feb. 8	March 19	March 23
1968 *	Feb. 26	Feb. 27	Feb. 28	April 7	April 11
1969	Feb. 17	Feb. 18	Feb. 19	March 30	April 3
1970	Feb. 9	Feb. 10	Feb. 11	March 22	March 26
1971	Feb. 22	Feb. 23	Feb. 24	April 4	April 8
1972 *	Feb. 14	Feb. 15	Feb. 16	March 26	March 30
1973	March 5	March 6	March 7	April 15	April 19
1974	Feb. 25	Feb. 26	Feb. 27	April 7	April 11
1975	Feb. 10	Feb. 11	Feb. 12	March 23	March 27
1976 *	March 1	March 2	March 3	April 11	April 15
1977	Feb. 21	Feb. 22	Feb. 23	April 3	April 7
1978	Feb. 6	Feb. 7	Feb. 8	March 19	March 23
1979	Feb. 26	Feb. 27	Feb. 28	April 8	April 12
1980 *	Feb. 18	Feb. 19	Feb. 20	March 30	April 3
1981	March 2	March 3	March 4	April 10	April 16
1982	Feb. 22	Feb. 23	Feb. 24	April 4	April 8
1983	Feb. 14	Feb. 15	Feb. 16	March 27	March 31
1984 *	March 5	March 6	March 7	April 15	April 19
1985	Feb. 18	Feb. 19	Feb. 20	March 31	April 4
1986	Feb. 10	Feb. 11	Feb. 12	March 23	March 27
1987	March 2	March 3	March 4	April 12	April 16

* Leap Year

TABLE OF EASTER DATES

And Movable Festivals Dependent Upon Easter to 1988

Good Friday	Easter	Ascension	Whit Sunday or Pentecost	Whit Monday	Year
April 4	April 6	May 15	May 25	May 26	1958
March 27	March 29	May 7	May 17	May 18	1959
April 15	April 17	May 26	June 5	June 6	1960 *
March 31	April 2	May 11	May 21	May 22	1961
April 20	April 22	May 31	June 10	June 11	1962
April 12	April 14	May 23	June 2	June 3	1963
March 27	March 29	May 7	May 17	May 18	1964 *
April 16	April 18	May 27	June 6	June 7	1965
April 8	April 10	May 19	May 29	May 30	1966
March 24	March 26	May 4	May 14	May 15	1967
April 12	April 14	May 23	June 2	June 3	1968 *
April 4	April 6	May 15	May 25	May 26	1969
March 27	March 29	May 7	May 17	May 18	1970
April 9	April 11	May 20	May 30	May 31	1971
March 31	April 2	May 11	May 21	May 22	1972 *
April 20	April 22	May 31	June 10	June 11	1973
April 12	April 14	May 23	June 2	June 3	1974
March 28	March 30	May 8	May 18	May 19	1975
April 16	April 18	May 28	June 7	June 8	1976 *
April 8	April 10	May 20	May 30	May 31	1977
March 24	March 26	May 5	May 15	May 16	1978
April 13	April 15	May 25	June 4	June 5	1979
April 4	April 6	May 16	May 26	May 27	1980 *
April 17	April 19	May 29	June 8	June 9	1981
April 9	April 11	May 21	May 31	June 1	1982
April 1	April 3	May 12	May 22	May 23	1983
April 20	April 22	May 31	June 10	June 11	1984 *
April 5	April 7	May 16	May 26	May 27	1985
March 28	March 30	May 8	May 18	May 19	1986
April 17	April 19	May 29	June 8	June 9	1987

GLOSSARY OF FESTIVAL TERMS

ADVENT

The term meaning the "arrival" or "coming" as applied to the four-week period preceding the birth of Christ. Advent, which starts the fourth Sunday before Christmas and continues through Christmas Eve, is regarded as a season of spiritual preparation for Christmas, just as Lent is for Easter.

ALL FOOLS' DAY

April first, when people customarily play all kinds of harmless jokes and tricks on friends and neighbors.

ALL SAINTS' DAY

November first. A feast that has been observed since the fourth century, in commemoration of all the martyrs and saints.

ALL SOULS' DAY (Called also *Day of the Dead*)

November 2. The day that commemorates the souls of all the faithful departed.

ANNUNCIATION (Known also as *Lady Day*)

March 25, the church feast in memory of the Angel Gabriel's announcement to the Virgin Mary that she was to become mother of Jesus.

ASCENSION (Called also *Ear of Wheat Thursday*)

The fortieth day after Easter, which falls on a Thursday. A church feast commemorating the physical passing of Jesus from earth, in his disciples' presence, on the fortieth day after his resurrection. Ascension is considered the oldest feast of the Christian Church.

FESTIVALS OF WESTERN EUROPE

ASSUMPTION OF THE VIRGIN

August 15, the feast that celebrates the Virgin's ascent to heaven.

BENEDICTION SUNDAY

The Sunday following Corpus Christi.

CABEZUDOS

The grotesque "dwarfs" who parade through the streets in Spain on festive occasions. The *cabezudos* are men in costume who wear immense false heads or faces, and caricature different professions, personalities, or historical characters. The Dwarfs accompany the Giants, in popular Spanish street processions. (See *Giants*).

CANDLEMAS

February 2. The fortieth day after Jesus' birth. The day celebrates the Presentation of the Infant Jesus in the Temple and the Purification of the Virgin Mary. The name comes from the custom of blessing candles in the church on this day and distributing them to worshipers.

CARNIVAL

In most Roman Catholic countries the last three days before Lent. The period is observed with all kinds of merrymaking, feasts, and public revelry to compensate for the forty days of Lenten abstinence.

CHRISTMAS

December 25, anniversary of the reputed date of the birth of Jesus in Bethlehem. This is the greatest feast of the Christian Church.

CORPUS CHRISTI

The Thursday following Trinity Sunday (fifty-seven days after Easter).

GLOSSARY

CRÈCHE

A miniature "Bethlehem," or Nativity scene, with figures of Jesus in the manger, Mary, Joseph, the shepherds, Kings and angels. The *crèche* is an important symbol of Christmas in every French home. The *nacimiento* of Spain and the *presepio* of Italy correspond to the *crèche* of France.

DAY OF THE DEAD (See *All Souls'*)

EAR OF WHEAT THURSDAY (See *Ascension*)

EASTER

A Sunday set apart by the Christian Church to commemorate Christ's resurrection. In the Gregorian calendar Easter is the first Sunday after the paschal full moon. If the full moon is on a Sunday, Easter falls on the following Sunday. Easter never is *before* March 22, or *after* April 25.

EASTER SEPULCHER

A recess in the north wall of the church chancel. This recess represents the tomb of Christ. In medieval times the Host and crucifix, placed in the tomb on Good Friday, were guarded until their removal on Easter morning, in symbol of the burial and resurrection of Christ.

EPIPHANY (Also called *Twelfth Night, Three Kings' Day, Festival of the Kings,* etc.)

January 6, the twelfth day after Christmas. Epiphany, meaning "manifestation," commemorates the star's leading of the Magi to the manger at Bethlehem, where Jesus was born.

EUCHARIST (Also called *Host* or *Holy Sacrament*)

The consecrated wafer and wine of the communion service. The term is also applied to the rite of the Lord's Supper.

FAST EVE (Also called *Shrove Tuesday*)

The Eve of Ash Wednesday, the first day of Lent.

FERIA

A popular Spanish fair which often is the occasion for animal markets and commercial exhibitions, but always for bullfights, parades in regional costume, folk dancing, eating, drinking and having a good time.

FESTA

A feast day or holiday celebration which usually includes a religious procession as well as all kinds of secular amusements, such as dancing, singing and eating regional foods.

FIESTA (*See Festa*)

GIANTS

The name given to the huge cardboard and canvas figures—often twenty to thirty feet tall—which are carried on the shoulders of a man concealed within. The men, who look out through little peepholes in front, make the figures dance, jig and perform different antics. The Giants are highly popular entertainment features of feast day parades in Spain, Belgium, and other European countries, where they represent kings, queens, historical or mythological characters. (See *Cabezudos*).

GOOD FRIDAY (Also called *Long Friday*)

The Friday preceding Easter. The day commemorates the crucifixion of Jesus.

HOLY INNOCENTS' DAY

December 28, the anniversary of King Herod's slaughter of Bethlehem's innocent children in his desire to be certain of killing Jesus.

GLOSSARY

HOLY SATURDAY

The Saturday preceding Easter.

HOLY THURSDAY

The Thursday before Easter. The day is also known as *dies mandati,* Maundy (or Mandate) Thursday, because Jesus washed his disciples' feet on this day and commanded them to do likewise.

HOLY WEEK

The week preceding Easter, beginning with Palm Sunday and ending with Holy Saturday.

KERMESS or KERMESSE

A local outdoor country fair, as celebrated in the Low Countries. Originally the kermess was held on the community's patronal feast day.

LADY DAY (See *Annunciation*)

LENT

The name given to the period of fasting and penitence that is widely observed in preparation for the Easter feast. In the Western Church Lent begins on Ash Wednesday and continues for the forty weekdays until Easter. Since Sundays are feast days, the six Sundays of the period are not included.

MARTINMAS

November 11, the feast of Saint Martin, celebrated in many European countries as a harvest feast. Often the new wine is tasted and harvest foods, including the traditional roast goose, are eaten in observance of the season.

MID-LENT

The fourth Sunday in Lent.

MIDSUMMER DAY (See *Saint John's Day*)

NACIMIENTO (See *Crèche*)

NEW YEAR'S DAY

The first day of the calendar year.

PALM SUNDAY

The Sunday immediately preceding Easter. The name Palm Sunday comes from the custom of carrying palms, in memory of the palms people waved before Jesus when he made his triumphal entry into Jerusalem. In many European countries where palms do not grow, branches of boxwood, olive, pussy-willow, or something else are substituted for the traditional palm.

PARDON

The term given in Brittany, France, to a pilgrimage.

PASSION (of Christ)

The term applied to the sufferings of Christ between the time of the Last Supper and the Crucifixion.

PENTECOST (Known also as *Whitsun*)

A feast observed by the Christian Church on the seventh Sunday and the fiftieth day after Easter. The occasion commemorates the descent of the Holy Ghost on the Apostles on the Day of Pentecost. (See *Whitsunday*).

PRESEPIO (See *Crèche*)

PURIFICATION OF THE VIRGIN MARY (See *Candlemas*)

GLOSSARY

ROGATION DAYS

The Monday, Tuesday and Wednesday preceding Ascension Thursday. On these days parish priests lead village processions to the fields, to ask God's blessing on crops, gardens, and all growing things.

ROMERÍA

In rural Spain a popular expedition, half-pilgrimage and half-picnic in character, which is made to some shrine or sacred spot. A *romería* often involves a journey of several days.

SAINT JOHN'S DAY (Known also as *Midsummer Day*)

June 24, birth anniversary of Saint John the Baptist, and approximate time of the summer solstice, when the sun is farthest from the equator.

SANTONS

Small painted figures, often of pottery, which are used in the Christmas *crèches* or miniature manger scenes of southern France. Originally *santons* were small images of saints. Now *santons* include familiar village characters, such as the old faggot woman, the baker, the fife player, who bring offerings to the Infant Jesus and mingle freely with figures of the Holy Family, the Kings and shepherds, in the charming household *crèches*. The art of *santon* making is traditional and is passed down from one generation to another in certain families.

SHROVE TUESDAY

The Tuesday before Ash Wednesday, or the last day before Lent. The day is generally celebrated with all kinds of feasting and merrymaking. (See *Fast Eve*)

SUMMER SOLSTICE (See *Midsummer Day, Saint John's Day*)

FESTIVALS OF WESTERN EUROPE

THREE KINGS' DAY (See *Epiphany*)

TRINITY

Fifty-seven days after Easter, or the Sunday following Pentecost (or Whitsun).

TWELFTH NIGHT (See *Epiphany*)

WALPURGIS NIGHT (Also called *May Day Eve*)

April 30, the night before May first. In popular Teutonic superstition witches ride broomsticks to a rendezvous, usually the Brocken, in the Harz Mountains, on this night, in order to hold high festival with their lord and master, the devil.

WANDERING JEW

According to medieval legend a Jew who treated Jesus with contempt when He was on his way to the Crucifixion. In the folklore of many European countries the Wandering Jew (who appears in various guises) is condemned to wander over the earth until Christ's second coming.

WHITSUN or WHITSUNDAY (See *Pentecost*)

A festival occurring on the seventh Sunday and the fiftieth day after Easter. The term *whit* is popularly thought to mean "white" and to refer to the white garments worn by converts who were baptized on this day.

WHITSUNTIDE (or PENTECOST)

The week beginning with Whitsunday but especially the first three days, which are called Whitsunday, Whit Monday and Whit Tuesday.

SOME HELPFUL BOOKS

GENERAL

Cocchiara, Giuseppe
Storia del Folklore in Europa. Torino, Einaudi, 1952.

Fehrle, Eugen
Feste und Volksbräuche im Jahreslauf Europäischer Volker. Kassel, Hinnenthal, 1955.

Folk-Lore: a Quarterly Review of Myth, Tradition, Institution and Custom.
London, Glaisher. Publication of the Folk-Lore Society (British).
See index to each volume for countries, festivals and customs.

Frazer, James George
The Golden Bough: A Study in Religion and Magic. 3d ed. London, Macmillan, 1911-26. 12v.
See name of country in volume 12, *Bibliography and General Index,* for festivals under each country.

BELGIUM

Delstanche, Albert
The Little Towns of Flanders. London, Chatto & Windus, 1906.
"Description of Mystery of the Passion, Furnes." p23-4.

Gibson, Hugh
Belgium. New York, Doubleday, 1939.
Excellent accounts of many festivals and medieval survivals.

Lierens, Charles
Belgian Folklore. 2d ed. (Art, Life and Science in Belgium, no7). New York, Belgian Government Information Service, 1948.

257

Marinus, Albert
Le Folklore Belge. Bruxelles, Les Éditions Historiques, n.d. 3v.
Comprehensive study of festivals by a leading folklorist. Well illustrated.

Poumon, Émile
Le Hainaut: Le Livre des Traditions. Vilvorde, Mees, 1953.
Excellent photographs. Short descriptions of festivals.

Reinsberg-Düringsfeld, Le Baron de
Traditions et Légendes de la Belgique. Bruxelles, Claassen, 1870. 2v.
Standard work on religious fêtes and saints' days as celebrated in the past.

Ryck, Paul de
Légendes et Contes Populaires Gantois. Gand, Service du Tourisme, 1955.

DENMARK

Ahrskov, Anders
"Seasonal Customs and Traditions." *Danish Foreign Office Journal,* Number 13, 1954. p 11-16.

Ellekilde, Hans L. ed.
Danmarks Folkenminder nr.44, Fra Dansk Folkeminder-samling, v1. København, Schonbergske, 1938.
Social life, folk customs, and songs.

Olrik, Axel
Nordens Trylleviser. Udgivet af Anders Bjerrum og Inger M. Boberg. Kobenhavn, Schultz, 1934.
Authoritative material collected by a leading folklorist.

Riis, Jacob A.
The Old Town. New York, Macmillan, 1909.
Old customs and home festivals delightfully described.

SOME HELPFUL BOOKS

FRANCE

Baïracli-Levy, Julia de
As Gypsies Wander. London, Faber, 1953.
"Gypsy Fiesta in Provence," p 147-58.

De L'Isle, G. Bidault
Vieux Dictions de nos Campagnes. Paris, Nouvelles
Éditions de la Toison d'Or, 1952. 2v.

Dumont, Louis
La Tarasque. (Published under patronage of Musée
des Arts et Traditions Populaires). Paris, Gallimard,
1951.
Interesting text and pictures of *Fête de la Tarasque.*

Le Braz, Anatole
Au Pays des Pardons. Paris, Calmann-Lévy, 1900.

Le Goffic, Charles
Fêtes et Coutumes Populaires. Paris, Colin, 1923.
French patronal feasts, *réveillon,* fires of Saint John, and
many other festival customs. Dances and music included.

Mistral, Frédéric
Mémoires. Tr. by C. E. Maud. London, Arnold, 1907.
"The Magi Kings," p32-7; "Journey to Les Saintes-
Maries," p235-49.

Mourey, Gabriel
Le Livre des Fêtes Françaises. Paris, Librairie de France,
1930.
Excellent illustrations. Historical development of festivals.

Robson, E. I.
A Guide to French Fêtes. London, Methuen, 1930.

Starkie, Walter
In Sara's Tents. New York, Dutton, 1953.
"From Sisteron to Les Saintes," p 153-95; "The Pilgrim-
age to Saint Sara," p248-312.

Vloberg, Maurice
Les Fêtes de France; Coutumes Religieuses et Populaires.
Grenoble, Arthaud, 1936.
Good material on festivals and customs.

Williams, Maynard Owen
"Carnival Days on the Riviera." *National Geographic Magazine,* volume 50, October 1926, p467-501.

GERMANY

Donnell, P. O.
"What Happened to These Children?" *Saturday Evening Post,* 228:26, December 24, 1955, p26-7; 54-5.
Modern interpretation of the old legend of the Pied Piper of Hamelin.

Fehrle, Eugen
Feste und Volksbräuche im Jahreslauf Europäischer Volker. Kassel, Hinnenthal, 1955.
Consult for German festivals.

Klodwig, Rudolf
Deutsche Sippenfeiern. Jauer, Queisser, 1943. 2v.

Rattelmüller, Paul E.
Festliches Jahr. Brauchtum im Bayerischen Alpengebiet. München, Callwen, 1953.
Excellent photographs.

Reichhardt, Rudolf
Die Deutschen Feste in Sitte und Brauch. Jena, Costenoble, 1908.
Good descriptions of folk customs connected with principal holidays.

LUXEMBOURG

Casey, Robert J.
Land of Haunted Castles. New York, Century, 1921.

SOME HELPFUL BOOKS

Clark, Sydney
All the Best in Belgium and Luxembourg. New York,
Dodd, Mead, 1956.
Echternach, p244-5; Vianden and Bildchen, p247.

Laport, George
Le Folklore des Paysages du Grand-Duché du Luxembourg.
(Folklore Fellows Communications). Helsinki, Suoma-
lainen tiedeakatemia, Academia scientiarum fennica, 1929.
Legends and folk origins: Bildchen, p8-9; Echternach,
p 15-17; Notre-Dame de Luxembourg, p38.

Taylor-Whitehead, W. J.
Luxembourg, Land of Legends. London, Constable, 1951.
Luxembourg-Ville: "Our Lady of Luxembourg," p39-44;
Bildchen: "The Madonna of Bildchen," p55-6; Echternach:
"The Fiddler of Echternach," p82-7.
References are to legends of the festivals occurring in these
places.

Renwick, George
Luxembourg, the Grand Duchy and Its People. New York,
Scribner's, 1913.
Contains some useful background material on Echternach,
Bildchen, etc.

ITALY

Handley, Marie Louise
"Siena's *Palio,* an Italian Inheritance from the Middle
Ages." *National Geographic Magazine,* volume 50, August
1926, p245-58.

Hume, Edgar Erskine
"The *Palio* of Siena." *National Geographic Magazine,*
volume 100, August 1951, p230-44.

Lancellotti, Arturo
Feste Tradizionali. Milano, Società Editrice Libraria, 1951.
2v.
Standard source, excellent illustrations.

Santi, Lionetto
Il Palio di Siena. 4th ed. Siena, Edizioni "Civitas Virginis," 1950.

Sitwell, Sacheverell
Primitive Scenes and Festivals. London, Faber, 1942.
"Festival at Nola," p259-78.

Toor, Frances
Festivals and Folkways of Italy. New York, Crown, 1953.
A good book on Italian festivals by an excellent folklorist.

NETHERLANDS

Graft, Dr. C. Cath. v. d.
Nederlandsche Volksgebruiken bij Hootijdagen. Amsterdam, de Lange, 1947.
Old folk ceremonials described by a leading authority. Well illustrated.

Halverhout, Heleen A. M.
Traditionele Recepten voor de Feestdagen. Bussum, van Dishoeck, 1955.
Descriptions of feast days, with recipes for the accompanying traditional foods. Useful conversion table for standard American measurements.

Haverkamp, Okke
En Nederland Lacht. . . Folkloristische Vreugden en Vreugdevolle Folklore. Naarden, Rutgers, 1946-49. 11v.
Illustrated. An excellent series on the folklore, customs, wit and humor of the following provinces: Volume 1, Drente; Volume 2, Groningen; Volume 3, Friesland; Volume 4, North Holland and West Friesland; Volume 5, Limburg; Volume 6, Gelderland; Volume 7, Overijsel; Volume 8, Zeeland; Volume 9, North Brabant; Volume 10, Utrecht; Volume 11, South Holland.

SOME HELPFUL BOOKS

Kruizinga, J. H.
Levende Folklore in Nederland en Vlaanderen. Assen, "De Torenlaan," 1953.
"Feesten en Feesttijden," p39-240.
Feast day celebrations and popular rhymes. Valuable source material.

Mok, Paul
"Folklore of the Netherlands." *New York Folklore Quarterly*, 6:4, Winter 1950. p221-33.
Holidays and customs.

NORWAY

Bosworth, Abbie L.
"Life in a Norway Valley." *National Geographic Magazine*, volume 67. May 1935, p627-48.
Christmas foods and customs.

Eriksen, Erling Vegusdal
Atterklang fra Gammeltida; Folkeminne fra Beiarn. (Norsk Folkeminnelag, nr.72) Oslo, Norsk Folkeminnelag, 1953. 1 v.
Folklore, songs, dialects, legends and festivals.

Gulbranssen, Trygve
Beyond Sing the Woods. Tr. by Naomi Walford, New York, Putnam's, 1936.

Solheim, Svale
Norsk Saetertradisjon. (Instituttet for Sammenlignende Kulturforskning, Oslo. Skrifter: Serie B, nr.47). Oslo, Aschehoug, 1952.

Undset, Sigrid
Kristen Lavransdatter: The Bridal Wreath, The Mistress of Husaby, The Cross, New York, Knopf, 1930.

PORTUGAL

Adams, Harriet Chalmers
"European Outpost: the Azores." *National Geographic Magazine,* 47:1. January 1955, p36 ff.

Braga, Theophilo
O Povo Portuguez; nos seus Costumes, Crenças e Tradições. Lisboa, Livraria Ferreira, 1885. 2v.
Volume 1, *Costumes e Vida Domestica;* Volume 2, *Crenças e Festas Publicas, Tradições e Saber Popular.*

Chaves, Luís
Do Barro se Faz a Louça; na Louça se Come o Trigo. Lisboa, Federação National dos Produtores de Trigo, 1953.
Cakes and loaves in religion and folklore.

Gallop, Rodney
Portugal; a Book of Folk Ways. London, Cambridge University Press, 1936.
Folk practices, festivals and music.

Lopes Dias, Jaime
Etnografia da Beira; Lendas, Costumes, Tradições, Crenças e Superstições. Lisboa, Livraria Morais, [1926]-53. 7v.
Folklore (Beira), folk songs, dances and dialects. Excellent source material.

Sampaio, Gonçalo
Canci Oneiro Minhoto. 2d ed. Porto, Livraria Educação Nacional, 1944.
Festival songs from many areas.

Sellers, Charles
Tales from the Lands of Nuts and Grapes. London, Field, 1888.
Spanish and Portuguese folklore.

SPAIN

Alford, Violet
The Singing of the Travels. London, Parrish, 1956.
Consult Index under name of festival.

Amades, Joan
Gegants, Nans i Altres Entremesos. Barcelona, La Neotipia, 1934.
Historical development of the Giants. Very fine illustrations.

Aubier, Dominique and Robert Delpire, ed.
Seville en Fête. Paris, Weber, 1954.
Magnificent photographs.

Caballé y Clos, Tomás
Folklore Catalán; Antiguas Tradiciones, Festividades Populares y Ferias. Barcelona, Editorial Frexinet, 1947.
Festivals, fairs, music and songs of Catalonia.

Capmany, Aureli
Calendari de Llegendes, Costums i Festes Tradicionals Catalanes. Barcelona, Jover, 1951.
Festivals and songs arranged by months. Quaint woodcuts.
El Libro Verde de Barcelona Añalejo. Barcelona, Casanova, 1945.
"Fiesta, Fun, and Fire in Old Valencia." *Life,* 38:18, May 2, 1955, p51-52; 54; 56.

Kany, C. E.
Fiestas y Costumbres·Españolas. Boston, Heath, 1929.

Sitwell, Sacheverell
Spain. London, Batsford, 1953.
"Romería del Rocío," p40-1; "Elche," p 107-8. Consult Index for references to other events.
"Spanish Fiesta." *Coronet,* volume 41, January 1957, p 114-21.
Description and photographs of *romería* to Virgin of Rocío, Almonte.

Starkie, Walter
In Sara's Tents. New York, Dutton, 1953.
"Mystery Play of Elche," p219-31; "Mummers and Dancers," p 199-247.

SWEDEN

Coombs, Anna Olsson
The Smörgåsbord Cookbook. New York, Wyn, 1949.
"Swedish Holidays," p 15-21. Interesting material on food lore and customs.

Cyriac, A. Kellgren
"Swedish Christmas Customs." *Folk-Lore,* volume 44, December 1923, p314-321.

Hagberg, Louise
"Old-Time Christmas in Sweden." *American-Scandinavian Review,* volume 14, December 1926, p744-50.

Holm, Thora
Svenska Helger: Högtider och Bemräkelsedagar i Svenska Hem. Stockholm, T. Holms Förlag, 1931.
Home customs and festivals, with foods appropriate to each season.

Nilsson, Martin P. N.
Arets Folkliga Fester. Stockholm, Gebers, 1915.
Well illustrated. Excellent material on festivals and customs.

Lagerlöf, Selma
Mårbacka. Tr. by Selma Swanston Howard. Garden City, Doubleday, 1925.
Recollections of the author's youth.
Memories of My Childhood; Further Years at Mårbacka. Garden City, Doubleday, 1934.
"The Easter Witch," p 163-73.
Gösta Berling's Saga. Tr. by Lillie Tudeer. New York, American Scandinavian Foundation, 1918.

Lloyd, L.
Peasant Life in Sweden. London, Tinsley, 1870.
An old but useful collection of peasant customs typical of different parts of Sweden.

SOME HELPFUL BOOKS

SWITZERLAND

Hasler, Hans
Bilder vom Zürisee. Zürich, Gut, 1949.

Hoffmann-Krayer, Eduard
Feste und Bräuche des Schweizervolkes. (Neubearbeitung durch Paul Geiger). Zürich, Atlantis, 1940.
Excellent work on social life and customs, festivals and folklore.
Kleine Schriften zur Volkskunde. Hrsg. von Paul Geiger. (Schriften der Schweizerischen Gesellschaft für Volkskunde. Bd. 30) Basel, Krebs, 1946.

Moser-Grossweiler, Fritz
Volksbräuche der Schweiz. Zürich, Scientia, 1940.
Highly recommended for study of festivals and saints' days. Good photographs.

INDEX OF FESTIVALS BY COUNTRY

FESTIVALS OF WESTERN EUROPE

INDEX

271

ALPHABETICAL INDEX OF FESTIVALS

INDEX

(6067)